T0301529

Entrepreneurship Research in Europe

EUROPEAN RESEARCH IN ENTREPRENEURSHIP

Series Editors: Alain Fayolle, *Professor of Entrepreneurship, EMLYON Business School and CERAG, France and Visiting Professor at Solvay Brussels School of Economics and Management, Belgium and* Paula Kyrö, *Professor of Entrepreneurship Education, Aalto University School of Economics, Finland*

This important series is designed to highlight the unique characteristics and rich variety of European research in entrepreneurship. It provides powerful lenses to help identify and understand the importance of European cultural roots within the international entrepreneurship landscape.

Titles in the series include:

Entrepreneurship Research in Europe
Outcomes and Perspectives
Edited by Alain Fayolle, Paula Kyrö and Jan Ulijn

The Dynamics between Entrepreneurship, Environment and Education
Edited by Alain Fayolle and Paula Kyrö

European Entrepreneurship and the Globalizing Economy
Edited by Alain Fayolle and Kiril Todorov

Entrepreneurship Research in Europe
Evolving Concepts and Processes
Edited by Odd Jarl Borch, Alain Fayolle, Paula Kyrö and Elisabet Ljunggren

Entrepreneurship Research in Europe

Evolving Concepts and Processes

Edited by

Odd Jarl Borch

Professor, Bodø Graduate School of Business, University of Nordland, Norway

Alain Fayolle

Professor of Entrepreneurship, EMLYON Business School, France and Visiting Professor, Solvay Brussels School of Economics and Management, Belgium

Paula Kyrö

Professor of Entrepreneurship Education, Aalto University School of Economics, Finland

Elisabet Ljunggren

Senior Researcher in Entrepreneurship, Nordland Research Institute, Norway

EUROPEAN RESEARCH IN ENTREPRENEURSHIP

Edward Elgar
Cheltenham, UK • Northampton, MA, USA

Published by
Edward Elgar Publishing Limited
The Lypiatts
15 Lansdown Road
Cheltenham
Glos GL50 2JA
UK

Edward Elgar Publishing, Inc.
William Pratt House
9 Dewey Court
Northampton
Massachusetts 01060
USA

A catalogue record for this book
is available from the British Library

Library of Congress Control Number: 2010941496

ISBN 978 0 85793 174 0

Typeset by Servis Filmsetting Ltd, Stockport, Cheshire
Printed and bound by MPG Books Group, UK

Contents

Contributors

Iiris Aaltio, University of Jyväskylä/Lappeenranta University of Technology, Finland

Sophie Bacq, Centre for Research in Entrepreneurial Change and Innovative Strategies (CRECIS), Louvain School of Management, Université catholique de Louvain, Belgium

Olga Belousova, Centre for Research in Entrepreneurial Change and Innovative Strategies (CRECIS), Louvain School of Management, Université catholique de Louvain, Belgium

Odd Jarl Borch, Bodø Graduate School of Business, University of Nordland, Norway

Sara Carter, Hunter Centre for Entrepreneurship, University of Strathclyde, Glasgow, UK

Mateja Drnovšek, Faculty of Economics, University of Ljubljana, Slovenia

Alain Fayolle, EMLYON Business School, France

Joaquín Guzmán, Dept Economía Aplicada I, University of Seville, Spain

Frank Janssen, Centre for Research in Entrepreneurial Change and Innovative Strategies (CRECIS), Louvain School of Management, Université catholique de Louvain, Belgium

Kalev Kaarna, University of Tartu, Centre for Entrepreneurship, Estonia

Norris Krueger, Max Planck Institute of Economics, Jena and Entrepreneurship Northwest, Boise, ID, USA

Paula Kyrö, Aalto University School of Economics, Finland

Francisco Liñán, Dept Economía Aplicada I, University of Seville, Spain

Elisabet Ljunggren, Nordland Research Institute, Norway

Tuija Mainela, University of Oulu, Department of International Business, Finland

Colin Mason, Hunter Centre for Entrepreneurship, University of Strathclyde, Glasgow, UK

Tõnis Mets, University of Tartu, Centre for Entrepreneurship, Estonia

Jarkko Mylläri, The University of Helsinki, Department of Teacher Education, Finland

Hannes Ottósson, University of Southern Denmark, Department of Entrepreneurship and Relationship Management, Denmark

Vesa Puhakka, University of Oulu, Department of Management, Finland

Juan C. Rodríguez-Cohard, Dept Economía Aplicada, University of Jaen, Spain

Thomas Schøtt, University of Southern Denmark, Department of Entrepreneurship and Relationship Management, Denmark

Jaana Seikkula-Leino, University of Turku, Lappeenranta University of Technology, Finland

Sakari Sipola, University of Oulu, Department of Management, Finland

Rok Stritar, Faculty of Economics, University of Ljubljana, Slovenia

Elisabeth Sundin, Linköping University, Department of Management and Engineering/Helix VINN Excellence Centre, Sweden

Stephen Tagg, Department of Marketing, University of Strathclyde, Glasgow, UK

Foreword

What makes great research? We all have a good sense of what makes good research, but what makes it great? Great questions.

This book should give the reader some ideas about the great questions that were embraced in August 2008 at the ESU conference at Høgskolen i Bodø.

At a recent Academy of Management research consortium, we asked a room full of past, present and future entrepreneurship scholars three simple questions:

1. What is the single most important question in entrepreneurship research (from your perspective)?
2. What is the one thing that you are most curious or most passionate about in entrepreneurship?
3. What is the number 1 thing on which you are focusing your research efforts?

Would you be surprised to know that almost everybody had three different answers to those questions? So my co-presenters and I asked 'Why?' (Note: this is a very good way to annoy your colleagues.)

In Bodø, if I had asked that question of the presenters, many (if not most) would have had similar answers. From their perspective, early stage as it might be, they were working on something they saw as very important to our understanding of entrepreneurship and a topic they were deeply curious (maybe even passionate) about.

I can still remember the fire in the eyes of some of the participants sharing their enthusiasm for their topic, whether Sophie Bacq on social entrepreneurship or Olga Belousova on corporate entrepreneurship (or the passion that Sara Carter and Jonathan Levie still have for their own work or even the joy of finally meeting Lars Kolvereid and seeing that his passion for entrepreneurship's Most Important Question remains unabated).

Part of this is to the credit of their advisers and mentors, but ultimately I think it speaks to the great potential of the students and junior faculty presenting. It also speaks to the faculty driving the conference (Jonathan,

Sara, Paula, Alain, Elisabet, Odd Jarl and the rest) who fostered an environment where we could all follow our passions, while insisting on rigour in both theory and method. Nevertheless, it was very clear to me that the next 'crop' of new colleagues in entrepreneurship will be exceptional.

The Bodø conference made me a big fan of ESU (the host institution, Høgskolen i Bodø, won my heart as well). I look forward to finding new ways to help ESU continue its fine work. How can I help?

Norris Krueger
Max Planck Institute of Economics, Jena
Entrepreneurship Northwest, Boise, ID, USA
Boise, Idaho
July 2010

Preface

This book series stems from a European university network of entrepreneurship researchers who annually arrange a conference for their entrepreneurship research groups and doctoral students (www.esu.fi). The mix between younger and more experienced researchers of this ESU community presents the most recent European entrepreneurship research in the combined workshop and conference, hence the articles in the book series represent this research front. It is characterized by great diversity and gives good promises for the future of European entrepreneurship research. This is also the aim for the book series: to share this diverse and interesting research with a larger audience.

Odd Jarl Borch
Alain Fayolle
Paula Kyrö
Elisabet Ljunggren

Acknowledgement

We would like to thank the INNOLA/INLAB Project funded by the European Social Fund (ESF) and the State Provincial Office of Southern Finland for their contributions to this book.

Introduction: becoming an entrepreneur and developing entrepreneurial behaviour

Paula Kyrö, Odd Jarl Borch, Alain Fayolle and Elisabet Ljunggren

EVOLVING CONCEPTS AND CONTEXTS OF ENTREPRENEURSHIP

The purpose of this third book in the series 'European Research in Entrepreneurship' is to demonstrate the importance of entrepreneurship research at a time of turbulent environments, to present important avenues of research, and to illustrate differences in entrepreneurship between countries and regions. We emphasize the questions of why, what and how to study entrepreneurship. By making links to the two previous books in this series we are able to illuminate some trends in European entrepreneurship research and to illustrate how European research on entrepreneurship has evolved since our first book in 2005. At that time we anticipated that the European entrepreneurship debate would gain in strength and find its own profile by revisiting its European roots in the global landscape. In the second book in 2008, these expectations were identified to gather around three research orientations. First, the European approach contextualizes rather than isolates research settings. Second, more than before it views entrepreneurship as a dynamic learning and developmental process whatever the context, and third, the new ideological dialogue of entrepreneurship has started to expand its scope from business to society.

In 2005 our expectations for the question 'why study entrepreneurship?' related to the role and value of entrepreneurial practices in society and economy, which concerns the need to provide new work and wealth for citizens in a complex and changing reality. In this respect our prediction is more than valid today. Social concepts and contexts have disembarked to theories, and complex and changing reality has inspired and strengthened opportunity-driven research. As anticipated, we have moved from the question of the entrepreneur's role in the economy towards the importance of entrepreneurial practices and processes in renewing society. This is the mainstreaming theme in this book.

The process approach is embedded in all parts of this book. It underlines various innovative and opportunity-driven processes as a complex inter-action between technology, environment and social practices, as indeed was anticipated in our previous books. Also, it became obvious that the individualistic-oriented approach has extended to collective and net-working activities and processes integrating theories from management, organization science, marketing and education as well as from philosophy and methodological fields of science. Thus the content of this book repre-sents a multi-disciplinary approach typical of the latest developments in entrepreneurship research. It borrows ideas from sociology, psychology, management, education, organization science and philosophy.

As regards what to study, the research, as anticipated, is enriched with action-bound theories and the theories understanding and modelling holistic complex and non-linear reality and practices. In this field, too, the focus of research has changed to the dynamics and processes of creating new economic activity in different contexts: individuals, small businesses, organizations and networks. Specific to the development of these proc-esses is the opportunity discovery and creation perspective that questions the traditional opportunity recognition approach.

From a methodological perspective, how to study, we highlighted how methodology affects and is dependent on the questions of why and what to study, and how recent developments assume methodological advance to gain access to the dynamic processes of these settings. As expected, the methodological development, as demonstrated in the chapters in this book, proceeds towards methods capturing the complex reality and the interaction between individual and collective human processes. Typically there is an effort to capture non-linear reality through individual expe-riences and perceptions as well as to find a way to reconceptualize the evolving concepts of entrepreneurship.

Now indeed we can say that these predictions are about to be validated. For this book we have chosen examples of all of these developments. The chapters present how these questions of *why*, *what* and *how* to study entre-preneurship have changed during these years. In Part I we focus on the process of becoming and learning to be an entrepreneur. Part II highlights how entrepreneurship as a social phenomenon and as a social process of becoming entrepreneurial has evolved. Finally Part III demonstrates how the process of creating and developing entrepreneurial organizations is about to take its rightful place in entrepreneurship research. These parts share the process orientation towards becoming an entrepreneur and developing entrepreneurial behaviour.

Together these 26 authors and research groups from ten countries representing applied economics, education, management, marketing, technology, economic and social sciences suggest that the evolving concepts and processes of entrepreneurship are complex, context-bound processes produced by human behaviour. They introduce the most recent developments in entrepreneurship research as process-oriented individual and social learning processes and arenas and provide the empirical contributions from a broad set of European countries.

PART I: THE PROCESS OF BECOMING AND LEARNING TO BECOME AN ENTREPRENEUR

Part I, with four chapters, starts by presenting the need for and challenges entailed in becoming and learning to be an entrepreneur and then demonstrates how processes and different phases of becoming an entrepreneur or entrepreneurial can be studied, and how the concept evolved through process-oriented research. The three last chapters deal with pre-intention, intention and opportunity creation and development phases, underlining the need to understand how individuals experience and perceive reality.

Chapter 1, 'Does education matter? The characteristics and performance of businesses started by recent university graduates', written by UK researchers Colin Mason, Stephen Tagg and Sara Carter, opens the arena to the need to better understand how to enhance entrepreneurship in graduate education. The authors summarize this need by showing that even if entrepreneurship education is a growing activity in universities, the evidence base which might support an emphasis on encouraging graduate entrepreneurship is extremely sketchy and without evidence; it is only an act of faith. By drawing on the largest survey of small businesses in the UK with 19 000 usable responses, they present evidence that graduates are starting businesses more quickly after leaving education than in the past and younger graduates are starting businesses more quickly after leaving education than non-graduates. Businesses of younger graduates have also grown faster than those of older graduates, and graduate business owners are more likely to be women than are non-graduate business owners. They argue that this compressed transition between leaving higher education and starting a business assumes a focus on experiential learning in entrepreneurship education and placements or internships in supporting graduate entrepreneurs to compensate for the lack of employment experience.

Chapter 2 supports these recommendations. 'Temporal stability of entrepreneurial intentions: a longitudinal study', written by the Spanish research group consisting of Francisco Liñán, Juan C. Rodríguez-Cohard and Joaquín Guzmán from Applied Economics at the University of Seville, analyses the temporal progression in intentions. Entrepreneurship is viewed as a process that occurs over time as the first step in the evolving process of venture creation. The authors argue that the intention to start up is a necessary precursor to performing entrepreneurial behaviours. Their results indicate that, after graduation, changes in intentions are rare and thus greater effort should be invested in enhancing the attractiveness of entrepreneurship at earlier stages in the education system. Developing the skills and values more closely linked to entrepreneurship (such as independence, self-realization, self-confidence, creativity, and so on) in younger students would contribute to more favourable personal attitudes towards this career option. The results also indicate that 'authentic experience' is essential to increase self-efficacy and entrepreneurial intention. According to the authors this calls for entrepreneurial pedagogy in authentic settings, as the UK researchers also recommended.

Chapter 3, 'Meta processes of entrepreneurial and enterprising learning: the dialogue between cognitive, conative and affective constructs', goes deeper into the dynamics of learning these competences. The authors Paula Kyrö, Jaana Seikkula-Leino and Jarkko Mylläri of the Finnish Aalto ENTRE Research Group adopt the tripartite constructs of personality and intelligence (Snow et al., 1996) distinguishing between the cognitive, conative and affective aspects of learning. Following Gibb's ideas, they argue that the affective aspects of values and attitudes should take a more explicit place in learning practices. Thus learning more about affective self-regulation processes, that is, an individual's active participation in his or her own learning process, would empower entrepreneurial and enterprising learning processes. The results indicate that all constructs appeared in entrepreneurship education learning interventions as well as in transitions between them, but the affective meta-process was hardest to identify and learn.

Chapter 4, by Rok Stritar and Mateja Drnovšek from Slovenia, focuses on 'Entrepreneurial opportunity identification: the case of Skype Technologies'. They argue that entrepreneurs do not discover opportunities; rather, they create them by taking advantage of technological change or innovation occurring in the economy. They follow Sarasvathy, who proposes that what are discovered are merely possibilities that have to be developed to become opportunities. The way an opportunity is developed is strongly connected to the individual, which means that two different entrepreneurs would not develop the same opportunity in the same way. They claim that even if the literature makes a notable distinction between the identification and development phase of the entrepreneurship process, it is less clear what the result of both phases is and where the process of identification ends and that of development starts. The results of their case study indicate that the way entrepreneurs want to develop an opportunity can also strongly influence the opportunity identification itself and emphasize the role of the individual in the identification and development of opportunities. Learning from these findings creates new and more specified demands of entrepreneurship education processes.

PART II: ENTREPRENEURSHIP AS A SOCIAL PROCESS OF BECOMING ENTREPRENEURIAL

The chapters in Part II demonstrate how social entrepreneurship has disembarked to entrepreneurship research along with its importance in society. This part of the book specifically shows how the new ideological dialogue of entrepreneurship has started to expand its scope from business to society. Belgian authors Bacq and Janssen (Chapter 7, this volume) argue, no doubt the growing interest in social entrepreneurship partly results from its innovativeness in addressing social problems that are becoming increasingly complex.

Chapter 5, by Iiris Aaltio, Paula Kyrö and Elisabeth Sundin representing a Swedish–Finnish research team, is entitled 'Heuristic method: insights into a conceptual understanding of women's entrepreneurship and social capital'. The authors claim that conceptual work that combines and investigates the multiple results of book compilations is still rare in the jungle of academic publishing. By introducing search and argument heuristics as an example of new openings in this field, they examine how conceptual thinking progresses through and enriches the conceptual understanding of the dialogue between women's entrepreneurship and social capital. They suggest that the lack of suitable concepts typically marginalizes women's entrepreneurship, and thus finding a way to enhance conceptualization in this field will advance the research on women's entrepreneurship and the practices of women entrepreneurs. Instead of 'marginalizing', they promote 'innovating' as an intrinsic line of women's entrepreneurship and social capital concepts. Thus a heuristic method explicates how social capital seems to be the field of innovations for women entrepreneurs. It seems to give access to the pursuit of opportunities and the gaining of access to resources needed for these activities. Thus it offers an opportunity to break the boundaries of 'otherness', paving the way of women's entrepreneurship so far. These findings also demonstrate new needs as to how to support women's entrepreneurship education and graduate entrepreneurs as Mason et al. recommended in the first chapter of this book.

In Chapter 6, 'Entrepreneurs' social capital enhancing performance and venture advancement', the Icelander Hannes Ottósson and the Dane Thomas Schøtt discuss social capital through the process perspective based on social capital at the crossroads of entrepreneurship theory and social network theory. They investigate the effects of networks on entrepreneurial performance and advancement. They claim that there is a need to increase the integration of outcome and process-oriented research and that many studies borrowing from sociology and economics have not succeeded in this. They conclude that by utilizing a dynamic panel research design that covers the whole entrepreneurial process, scholars can stop asking 'whether' questions and start asking 'when' and 'how' questions.

Chapter 7 by Sophie Bacq and Frank Janssen, 'Structuring the field of social entrepreneurship: a transatlantic comparative approach', concludes this part with a conceptual comparative study. The authors claim that the lack of a unifying paradigm in the field of social entrepreneurship has led to a proliferation of definitions. Therefore, there is a need to clarify the concepts of 'social entrepreneurship', 'social entrepreneur' and 'social enterprise', and to identify the different schools and practices. Their in-depth literature review identifies three main directions: in the USA (1) the Social Innovation and (2) the Social Enterprise Schools, and (3) the European School, and their findings indicate that there are no geographical differences between the concepts but, even within the United States, different conceptions exist concurrently.

PART III: THE PROCESS OF CREATING AND DEVELOPING ENTREPRENEURIAL ORGANIZATIONS

The third part of the book contains three chapters, all of which demonstrate how entrepreneurial processes have developed in different organizational contexts. They seek to understand and conceptualize how these processes have evolved and how they could be developed further.

In Chapter 8, 'Mapping internationalization paths of technology-based SMEs: cases of Estonian ICT and biotechnology companies', Kalev Kaarna and Tõnis Mets from Estonia combine international studies with entrepreneurship by modelling the internationalization paths of the firms. They argue that researchers like Shane and Venkataraman, Coviello and Mathews and Zander have tried to add the dynamic process component to the definition of international entrepreneurship, but these attempts have gone unnoticed by most empirical studies. Accordingly they suggest that the internationalization process should be broadened to emphasize the dynamic nature of the process of recognizing and exploiting entrepreneurial opportunities across national borders.

Finnish researchers Tuija Mainela, Vesa Puhakka and Sakari Sipola, in their chapter 'Exploring firm growth as a process of creation', criticize prior studies on firm growth due to their positivistic, variance-based methods. Instead of explaining and predicting what happens in a social reality by looking for natural laws implying regularities and causality, they suggest that the conceptualization of firm growth should emphasize the multidimensionality, emergent nature and context-dependence of firm growth. They propose a conceptual framework for studying firm growth as a process of creation building on four primary and intertwined elements: (1) types of opportunities; (2) types of growth behaviours; (3) contextual issues of resources, strategizing practices and environment; and (4) the outcome of the process. Thus the growth behaviour of a firm can be expressed in many ways. What is essential for a firm is to recognize different mechanisms such as organizational learning, various information-gathering behaviours and to build an organization where these are catered for. This contributes to a starting point and an environment where growth can take place. Thus it also presents some ideas regarding the need to educate young growth-orientated students.

The book concludes with a chapter by Belgian Olga Belousova, 'The influence of organizational characteristics on intentions of employees towards corporate entrepreneurship'. The author is interested in learning more about the way organizations become more innovative and entrepreneurial and stimulate such behaviours among the employees. Being innovative, risk-taking and ready to pioneer has proved to contribute well to the financial performance and strategic value of big corporations as it has also to small and medium sized enterprises, and individual innovation behaviour is recognized as crucial in fostering continued entrepreneurship. Thus this concluding chapter leaves us with a challenge to improve these competences in education regardless of the context students choose in their careers.

From the methodological perspective these ten chapters share a tendency to overcome the problems of linearity and find a way to reconceptualize the complex processes and evolving concepts of entrepreneurship. This is done by emphasizing a longitudinal approach, conceptual methods and individual experiences and perceptions. The chapters also show the multitude of methodologies applied within the entrepreneurship research field.

A longitudinal approach is chosen, for example, by Liñán, Rodríguez-Cohard and Guzmán in their intention study and Kaarna and Mets in their internationalization research. The first of these adopts a two-wave, approximately three-year longitudinal analysis through a questionnaire to 336 final-year undergraduate students in three public universities in Andalusia. Kaarna and Mets use a longitudinal case study approach to evaluate the model for mapping internationalization paths over 15–18 years. As they argue, such a longitudinal approach is not common in international entrepreneurship research, but is needed to gain better insight into the processes.

A longitudinal approach is also evident in two Grounded Theory studies. The research of 'Meta processes of entrepreneurial and enterprising learning' applies Straussian Grounded Theory with the coding outcomes of open, axial and selective phases followed by the concept map method. It consists of the two-year follow-up reflections of 18 university students who participated in two consecutive study programmes in entrepreneurship education. 'The case of Skype Technologies' written by Rok Stritar and Mateja Drnovšek also adopts a Grounded Theory approach by collecting secondary data in the form of written and video interviews with the Skype business founder. The authors systematically coded the data and built a grounded emergent model of opportunity identification and development for the venture.

The conceptual study by Aaltio, Kyrö and Sundin demonstrates how a heuristic method of discovery, a method rarely used in entrepreneurship research, can help to provide new insights on how to conceptualize. After employing a heuristic search, that is finding an analogy and borrowing a heuristic method from sociology, they adopt argument heuristics by problematizing the obvious with the question, 'What if the social capital for women entrepreneurs represents something other than social capital as it is generally defined?', then by making a reversal: 'What if women entrepreneurs are not only constructed by social capital but rather construct it for some purpose?' New concepts for the interplay between social capital and women's entrepreneurship were generated.

The comparative conceptualizing study by Sophie Bacq and Frank Janssen provides new insights into social entrepreneurship through an in-depth literature review often needed in the nascent phase of evolving concepts. A similar approach is used by Belousova to generate new hypotheses for studying corporate entrepreneurship. She argues that entrepreneurship – and in particular, corporate entrepreneurship – is a multidimensional and complex phenomenon that cannot be easily described. Hence it is necessary to avoid blind usage of concepts and tools from other domains without properly adapting them to the field. Therefore, to capture this conceptual diversity several approaches towards the intentions of employees to engage in entrepreneurship were needed to reconceptualize corporate entrepreneurship.

Another example of reconceptualizing is Mainela, Puhakka and Sipola's exploration of firm growth as a process of creation. They claim that this kind of processual and cross-disciplinary viewpoint is needed to develop growth as an opportunity-driven behavioural process embedded in a particular, dynamic context. Their in-depth literature review represents a research design that models firm growth as processes of individuals' actions for growth. They argue that there are few studies which aim to build such a comprehensive view of firm growth. They depict firm growth as a process of creation instead of focusing on the relationships between single variables.

Finally, the research by Hannes Ottósson and Thomas Schøtt is an example of a quantitative study of potential entrepreneurs' self-perceived effectiveness in the three stages of the venture process. The original data was collected in 2006 in the Danish participation in the international research project Global Entrepreneurship Monitor (GEM). Ten thousand randomly selected adults were contacted and interviewed over the telephone about their entrepreneurial activities. The authors moreover surveyed a panel of 714 entrepreneurs in Denmark. Through multiple regression modelling they found that social capital positively affects performance in terms of venture emergence and the perceived effectiveness of entrepreneurs.

Together these methodological choices are examples of how to study changes in processes, how to conceptualize, and how the changing and complex non-linear reality can be understood rather through individuals' experiences and perceptions than by studying reality as it is. Thus they present examples of methodological advance in gaining access to the dynamic processes of entrepreneurship as proclaimed in our previous books in this series.

We can now therefore give an answer to our question 'Is there any room for newness and innovation in entrepreneurship research?' in the first book in the 'European Research in Entrepreneurship' series. Even though the chapters in this book only present some examples of the European entrepreneurship research field, they clearly demonstrate how European research seems to follow the path we predicted. There is a clear tendency to proceed further from the linear understanding of entrepreneurial processes, there are promising initiatives for reconceptualizing, and new concepts are developed by adopting both conceptual and methodological views from neighbouring fields of science. We hope that researchers, practitioners and policymakers will recognize this as an opportunity to adopt these new ideas and develop them further in renewing their practices. We further hope that this book will provide educators with some new ideas to be adopted in their teaching in order to help their students to acquire entrepreneurial competences. For us it has been a privilege to work with so many junior and senior researchers in the European university network on entrepreneurship research in editing this book. These new ideas also give us positive prospects to develop the ESU network further.

REFERENCES

Fayolle, A. and P. Kyrö (eds) (2008), *Entrepreneurship Research in Europe: the Dynamics between Entrepreneurship, Environment and Education*, Cheltenham, UK and Northampton, MA, USA: Edward Elgar.
Fayolle, A., J. Uljin and P. Kyrö (eds) (2005), *Entrepreneurship Research in Europe: Perspectives and Outcomes*, Cheltenham, UK and Northampton, MA, USA: Edward Elgar.
Snow, R.E., L. Corno and D. Jackson (1996), 'Individual differences in affective and conative functions', in D.C. Berliner and R.C. Calfee (eds), *Handbook of Educational Psychology*, New York: Simon & Schuster Macmillan, pp. 243–310.

PART I

The Process of Becoming and Learning to
Become an Entrepreneur

1. Does education matter? The characteristics and performance of businesses started by recent university graduates

Colin Mason, Stephen Tagg and Sara Carter

INTRODUCTION

> In England, there are almost no famous entrepreneurs who went to university. Almost all left school at 15 or 16.
>
> (Sir Richard Branson, quoted in *The Globe and Mail (Canada)*, 14 September 2006)

Encouraging graduate entrepreneurship has emerged as a key element in the UK government's enterprise agenda throughout the present administration. The Dearing Report (1997) was the first to suggest that Higher Education Institutes (HEIs) should consider the scope to encourage entrepreneurship through their educational programmes. This proposal was reinforced by the Lambert Review (2003) which noted the importance of entrepreneurial skills especially for science and technology students. The Department of Trade and Industry's Science Enterprise Challenge Fund in 1999 provided universities with funding for entrepreneurship education for science and engineering students (as well as for other knowledge transfer activities). Several business schools offer entrepreneurship courses to their own students. There are growing calls for entrepreneurship education in the disciplines that comprise the creative industries (DCMS, 2006). Within the context of graduate employability, the Higher Education Academy has supported a number of pilot projects introducing enterprise and entrepreneurship into mainstream curricula including subjects such as engineering, languages, religious studies and the performing arts. To promote graduate entrepreneurship across the board, the National Council for Graduate Entrepreneurship (NCGE) was established in 2004 with funding from the Small Business Service and Department for Education and Skills. Its mission is, first, to increase the number of graduates giving serious thought to starting a business and second, to increase the number and sustainability of graduate start-up businesses.

The consequence of these developments is that 'entrepreneurship is now part of the Higher Education landscape' (Hannon, 2006a: 297). A recent survey found that 86 out of 102 UK HEIs offered entrepreneurship courses or 'experiences', 79 of them at undergraduate level (McKeown et al., 2006). The focus of these activities is primarily business and science and engineering students (Bilen et al., 2005) and, occasionally, vocational studies students (Hynes, 1996). Many courses are based around action learning (Rasmussen and Sørheim, 2006) and placements which give students experience of working in a small business (Greenbank, 2002; Cooper et al., 2004). In some universities it is possible to take an entrepreneurship major (Kolvereid and Moen, 1997). Some universities offer specific postgraduate courses for graduates who intend to start their own business (Jones-Evans et al., 2000). There are also extensive extra-curricular activities (for example entrepreneurship clubs) (Edwards and Muir, 2005) and a range of other programmes that students participate in, such as STEP (a small business placement scheme) (Westhead et al., 2000), business plan competitions and summer schools (Collins and Robertson, 2003). These courses and associated activities have two main objectives: first, to increase entrepreneurial aspirations amongst students by promoting the notion that starting your own business is a legitimate career path for graduates; and second, to develop entrepreneurial competences amongst students. Some proponents would add a third objective: to enhance the employability of their students (Botham and Mason, 2007).

However, it is extremely difficult to find any explicit justification for this emphasis on encouraging graduate entrepreneurship. From the government's perspective, encouraging graduate entrepreneurship is simply one way in which the UK's enterprise culture can be enhanced. Entrepreneurial skills and motivation are seen as being central to the dynamism of a commercial society (Gavron et al., 1998). One specific concern is the preponderance of sole traders and single person businesses, and the lack of SMEs that achieve significant growth. Although the point is not made explicit there is a clear inference that graduate entrepreneurs are expected to start better quality businesses, and specifically ones which grow. Graduate entrepreneurs are also seen as essential if the UK is to compete effectively in the knowledge economy (Department of Trade and Industry, 2001). Founders of knowledge-intensive and technology-based firms are likely to require graduate education in science, engineering and life sciences. But the evidence base which might support an emphasis on encouraging graduate entrepreneurship is extremely sketchy. In summary, it is not possible with our present knowledge base to argue that support-ing graduate entrepreneurship is justified on the grounds that businesses started by graduates have greater economic impact. Without an evidence base the emphasis that is currently being placed on support for graduate enterprise is an act of faith. This need for an improved evidence base is also emphasized by the NCGE (Hannon, 2006b).

The aim of this chapter is to apply some empirical evidence to this issue by drawing on the most recent (2006) Federation of Small Business mem-bership survey, *Lifting the Barriers to Growth in UK Small Business* (Carter et al., 2006), the largest survey of small businesses in the UK, with 19 000 usable responses. This sample size allows considerable scope for com-parative analysis. It presents evidence on two key issues. First, whether the businesses which recent graduates start are distinctive from businesses owned both by young non-graduates and by older graduates (in terms of sectors, size, gender, location, route into business, ownership form, family involvement). Second, whether businesses run by recent graduates perform better than other businesses. This evidence will allow a rather more informed judgement on the appropriateness of specifically targeting university graduates to become entrepreneurs.

ENTREPRENEURSHIP AND HIGHER EDUCATION

The available evidence which might support a policy of fostering graduate entrepreneurship is remarkably limited. There is no empirical evidence in the entrepreneurship literature to support the claim that there is a posi-tive relationship between education and entrepreneurship. Indeed, several studies, particularly US studies, suggest that in developed countries the relationship may be non-linear (Davidsson and Honig, 2003; Wiklund and Shepherd, 2005). In other words, some education has a positive impact on entrepreneurship but there comes a point when 'too much' education discourages entrepreneurial activity (Reynolds, 1997; Wagner, 2006). This may be because higher education offers greater employment oppor-tunities. So, as Reynolds (2007: 24) comments, 'it is not clear that more education will increase the tendency to enter into the start-up process'. However, this conclusion does not hold everywhere, since evidence from both Sweden and Scotland suggests that education has a positive impact on entrepreneurship along the entire educational spectrum (Delmar and Davidsson, 2000; Davidsson, 2006; Levie, 2006). Moreover, US studies indicate that the impact of education on entrepreneurship is affected by ethnicity, with black and Hispanic graduates being more than twice as likely to be involved in a start-up than their white counterparts (Reynolds,

2007). Finally, the effect of education on entrepreneurship is also shown to have sector-specific effects (Wiklund and Shepherd, 2005).

The propensity for graduates to start businesses is very low. UK statistics on the status of graduates at the end of the year in which they graduate indicate that only 2.3 per cent are self-employed (2.9 per cent if only first degree graduates are considered). Creative arts and design graduates are the most likely to be self-employed (Graduate Prospects, 2006). This compares with two-thirds of graduates who are in employment, and a further 20 per cent who are engaged in further study. However, this evidence is of limited value as many new graduates are still considering their future and so are often engaged in activities which they regard as temporary or stop-gap. More significantly, it is probable that those graduates who are intent on an entrepreneurial career will seek business experience before starting a business. Indeed, tracking of the 'class of '99' found that the rate of self-employment increased from 1.44 per cent in July 1999 to 2.5 per cent in November 2004 (Greene and Saridakis, 2007). Canadian evidence has also indicated that graduate self-employment rates for both males and females rise between the second and fifth year after graduation (Finnie and Laporte, 2003). Thus, the low proportion of graduates who are classified as self-employed at the end of the year in which they graduated would not seem to be a problem which, on its own, justifies policy intervention.

Cross-sectional data indicates that graduates are more likely to start businesses than non-graduates. Analysis of the 2004 Global Entrepreneurship Monitor (GEM) for the UK indicates that the total entrepreneurial activity (TEA) rate[1] amongst graduates is 8.1 per cent compared with 5.3 per cent for non-graduates. Although there are regional variations in the graduate TEA rate, it is higher than that for non-graduates in every region. Both male graduates and female graduates have higher TEAs than their non-graduate counterparts (11.0 per cent vs 7.2 per cent for males and 4.6 per cent vs 3.6 per cent for women), although the difference is smaller amongst women. Separating the TEA into its component parts reveals that graduates are more likely than non-graduates to be nascent entrepreneurs (4.5 per cent vs 2.7 per cent) and are also more likely to have recently started a new business (3.9 per cent vs 2.7 per cent) (Brooksbank and Jones-Evans, 2005).

The higher rate of entrepreneurial activity amongst graduates is supported by other evidence. The Labour Force Survey indicates that 12.6 per cent of first degree graduates and 12.7 per cent of those with postgraduate qualifications were self-employed in the December 2003–February 2004 period. However, this includes graduates who are running or are partners in professional practices (for example, accountants, lawyers, chartered engineers). It also includes sole traders, sub-contractors and freelancers who together account for close to half of the graduate self-employed (ISBA Consortium, 2004). The British Social Attitudes Survey found that 12 per cent of graduates were self-employed – a higher proportion than for the non-degree population. However, Levie et al. (2003) found that alumni of the University of Strathclyde were no more likely than the Scottish adult population as a whole to start their own business or to have recently started one. Their study also found that there were significant differences in entrepreneurial activity by discipline, with the highest TEA rate for engineers and the lowest for scientists.

GEM also indicates that graduates are more likely than non-graduates to know an entrepreneur, more likely to think that there are good start-up opportunities, and more likely to think they have the skills to start a business, all factors which are associated with entrepreneurship. However, this is offset by evidence that graduates are more deterred than non-graduates by fear of failure, are less likely to think that starting a business is a good career move, and less likely to think that entrepreneurs have high status. Nevertheless, graduates are more likely than non-graduates to expect to start a business in the next three years.

GEM further reveals that graduates are more entrepreneurial than non-graduates in every age band except 25–34, although the difference is not significant. The most entrepreneurial age bands for graduates are 35–44 and 45–54, whereas for non-graduates it is 25–34 and 35–44 (Brooksbank and Jones-Evans, 2005). The Strathclyde alumni study found that entrepreneurial activity was more evenly concentrated across the age groups amongst the alumni sample whereas it was biased towards the younger age groups (< 35 years old) in the general population (Levie et al., 2003). This evidence suggests that graduates and non-graduates have different routes into entrepreneurship. It may also suggest that graduates are often working for between 10 and 20 years before starting a business, by which time any university influence is likely to have worn off.

But evidence on the quality of the businesses started by graduates and non-graduates is conspicuous by its absence. Specifically, we do not know whether graduate entrepreneurs are distinctive in terms of the types of businesses that they start or how these businesses perform. Only one-third of self-employed graduates (4 per cent of all graduates) are running businesses which employ other people (cited in ISBA Consortium, 2004). However, this feature is a characteristic of the small business sector as a whole. In terms of sector, GEM data indicates that graduate entrepreneurs are concentrated in business services (34 per cent) and health, education and social services (28 per cent). These sectors are less significant for non-graduate entrepreneurs. Non-graduates are more likely to be in retail (22 per cent), agriculture, construction and consumer services (Brooksbank and Jones-Evans, 2005). Businesses started by Strathclyde alumni were biased towards the business services sector (61 per cent vs 42 per cent in the general population sample) where many operate as small professional consultancies. Perhaps for this reason the study also found only partial support for the hypothesis that graduate entrepreneurs would have higher growth ambitions for their business (Levie et al., 2003).

There is very little qualitative evidence to complement these statistics. McLarty (2005) reported on a small scale (n = 39) of graduate entrepreneurs in the east of England. Most started within two years of graduation.[2] The degree was a strong influence on the business idea (74 per cent) and the decision to become an entrepreneur was made before leaving university. Family influence, including self-employed parents or other close relatives, and support were important. Both Fletcher (1999) and Rosa (2003) have tracked graduate entrepreneurs who participated in the Scottish Graduate Enterprise Programme (which ran from 1983–91). This is an elite group of graduate entrepreneurs who had received intensive training and support. Nevertheless, according to Rosa (2003: 451) those who started businesses were 'far removed as a group from the ideal of high performance enterprises. Most of the businesses started were small, and were often self-employed businesses at the time . . . The types of businesses were unimaginative and routine, and did not access the "cutting edge" knowledge area . . . flowing from universities . . . '.

In summary, the existing knowledge base provides little support for the present emphasis on graduate entrepreneurship. Graduates are already more likely than non-graduates to start businesses, although there is probably scope to raise the level of entrepreneurial activity among women graduates. The lower TEA rate amongst graduates in the 25–34 year age band, which is some 30 per cent below the rate for the 35–44 and 45–54 year age groups, might give grounds for attempting to raise the entrepreneurship rate amongst recent graduates. But crucially, there is no evidence that businesses started by graduates have greater economic impact.

METHODOLOGY AND DATA

This chapter is based on responses to the 2005–06 biennial survey of the Federation of Small Businesses' (FSB) membership (Carter et al., 2006). The FSB biennial surveys are among the largest non-government business surveys in the UK, and they are designed to reflect the attitudes

Table 1.1   Young graduate and young non-graduate business owners: age and qualifications

Age group	Degree level or above (%)	Professional qualifications below degree level (%)	Age 16 school qualifications (%)	Age 18 school qualifications (%)	No educational qualifications (%)
Under 21	29	8	29	38	4
22–34	37	25	24	23	6
35–44	31	24	28	17	8
45–54	29	27	24	17	11
55–64	26	27	21	13	19
65+	23	29	17	14	21
No response	31	33	22	14	9
Total	29	26	24	16	13

and opinions of small business owners and inform local, regional and national policy towards the small business sector. Data were collected by a postal survey questionnaire distributed to 169418 FSB members in September 2005. The questionnaire was also available to complete on the Internet, and was available on request in six languages. In total, 18939 usable responses were received by the cut-off date, a response rate of 11.17 per cent. Comparison with VAT statistics indicates that FSB respondents are fairly typical in terms of region and sector (agriculture is under-represented, manufacturing is over-represented). Some deviation is expected since only 77 per cent of FSB respondents are registered for VAT.

The survey included 5230 graduate business owners, 27.6 per cent of the total respondents. This comprises 453 young graduates (under 35) who make up 39.2 per cent of all respondents under 35 years old, and 4777 older graduates (35+). The 703 young non-graduate business owners and 11160 older non-graduate business owners provide comparisons. Graduates are slightly over-represented amongst the younger age groups. However, the association between age and educational qualifications is not dramatic (Table 1.1). The 22–34 year age band includes 37 per cent of graduates, compared with 31 per cent in the 35–44 year age band, 29 per cent in the 45–54 year age band and 26 per cent in the 55–64 year age band. There is a rather stronger relationship between age and lack of qualifications, with the proportion of business owners with no educational qualifications ranging from under 10 per cent amongst those under 45 to around 20 per cent in the over-55 group.

COMPARING YOUNG GRADUATE AND YOUNG NON-GRADUATE BUSINESS OWNERS

There are clear differences between young graduate and young non-graduate business owners in terms of the number of years as a business owner and the length of time that they have owned their present business. Young non-graduates have been in business for longer and have owned their present business for longer (Table 1.2). Similar proportions of young graduate and young non-graduate business owners started their businesses immediately after leaving education (69 per cent in each case).

However, graduate business owners are statistically more likely to start their business more quickly after leaving full-time education than non-graduates (Table 1.3). Thus, the longer period of time that non-graduates have been in business is entirely attributable to their greater number of years in the labour market. Moreover, young non-graduates have had more jobs than young graduate business owners (59 per cent more than five jobs, compared with 44 per cent for graduates). There are no differences in routes into business, with identical proportions of graduates and non-graduates starting their business from scratch (79 per cent) and buying a going concern (12 per cent).

When measured in terms of employment, businesses owned by young graduates employ slightly more people (Table 1.4). However, there are no significant differences in the size of businesses owned by young graduates

Table 1.2 *Young graduate and young non-graduate business owners: time in business*

	Years as a business owner*				Years owning present business*			
	Young graduate		Young non-graduate		Young graduate		Young non-graduate	
	Count	%	Count	%	Count	%	Count	%
Less than 1 year	56	12	88	13	67	15	120	17
1–3 years	199	44	255	36	237	52	280	40
4–5 years	78	17	132	19	75	17	126	18
6–10 years	91	20	145	21	60	13	115	16
Over 10 years	26	6	81	12	11	2	58	8
Total	450	100	701	100	450	100	699	100

Note: * The chi-square statistic is significant at the 0.05 level.

Table 1.3   Young graduate and young non-graduate business owners: length of time after leaving full-time education before starting their business

Elapsed years	Young graduates		Young non-graduates	
	Count	%	Count	%
No break	64	14	62	9
1	34	8	29	4
2	46	10	39	6
3–5	119	26	95	14
6–10	147	33	238	34
11 and above	35	8	228	32
Total	445	100	691	100

Note: The chi-square statistic is significant at the 0.05 level.

Table 1.4   Businesses of young graduates and young non-graduates: current employment

Number of employees	Young graduates		Young non-graduates	
	Count	%	Count	%
0	27	6	55	8
1	67	15	92	13
2–4	181	40	263	37
5–9	74	16	164	23
10–49	95	21	122	17
50–99	8	2	4	1
100+	1	0	3	0
Total	453	100	703	100

Note: The chi-square statistic is significant at the 0.05 level.

and young non-graduates when measured in sales, with 51 per cent of businesses owned by young graduates having a turnover of £100 000 or less, compared with 53 per cent of businesses owned by young non-graduates. At the other end of the size distribution the proportion of businesses with a turnover of over £1 million was the same for both groups (5 per cent). Businesses owned by young graduates are more likely to be Limited Liability Companies (56 per cent vs 44 per cent), which the UK Treasury interprets as indicating a 'serious' small business, whereas businesses

Table 1.5   Businesses owned by young graduates and young non-graduates: sector differences

Sector	Young graduates		Young non-graduates	
	Count	%	Count	%
Agriculture	8	2	18	3
Mining and utilities	1	0	9	1
Manufacturing	27	6	79	11
Construction	38	8	76	11
Retail, wholesale and motor trades	96	21	202	29
Hotels and restaurants	38	8	41	6
Transport and communications	6	1	32	5
Financial services	17	4	22	3
Business services	154	34	135	19
Education	10	2	9	1
Health and social work	20	4	13	2
Personal services	8	2	44	6
Non-responses	30	7	23	3
Total	453	100	703	100

Note: The chi-square statistic is significant at the 0.05 level.

owned by non-graduates are more likely to be sole traders (41 per cent vs 31 per cent) or partnerships (14 per cent vs 11 per cent). Differences in the proportion of businesses registered for value-added tax (71 per cent for graduate businesses and 69 per cent for non-graduate businesses) are not statistically significant.

Turning to sector, the differences between young graduate and young non-graduate-owned businesses are unambiguous. Non-graduate business owners are more prominent in manufacturing, construction, retail and personal services, whereas graduate business owners are much more prominent in business services (Table 1.5). These differences are also reflected in the type of business premises. Graduate-owned businesses are more likely to be located in offices (25 per cent vs 15 per cent), whereas non-graduate-owned businesses are more likely to be located in a factory, workshop or business unit (9 per cent vs 19 per cent). Despite these sectoral differences there are no differences between graduates and non-graduates in terms of their self-evaluation of the strengths and weaknesses of their businesses: product/service quality, customer service, reputation and quality of staff were rated as strengths while distribution channels and cash flow/financial performance were regarded as the greatest weakness.

Table 1.6   Businesses owned by young graduates and young non-graduates: ownership by gender

Ownership	Young graduates		Young non-graduates	
	Count	%	Count	%
Male 100%	182	40	369	52
Male majority (51–99%)	38	8	52	7
Equal male and female ownership	122	27	141	20
Female majority (51–99%)	12	3	13	2
Female 100%	95	21	124	18
Total	449	100	699	100

Note: The chi-square statistic is significant at the 0.05 level.

Comparing businesses owned by young graduates and young non-graduates reveals an important gender effect, with graduate businesses less likely to be 100 per cent male owned and more likely to be equal male–female ownership or female owned (Table 1.6). However, there are no statistically significant differences between businesses owned by graduates and non-graduates in terms of the involvement of family members in either the ownership or management of the business.

The majority of both young graduates and young non-graduates owned only one business (78 per cent vs 80 per cent). Only a minority, 23 per cent of graduates and 25 per cent of non-graduates, had previously owned a business. For the majority, the business is their only source of income (74 per cent). One in ten respondents has income from another business and a further one in ten has income from employment (11 per cent of graduate entrepreneurs and 9 per cent of non-graduates). The only significant difference in income sources is that 13 per cent of non-graduate business owners, but only 4 per cent of graduate business owners, have income from family tax credit, suggesting that a higher proportion of non-graduates are running businesses which generate low incomes for their owners.

There is no difference between young graduate and young non-graduate-owned businesses in terms of their recent (two-year) growth in sales, profitability or employment. However, a higher proportion of graduates report that the income that they have taken from the business has gone up (26 per cent vs 16 per cent). Differences in growth may emerge in the future with graduate business owners significantly more growth oriented: 23 per cent want their business to grow rapidly and 61 per cent want to expand moderately (compared with 20 per cent and 58 per cent for non-graduate business owners). This is reflected in employment projections,

Table 1.7   Businesses owned by young graduates and young non-graduates: proportion of sales to the local and UK market

	% annual sales to local area*				% annual sales to UK market*			
	Young graduates		Young non-graduates		Young graduates		Young non-graduates	
	Count	%	Count	%	Count	%	Count	%
None	24	6	22	3	40	11	89	18
1–25%	116	29	127	20	110	32	171	35
26–50%	69	17	92	14	33	9	36	7
51–75%	82	21	155	24	41	12	42	9
76–100%	107	26	248	39	125	36	147	30
Total	398	100	644	100	349	100	485	100

Note: * The chi-square statistic is significant at the 0.05 level.

with graduate business owners more likely to anticipate a definite increase in employment (26 per cent vs 20 per cent). Businesses owned by graduates are also less dependent on their local market and more likely to be serving the UK market (Table 1.7). However, there are no differences in the proportion of graduate and non-graduate businesses with sales in the EU or rest of the world.

There are differences in the sources of financing used by young graduate-owned and young non-graduate-owned businesses. Graduate-owned businesses more likely to use their own savings (51 per cent vs 47 per cent), retained profits (26 per cent vs 19 per cent) and grants (12 per cent vs 6 per cent). Non-graduate business owners are more likely to use personal credit card (29 per cent vs 25 per cent), bank loan (36 per cent vs 33 per cent) and supplier credit (19 per cent vs 13 per cent). There is no difference in the proportion of graduate and non-graduate-owned businesses seeking a bank loan in the previous two years (32 per cent). Graduates are more likely to have had their loan approved (87 per cent vs 84 per cent) but the difference is not statistically significant. However, non-graduates are more likely to be deterred from seeking a bank loan for fear of rejection (21 per cent vs 13 per cent), a difference which is statistically significant.

The sources of advice used by young graduate and young non-graduate business owners are remarkably similar, notably their accountant (52 per cent in both cases), family (46 per cent of graduates, 40 per cent of non-graduates), solicitor (32 per cent in both cases) and other business owners (23 per cent in both cases). Graduates and non-graduates tended to have similar levels of satisfaction with the sources of advice used. However, some

Table 1.8   Young graduate and young non-graduate business owners: proportion of household wealth invested in their business

	Young graduates		Young non-graduates	
	Count	%	Count	%
Up to 25%	243	58	340	54
26–50%	76	18	131	21
51–75%	46	11	88	14
76–100%	52	12	74	12
Total	417	100	633	100

Note: Differences not statistically significant.

differences are apparent. Specifically, graduate business owners were more satisfied than non-graduates with government-funded business support (19 per cent vs 13 per cent) and with advice from their family (19 per cent vs 13 per cent), whereas non-graduate business owners were more satisfied with the advice that they got from their banks (25 per cent vs 19 per cent). Non-graduate business owners were significantly less aware than graduates of government business support services (52 per cent vs 47 per cent). Otherwise, the reasons for not using government-funded business support services were similar in each case – confusion over service provision, no need of support, inappropriate for my business and better advice from elsewhere.

By investing their own personal wealth in their business, business owners expose themselves and their family to some degree of potential personal financial risk. Both young graduate and young non-graduate business owners had very similar levels of household wealth invested in the business, with only a minority (12 per cent in each case) being significantly exposed, with more than 75 per cent of their household wealth invested in their business (Table 1.8).

However, the consequences of becoming insolvent are likely to be more severe for non-graduates, with 17 per cent anticipating bankruptcy in such circumstances, compared with 11 per cent of graduate business owners (Table 1.9).

Both young graduates and young non-graduates have polarized views on their financial status as business owners. Among graduate business owners 23 per cent think their financial status is a lot worse, and 23 per cent think it is a little worse, than their non-business-owning contemporaries. The proportions for non-graduate business are similar, at 19 per cent and 25 per cent respectively. At the other extreme, only 15 per cent of graduate business owners and 12 per cent of non-graduates think that their financial

Table 1.9   Young graduate and young non-graduate business owners: consequences of business insolvency

	Young graduates		Young non-graduates	
	Count	%	Count	%
My standard of living would remain unaffected	53	12	85	12
I would have to scale down my lifestyle	176	39	208	30
My basic survival and home would be under threat	165	36	273	39
I would lose everything, become bankrupt	52	11	118	17
Total	446	100	684	100

Note: The chi-square statistic is significant at the 0.05 level.

Table 1.10   Young graduate and young non-graduate business owners: perceived financial status and quality of life as a business owner

	Financial status as a business owner				Quality of life as a business owner			
	Young graduates		Young non-graduates		Young graduates		Young non-graduates	
	Count	%	Count	%	Count	%	Count	%
A lot worse	104	23	135	19	39	9	82	12
A little worse	104	23	174	25	82	18	153	22
About the same	85	19	164	23	90	20	170	24
A little better	87	19	138	20	163	36	178	25
A lot better	68	15	85	12	71	16	114	16
Total	448	100	696	100	445	100	697	100

Note: Differences are not significant at the 0.05 level.

status is a lot better as a consequence of owning their own business (Table 1.10). However, graduate business owners are more positive than non-graduates about their quality of life as business owners, with more than half thinking it is a little (36 per cent) or a lot (16 per cent) better, compared with 41 per cent of non-graduate business owners (Table 1.10).

Overall, therefore, there are surprisingly few differences between the businesses started by young (under 35 years old) graduates and non-graduates. Indeed, just five differences emerge. First, graduates become business owners more quickly after leaving education than non-graduates. The corollary of this is that graduates have less business experience (years as employees, number of jobs) than their non-graduate counterparts. Second, graduate businesses are more likely to be owned or co-owned by women. Third, graduate-owned businesses are more 'serious' in the sense that they are more likely to be limited companies. They also employ more people but there are no differences on other size measures. Fourth, there are clear sectoral differences, with over one-third of graduate-owned businesses in the business services sector. Fifth, graduate-owned businesses are less dependent on their local market. But whether these differences justify the promotion of graduate businesses is debatable when there is no consistent evidence that graduate-owned businesses have a greater economic impact than those started by non-graduates. Indeed, what is more striking from this comparison is that there is a significant minority of non-graduate businesses that appear to be marginal as indicated by the higher proportion of non-graduate owners with income from family tax credit, the greater proportion of non-graduate business owners who would experience financial hardship in the event that their business became insolvent, and the higher proportion of non-graduate business owners who are dissatisfied with their quality of life. Arguably this could justify an emphasis on helping non-graduate business owners.

COMPARING YOUNGER AND OLDER GRADUATE BUSINESS OWNERS

The second part of the analysis compares younger (under 35) and older (over 35) graduates in order to see whether there has been any change in the nature of graduate entrepreneurship. As expected, younger graduate business owners have been in business for a much shorter period of time than their older counterparts and have owned their current business for a much shorter time. There are no significant differences in terms of the route into business (started from scratch, inherited, bought, and so on). However, younger graduates are starting businesses more quickly after graduating. They are twice as likely to start their business immediately (14 per cent vs 7 per cent) or within three years (18 per cent vs 4 per cent) after leaving education. Younger graduates have also had fewer jobs (9 per cent none, 24 per cent one, compared with 3 per cent and 13 per cent).

As would be expected, businesses owned by older graduates are larger in terms of sales and employment than those started by younger graduates. However, there are some qualitative differences between the two cohorts. First, the businesses of older graduates are more likely to be partnerships (14 per cent vs 11 per cent) whereas younger graduates are more likely to be sole traders (31 per cent vs 28 per cent). The businesses of older graduates are also more likely to be registered for VAT (77 per cent vs 71 per cent). Second, businesses owned by older graduates are more likely to be home-based (39 per cent vs 35 per cent). Third, businesses owned by older graduates are more likely to be in manufacturing (9 per cent vs 6 per cent) and construction (10 per cent vs 8 per cent) sectors and less likely to be in retail, wholesale and motor trades (16 per cent vs 21 per cent), hotels and restaurants (8 per cent vs 5 per cent) and business services (34 per cent vs 31 per cent). There are no significant differences in the competitive strengths of businesses owned by younger and older graduates nor in terms of their involvement in e-commerce.

Businesses owned by younger graduates are more likely to be 100 per cent female-owned (21 per cent vs 13 per cent). In terms of family ownership, businesses owned by older graduates are more likely to have the spouse as co-owner (41 per cent vs 25 per cent) and co-manager (29 per cent vs 23 per cent). Businesses owned by younger graduates, in contrast, are more likely to have parents and siblings as co-owners or co-managers, although in all cases the proportions are below 10 per cent. Older graduates are more likely to be portfolio business owners (31 per cent vs 22 per cent) and have been serial entrepreneurs (that is owning more than one business) (46 per cent vs 23 per cent). Older graduates are also more likely to have other income sources, including income from other businesses (17 per cent vs 10 per cent).

The businesses owned by younger graduates are clearly more growth-oriented than those owned by older graduates, with more young graduate businesses reporting significantly increased sales in the previous two years (42 per cent vs 29 per cent), increased profits (29 per cent vs 22 per cent) and income (26 per cent vs 16 per cent). However, there are no differences in employment growth. Younger graduate business owners are also more likely to anticipate future growth than their older counterparts, with 23 per cent wanting to grow rapidly and 61 per cent wanting to grow moderately, compared with 14 per cent and 52 per cent respectively of older graduates. Businesses owned by younger graduates are more oriented to local markets and less oriented to the UK market. The businesses of younger graduates are also less likely to be selling into the EU and the rest of the world.

Younger graduate business owners use more sources of funding than older graduates, including both a range of personal sources, notably family (29 per cent vs 11 per cent), personal credit card (25 per cent vs 19 per cent) and own savings (51 per cent vs 41 per cent), and formal sources, notably bank overdraft (47 per cent vs 38 per cent), company credit card (21 per cent vs 16 per cent) and bank loan (33 per cent vs 24 per cent). Older graduates are more likely to use retained profits (40 per cent vs 26 per cent). Younger graduate business owners are also more likely to have sought a bank loan in the previous two years (33 per cent vs 26 per cent). There is no significant difference in loan approval (87 per cent vs 90 per cent). However, younger graduate business owners are significantly more likely to be deterred from seeking a bank loan for fear of rejection (13 per cent vs 9 per cent).

Younger graduate business owners make greater use of most of the available advice sources. Their main sources of advice are their account-ant, family and lawyer, with their use of family being significantly greater than for older graduates (46 per cent vs 18 per cent) (see McLarty, 2005). Younger graduates were more likely to give lack of awareness as the main reason for not using government-supported sources of business advice (29 per cent vs 22 per cent), whereas older graduates were more likely to give inappropriateness and better advice offered elsewhere as reasons. Younger graduate business owners are generally more satisfied with sources of advice than older graduates, notably other business owners (39 per cent vs 26 per cent), family (37 per cent vs 17 per cent) and customers (30 per cent vs 22 per cent). Younger graduate business owners are also more satisfied than their older counterparts with government-funded business support.

There is no difference between younger and older graduates in terms of the proportion of household wealth which they have committed to the business. However, the proportion of business owners who would become bankrupt if their business went into insolvency is slightly higher among younger graduates than older ones (11 per cent vs 7 per cent). The net balance of both younger and older entrepreneurs who consider their financial position to be worse as a business owner is negative in both cases (−12 and −5), although the differences are not significant. In contrast, the net balance for quality of life is positive in both cases (+25 and +23), and the differences are again not significant.

The kinds of differences between the businesses of younger and older graduates are largely those which would be anticipated and relate to the length of time in business, age of the business and involvement in multiple business ventures. However, there are four differences of note. First, grad-uates are going into business for themselves sooner after completing their university studies, but with less employment experience. Second, more women graduates are now becoming business owners. Third, younger graduate business owners make significant use of their family, particularly as a source of business advice and for funding, and less often as a co-owner or partner. This is an important finding its own right but because of the effect of time on the older graduate cohort it is not clear whether it reflects a departure from the past. Finally, businesses owned by young graduates have recorded greater growth in the recent past and have greater growth ambitions.

CONCLUSIONS

Entrepreneurship education is a growing activity in UK universities as well as in many other countries, although it is still well below US levels (Finkle et al., 2006; Kuratko, 2005), prompted largely by government exhortation and funding initiatives. However, the rationale for singling out university students as a specific target has never been articulated and the implicit assumption that graduates will create 'better' businesses is unproven. This chapter, which accesses the largest SME survey in the UK, is an attempt to improve the evidence base on this highly relevant topic.

Graduates are clearly starting different types of businesses from those of non-graduates, in terms of sector. However, although graduates are more likely to start Limited Liability Companies, this does not translate into size or growth differences. The businesses owned by younger graduates have grown faster than those of older graduates, but this might be explained in terms of the greater significance of consultancy-type businesses owned by older graduates.

Graduate business owners are more likely to be women than non-graduate business owners. Younger women graduates are also more likely than older women graduates to be business owners. However, whether this is because younger women graduates are more likely to start businesses or because women entrepreneurs have a higher exit rate cannot be determined from this data. Moreover, these contrasts are also likely to be influenced by the increase in higher education opportunities for women over the past twenty years which has resulted in an increase in the supply of women graduates.

Finally, and perhaps most importantly, graduates are starting businesses more quickly after leaving education than in the past and younger graduates are starting businesses more quickly after leaving education than non-graduates. Moreover, there is no evidence that this trend is likely to be affected by rising student debt (NCGE, 2006; Greene and Saridakis, 2007). The consequence is that many graduates lack what Timmons (1999: 46) terms 'the 50 000 chunks of business experience' which he argues is essential for successful entrepreneurship. This compressed transition between leaving higher education and starting a business has several implications for both entrepreneurship education and the way in which graduate entrepreneurs are supported. The main implication for entrepreneurship education is the need to focus on experiential learning and placements or internships to compensate for the lack of employment experience. This could include encouraging students to start part-time businesses while studying. In this regard, Canada's government-funded 'summer companies' programme, which supports students to establish their own businesses in the summer vacation, may be worth consideration. It also suggests that universities need to be more engaged in supporting their young graduate entrepreneurs, notably, by linking them to more experienced alumni to provide coaching, mentoring and advice.

NOTES

1. The Total Entrepreneurial Activity (TEA) index indicates the percentage of the labour force actively involved in setting up a business, or being the owner/manager of a business which is less than 42 months old.
2   This may be influenced by the use of the Prince's Youth Business Trust as one means of identifying the sample. The age profile which ranged from 20–38 was skewed towards younger graduates.

REFERENCES

Bilen, S.G., E.C. Kisenwether, S.E. Rzasa and J.C. Wise (2005), 'Developing and assessing students' entrepreneurial skills and mindset', *Journal of Engineering Education*, **94**(2), 233–43.
Botham, R. and C. Mason (2007), 'Good practice in enterprise development in UK higher education', NCGE Report 004/2007.
Brooksbank, D. and D. Jones-Evans (2005), 'Graduate entrepreneurship in the UK 2004: a preliminary policy paper based on GEM 2004 data', NCGE Research Report 002/2005.
Carter, S., C. Mason and S. Tagg (2006), *Lifting The Barriers to Growth in UK Small Businesses,* London: Federation of Small Business.
Collins, A. and M. Robertson (2003), 'The entrepreneurial summer school as a successful model for teaching enterprise', *Education and Training*, **45**(6), 324–30.
Cooper, S., C. Bottomley and J. Gordon (2004), 'Stepping out of the classroom and up the ladder of learning: an experimental learning approach to entrepreneurship education', *Industry and Higher Education*, **18**(1), 11–22.
Davidsson, P. (ed.) (2006), 'Nascent entrepreneurship', *Foundations and Trends in Entrepreneurship*, **2**(1), 1–179.
Davidsson, P. and B. Honig (2003), 'The role of social and human capital among nascent entrepreneurs', *Journal of Business Venturing*, **18**, 301–31.

DCMS (2006), *Developing Entrepreneurship for the Creative Industries: The Role of Higher and Further Education*, London: Department for Culture, Media and Sport, Creative Industries Division.

Dearing, R. (1997), *Higher Education in the Learning Society*, London: Department for Education and Science.

Delmar, F. and P. Davidsson (2000), 'Where do they come from? Prevalence and characteristics of nascent entrepreneurs', *Entrepreneurship and Regional Development*, **12**, 1–23.

Department of Trade and Industry (2001), *Prosperity for All*, London: DTI.

Edwards, L.-J. and E.J. Muir (2005), 'Promoting entrepreneurship at the University of Glamorgan through formal and informal learning', *Journal of Small Business and Enterprise Development*, **12**(4), 613–26.

Finkle, T.A., D.F. Kuratko and M.G. Goldsby (2006), 'An examination of entrepreneurship centres in the United States: a national survey', *Journal of Small Business Management*, **44**(2), 184–206.

Finnie, R. and C. Laporte (2003), 'Setting up shop: self-employment among Canadian college and university graduates', *Relations Industrielles/Industrial Relations*, **58**(1), 3–32.

Fletcher, M. (1999), 'Promoting entrepreneurship as a career option', *Journal of European Industrial Training*, **23**(3), 127–39.

Gavron, R., M. Cowling, G. Holtham and A. Westall (1998), *The Entrepreneurial Society*, London: IPPR.

Graduate Prospects (2006), 'Graduates in self-employment', NCGE Research Report 001/2006.

Greenbank, P. (2002), 'Undergraduate work experience: an alternative approach using micro businesses', *Entrepreneurship and Training*, **44**(6), 261–70.

Greene, F.J. and G. Saridakis (2007), 'Understanding the factors influencing graduate entrepreneurship', Birmingham: NCGE Research Report 001/2007.

Hannon, P.D. (2006a), 'Teaching pigeons to dance: sense and meaning in entrepreneurship education', *Entrepreneurship and Training*, **48**(5), 296–308.

Hannon, P.D. (2006b), 'Graduate entrepreneurship in the UK: defining a research and education policy framework', NCGE Research Report, 012/2006.

Hynes, B. (1996), 'Entrepreneurship education and training: introducing entrepreneurship into non-business disciplines', *Journal of European Industrial Training*, **20**(8), 10–17.

Institute for Small Business Affairs Consortium (2004), 'Making the journey from student to entrepreneur: a review of the existing research into graduate entrepreneurship', NCGE Research Report 001/2004.

Jones-Evans, D., W. Williams and J. Deacon (2000), 'Developing entrepreneurial graduates: an action learning approach', *Education and Training*, **42**, 282–8.

Kolvereid, L. and O. Moen (1997), 'Entrepreneurship amongst business graduates: does a major in entrepreneurship matter?', *Journal of European Industrial Training*, **21**(4), 154–60.

Kuratko, D.F. (2005), 'The emergence of entrepreneurship education: development, trends and challenges', *Entrepreneurship Theory and Practice*, **29**(5), 577–98.

Lambert, R. (2003), *Lambert Review of Business–University Collaboration*, London: HM Treasury.

Levie, J. (2006), 'GEM Scotland 2005', Glasgow: Hunter Centre for Entrepreneurship, University of Strathclyde.

Levie, J., W. Brown and L. Galloway (2003), 'How entrepreneurial are university alumni? A Scottish and international comparison', in M.C. Jones and P. Dimitratos (eds), *Emerging Paradigms in International Entrepreneurship*, Cheltenham, UK and Northampton, MA, USA: Edward Elgar, pp. 342–64.
McKeown, J., C. Millman, S.R. Sursani, K. Smith and L.M. Martin (2006), 'UK Graduate Entrepreneurship Education in England, Scotland and Wales', Birmingham: NCGE Working Paper 030/2006.
McLarty, R. (2005), 'Entrepreneurship among graduates: towards a measured response', *Journal of Management Development*, 24, 223–38.
NCGE (2006), 'Nascent graduate entrepreneurship', Birmingham: National Council for Graduate Entrepreneurship.
Rasmussen, E.A. and R. Sørheim (2006), 'Action-based entrepreneurship education', *Technovation*, 26(2), 185–94.
Reynolds, P.D. (1997), 'Who starts new firms? Preliminary explorations of firms-in-gestation', *Small Business Economics*, 9, 449–62.
Reynolds, P.D. (2007), 'New firm formation in the United States: a PSEDI overview', *Foundation and Trends in Entrepreneurship*, 3(1), 1–155.
Rosa, P. (2003), '"Hardly likely to make the Japanese tremble". The businesses of recently graduated university and college "entrepreneurs"', *International Small Business Journal*, 21, 435–59.
Timmons, J. (1999), *New Venture Creation: Entrepreneurship in the Twenty-first Century*, Boston: Irwin-McGraw Hill.
Wagner, J. (2006), 'Nascent entrepreneurs', in S.C. Parker (ed.), *The Life Cycle of Entrepreneurial Ventures*, New York: Springer, pp. 15–37.
Westhead, P., D.J. Storey and F. Martin (2000), 'The Shell Technology Enterprise Programme: student outcomes', *Education and Training*, 42(4), 272–81.
Wiklund, J. and D. Shepherd (2005), 'Entrepreneurial orientation and small business performance: a configurational approach', *Journal of Business Venturing*, 20(1), 71–91.

2. Temporal stability of entrepreneurial intentions: a longitudinal study

Francisco Liñán, Juan C. Rodríguez-Cohard and Joaquín Guzmán

INTRODUCTION

Entrepreneurship is considered as a process that occurs over time (Bygrave, 2003; Dubini and Aldrich, 1991; Gartner, 2004; Jack and Anderson, 2002; Liñán, 2007). More recently, cognitive models have received considerable attention (Busenitz and Lau, 1996; De Carolis and Saparito, 2006; Shepherd and Zacharakis, 2003; Westhead et al., 2005). According to authors such as Baron (1998, 2004), the cognitive perspective has much to offer in the understanding of the entrepreneurial process. Entrepreneurial cognition is quite a broad concept and may include many different topics. In this sense, Baron and Ward (2004) specifically include the study of entrepreneurial intentions within it.

Several studies have applied intention models to explain the decision to start a firm. In particular, the applicability of the planned behaviour approach (Ajzen, 1991) to entrepreneurship has been consistently corroborated. A number of studies have tried to explain the factors and variables that explain intention. Empirical analyses of entrepreneurial intentions are increasingly common (Autio et al., 2001; Erikson, 1999; Kolvereid, 1996; Krueger, 1993; Krueger et al., 2000; Lee and Wong, 2004; Liñán and Chen, 2009; Peterman and Kennedy, 2003; Tkachev and Kolvereid, 1999; Veciana et al., 2005).

However, very few attempts have been made to date to analyse the temporal progression in intention (whether intention is stable over time); or the intention–behaviour link. Only in relation to effectiveness of education have changes in attitudes and intentions been measured. In this sense, Souitaris et al. (2007) used a longitudinal design to measure the effectiveness of an entrepreneurship education programme. Correspondingly, though, their study covered only a relatively short time span (five months from the first wave to the second). Similar research was carried out by Audet (2000). Longitudinal research over a longer time frame has been used in some entrepreneurship research (Aspelund et al., 2005; Hansemark, 2003; Menzies et al., 2006), but it does not test the entrepreneurial intention model.

Therefore, there is a notable lack of longitudinal long-term studies of entrepreneurial intentions. This chapter tries to fill this substantial gap in the literature. In 2004, an initial sample of final-year university students served to study the antecedents of the entrepreneurial intention (Liñán and Chen, 2009). On that occasion, results confirmed once more the applicability of the entrepreneurial intention model to entrepreneurship, explaining more than 50 per cent of the variance in the dependent variable (Liñán et al., 2005; Liñán and Santos, 2007). Contact data were requested so that a follow-up of respondents could be carried out; 84 per cent of the original sample provided those contact data. No relevant statistical differences were found between both groups (providing and not providing contact data). After three years, a new questionnaire was sent to those students measuring key intention-model constructs and inquiring about self-employment experience.

In this chapter, we address two specific research questions. The first one relates to the temporal stability of entrepreneurial intention and its motivational antecedents (attitude, subjective norm and perceived behavioural control). Since respondents to the first survey were in their final year of studies, a major change had taken place in their lives. Therefore, their perceptions might have suffered substantial variations. The temporal stability of entrepreneurial intention in this situation is a major issue. The second research question refers to the capacity of entrepreneurial intention to predict entry into self-employment. In this sense, a logistic regression model will be used to carry out a tentative analysis of the intention–behaviour link.

The chapter is organized in five additional sections. After this introduction, the next section revises the relevant theory. Section 3 describes the empirical analysis. The following section presents the results. A discussion of our findings is included in section 5. Finally, the chapter ends with a brief conclusion.

THEORETICAL BACKGROUND

The decision to become an entrepreneur may plausibly be considered as voluntary and conscious (Krueger et al., 2000). Therefore, it seems reasonable to analyse how that decision is taken. Entrepreneurship may be viewed as a process that occurs over time (Gartner et al., 1994; Kyrö and Carrier, 2005). In this sense, entrepreneurial intentions would be the first step in the evolving and, sometimes, long process of venture creation (Lee and Wong, 2004). The intention to start up, then, would be a necessary precursor to performing entrepreneurial behaviours (Fayolle et al., 2006; Kolvereid, 1996). Intention is considered the single best predictor of behaviour (Ajzen, 1991, 2001; Fishbein and Ajzen, 1975).

In turn, the intention of carrying out entrepreneurial behaviours may be affected by several factors, such as needs, values, wants, habits and beliefs (Bird, 1988; Lee and Wong, 2004). In particular, the cognitive variables influencing intention are called motivational 'antecedents' by Ajzen (1991). More favourable antecedents would increase the start-up intention (Kolvereid, 1996; Kolvereid and Isaksen, 2006; Krueger and Carsrud, 1993; Krueger et al., 2000; Liñán, 2004). Obviously, situational factors also influence entrepreneurial intentions (Ajzen, 1987; Boyd and Vozikis, 1994; Tubbs and Ekeberg, 1991). These external factors influence one's attitudes toward entrepreneurship (Krueger, 1993). Variables such as time constraints, task difficulty, and the influence of other people through social pressure could be examples of these situational factors (Lee and Wong, 2004).

According to the theory of planned behaviour (TPB), entrepreneurial intention indicates the effort that the person will make to carry out that entrepreneurial behaviour. And so it captures the three motivational factors, or antecedents, influencing behaviour (Ajzen, 1991; Liñán, 2004):

- *Attitude towards start-up (personal attitude, PA)* refers to the degree to which the individual holds a positive or negative personal valuation about being an entrepreneur (Ajzen, 2001; Autio et al., 2001; Kolvereid, 1996). It includes not only affective (I like it, it is attractive), but also evaluative considerations (it has advantages).
- *Subjective norm (SN)* measures the perceived social pressure to carry out – or not – entrepreneurial behaviours. In particular, it refers to the perception that 'reference people' would approve the decision to become an entrepreneur, or not (Ajzen, 2001).
- *Perceived behavioural control (PBC)* is defined as the perception of the ease or difficulty of becoming an entrepreneur. It is, therefore, a concept quite similar to *self-efficacy (SE)* (Bandura, 1997), and to perceived feasibility (Shapero and Sokol, 1982). All three concepts refer to the sense of capacity regarding the fulfilment of firm-creation behaviours. Nevertheless, recent work has emphasized the difference between PBC and SE (Ajzen, 2002). PBC would include not only the feeling of being able to, but also the perception about the controllability of the behaviour.

The relative contributions of these three motivational factors to explaining entrepreneurial intention are not established beforehand. The specific configuration of relationships between those constructs would have to be empirically determined for each specific behaviour (Ajzen, 1991, 2002).

There would be three relevant conditions for accurate behavioural prediction (Ajzen, 1991). First, the measured behavioural intention should correspond with the behaviour to be predicted. In this sense, the measures of intention and attitudinal constructs used here closely correspond to the behaviour of interest (starting a firm) and, therefore, this should not be a major problem. Secondly, intentions must remain stable in the interval between their assessment and observation of the behaviour. Thirdly, perceptions of behavioural control (PBC) should realistically reflect actual control over behaviour performance.

Very little research analyses the stability of intentions. One of the few exceptions is Sheeran et al. (1999), although this is not specifically related to starting up a firm. They found that the stability of intentions does play a very significant moderating role in explaining the intention–behaviour link. Nevertheless, the time interval for the two waves was very short (five weeks). Audet (2004), within an 18-month time frame, tries to assess the temporal stability of entrepreneurial intentions, concluding that it is relatively weak. Unfortunately, she did not perform any statistical test to verify her impressions. Cooper and Lucas (2007) tested the effect of two training programmes in the UK on self-efficacy, desirability and intention after six months. Each programme had effects on some of these elements, but not all. We have not found any longer-term analysis of the temporal stability of intentions.

In a meta-analysis carried out by Schuerger et al. (1989) for the somewhat similar psychological concept of personality traits, reliability was found to decline consistently over time. Thus, correlation coefficients between measures decreased asymptotically towards 0.50. However, it has been argued that attitudes are less stable than personality traits (Wiklund et al., 2003). In this sense, Souitaris et al. (2007), after five months, found correlations ranging from 0.51 (for subjective norms at T1 and T2) to 0.71 (for entrepreneurial intention). Besides, given the major change that happened to our respondents' careers and the long time-frame of our study, stability could be expected to be relatively low.

On the other hand, human capital and other demographic external factors have an influence on intentions (Boyd and Vozikis, 1994; Lee and Wong, 2004; Tubbs and Ekeberg, 1991). In particular, a greater knowledge of different entrepreneurial aspects will surely contribute to more realistic perceptions about entrepreneurial activity (Ajzen, 2002), thus indirectly influencing intentions. The relevance of experience and education has been widely highlighted, especially for the increased knowledge it provides (Cooper, 1985, 1993). In general, greater knowledge will also directly provide a greater awareness about the existence of the entrepreneurial career option (Liñán, 2004), as may be inferred by the importance attached to the existence of role models (Carrier, 2005; Matthews and Moser, 1995; Rondstadt, 1990). This latter element would have an influence on PBC and possibly on PA and SN as well (Scherer et al., 1991).

In particular, labour experience would act as a major source of practical entrepreneurial knowledge (Cooper, 1993). A major career change after graduation is, most often, acquiring labour experience. Therefore, it might be expected that this change would have affected the individual's attitudes towards entrepreneurship. The effect of these changes (and particularly acquiring labour experience) could help individuals have a more realistic PBC. This effect may, to a lesser extent, also be felt with regard to the other motivational antecedents.

Based on the theory, we expect the following hypotheses to hold:

H1:   Individuals not having labour experience at Time 1, but acquiring it after graduation will change their attitudes and intention levels at Time 2 more than those who had already labour experience at Time 1.

H2:   Individuals not having labour experience at Time 1, but acquiring it after graduation will have lower temporal stability of attitudes and intention compared to those that had already labour experience at Time 1.

H3:   Entrepreneurial intention at Time 1 significantly explains start-up behaviour of respondents.

H4:   The relationship between entrepreneurial intention at Time 1 and start-up behaviour is moderated by acquiring labour experience after graduation.

H5:   The relationship between entrepreneurial intention at Time 1 and start-up behaviour is moderated by the temporal stability of intentions.

EMPIRICAL ANALYSIS

The longitudinal analysis has been designed as a two-wave study (Raykov, 1999). Time 1 (T1) was November 2004, while Time 2 (T2) corresponds to the second half of 2007. Therefore, the time interval ranges from 33 to 37 months. For the purposes of this study, we will refer to T1 as 2004 and to T2 as 2007, assuming a three-year interval.

The T1 survey was carried out through a questionnaire administered to final-year undergraduate students. There were three reasons for the selection of this target population. First, this kind of population is commonly used in entrepreneurship research (Autio et al., 2001; Tkachev and Kolvereid, 1999; Krueger et al., 2000; Fayolle et al., 2006; Veciana et al., 2005). Secondly, according to Reynolds et al. (2002), university graduates from 25 to 34 years old make up the segment of the population showing higher probability of becoming entrepreneurs. Finally, these students are at the point of facing their own choice of professional career. Therefore, their answers could be expected to be more careful and thoughtful.

The sample at T1 was obtained from three public universities in Andalusia. This is one of the most backward regions in Spain, with per capita income below 80 per cent of the national average. Traditional culture has not favoured entrepreneurial activity, but some encouraging changes have been taking place in recent years (Maestre, 1999). Recent data show that start-up activity is comparable to other more developed regions in the country (De la Vega et al., 2007), but the relative presence of necessity entrepreneurs is larger than that of opportunity entrepreneurs.

Two of the universities (Seville and Pablo Olavide) are located within the Seville metropolitan area, with more than 1.2 million inhabitants. The third one is Jaen University, located in a middle-sized rural-area town. The final T1 sample was made up of 400 students: 46 from Jaen University, 31 from Pablo Olavide University, and the 323 remaining from Seville University. This distribution of the sample roughly corresponds to the total number of students at each university; 69.2 per cent of the sample corresponds to Management students and the rest to Economics. In particular, all the questionnaires from Jaen and Pablo Olavide Universities correspond to Management students, because the Economics degree is not on offer there. Women comprise 55 per cent of respondents, while the average age is 23.7 years old. These percentages broadly correspond with the general characteristics of the students in both degrees. Therefore, the sample can be considered as representative.

Questionnaires were administered in class, with prior permission from the lecturer. Students were briefed on the purpose of the study by a member of the research team, and then asked to volunteer to fill in the entrepreneurial intention questionnaire (EIQ). Questionnaires were in principle anonymous, but contact data were asked for if students wanted to participate in the project follow-up. A total of 336 students provided these contact data (84.0 per cent). A comparison was carried out between both groups (providing and not providing contact data), with regard to demographic variables and their scores in the scales of the constructs. The only significant differences found relate to age and labour experience.

Those providing contact data were younger (23.37 years of age vs 24.95), and had more labour experience (45.8 per cent of them had experience, versus 31.3 per cent of those not willing to participate in the follow-up). There were no differences regarding gender, degree studied, role models, parents' level of studies, parents' occupations and income level.

At T2, a new and shorter questionnaire was developed. The key constructs measuring motivational antecedents and intention were identical; some items were included to measure demographic information, employee or self-employed experience, and an update of contact data was asked for future follow-ups. In July 2007 this new questionnaire was sent by post to all participants who had provided a postal address. In September a Word version was emailed to those not providing addresses or not found (the post was returned). Finally, phone calls were made at regular intervals to non-repliers. In December 2007 we stopped accepting more answers.

A total of 118 matched questionnaires were received, but seven of them had to be discarded due to missing data. Therefore, a 33.04 per cent response rate was obtained (111 out of 336). This rate is certainly not high, but it has to be borne in mind that the time frame is three years. As a reference, Audet (2004) reports a 35.3 per cent response rate over 18 months. Similarly, Souitaris et al. (2007) report a 55.3 per cent response rate over a five-month period over a sample of students taking a course (questionnaires administered in class both at T1 and T2). Given these antecedents, we are fairly satisfied. When we look for possible statistical differences between T2 respondents and the rest, we found that only age (23.0 years of age vs 23.86 for all others) and parents' level of studies (T2 respondents have parents with a lower study level; 45.2 per cent of fathers and 56.1 per cent of mothers had only primary studies, vs 31.9 per cent and 43.2 per cent respectively for all other participants) were significant. No differences were found with respect to gender, degree studied, labour experience, role models, parents' occupations and income level, all of which were measured at T1.

Following Sheeran et al. (1999), temporal stability of non-observable variables has been measured as the within-participants Pearson correlation between scale items at T1 and T2. A correlation coefficient has been computed for each of the three motivational antecedents, plus an additional one for the intention scale. Complementarily, correlation coefficients among construct averages at T1 and T2 have also been computed.

Measures

Although results have supported the applicability of the TPB to entrepreneurship, some conflicts between the various studies have emerged. A good part of these differences may have been due to measurement issues

(Chandler and Lyon, 2001). In fact, measuring cognitive variables implies considerable difficulty (Baron, 1998). Thus, empirical tests have differed widely. Krueger et al. (2000) used single-item variables to measure each construct. Kolvereid (1996) used a belief-based measure of attitudes. More recently, Kolvereid and Isaksen (2006) have used an aggregate measure for attitudes, but a single-item one for intention. Similarly, some of these studies used an unconditional measure of intention (Autio et al., 2001; Kickul and Zaper, 2000; Kolvereid and Isaksen, 2006; Krueger et al., 2000; Zhao et al., 2005), while others forced participants to state their preferences and estimated likelihoods of pursuing a self-employment career 'as opposed to organizational employment' (Erikson, 1999; Fayolle et al., 2006; Kolvereid, 1996). Therefore, there is work to be done to produce a standard measurement instrument for entrepreneurial intention and its antecedents. In this sense, the entrepreneurial intention questionnaire (EIQ) used in this chapter is based on an integration of psychology and entrepreneurship literature, as well as previous empirical research in this field. The EIQ tries to overcome the main shortcomings of previous research instruments. The scales measuring central constructs of the planned behaviour theory are included in the appendix. The full questionnaire is available from the authors upon request. For entrepreneurial intention and its three motivational antecedents, the aggregate measure for each construct has been computed as the simple average of the items comprising each scale.

The entrepreneurial intention questionnaire (EIQ) was previously used by Liñán and Chen (2009), who validated it and assessed its psychometric properties. Entrepreneurial intention has been measured through a Likert-type scale with five items. These are general sentences indicating different aspects of intention. A similar system had already been used by Chen et al. (1998) and Zhao et al. (2005). However, Armitage and Conner (2001) identified three distinct kinds of intention measures: desire (I want to . . .), self-prediction (How likely it is . . .) and behavioural intention (I intend to . . .). This latter type seems to provide slightly better results in the prediction of behaviour (Armitage and Conner, 2001: 483). In this sense, Chen et al. (1998) use a mix of self-prediction and pure-intention items, whereas Zhao et al. (2005) use 'interest' measures (How interested are you in . . .). In our opinion, the similarity between interest and intention may not be so clear. For this reason we have chosen a pure-intention measure.

Personal attitude has also been measured through an aggregate attitude scale. This is an important difference compared to other studies, such as those of Kolvereid (1996) and Fayolle et al. (2006), where a belief-based measure of personal attitude was used. However, Ajzen (1991, 2001) states that beliefs are the antecedents of attitudes, and suggests using an aggregate measure for attitudes (beliefs would explain attitude, while attitude would explain intention). In this sense, Krueger et al. (2000) use such a design, with beliefs explaining an aggregate measure of attitude, while this latter variable was used to explain intention. Similarly, in Kolvereid and Isaksen's (2006) study, both kinds of measures were included together in a linear regression with entrepreneurial intention as the dependent variable. Aggregate attitude was a significant regressor, while beliefs were not. Correlations between the aggregate and belief-based measures are sometimes disappointing (Ajzen, 1991: 192). For this reason, we have chosen an aggregate measure of personal attitude in the EIQ.

The SN, according to Ajzen (1991), should be approached through an aggregate measure of the kind 'what do reference people think?' In practice, however, some researchers simply omit this element from the model (Krueger, 1993; Chen et al., 1998). On the other hand, others have posited answers to this question with their respective 'motives to comply' (Kolvereid, 1996; Kolvereid and Isaksen, 2006; Tkachev and Kolvereid, 1999). Nevertheless, Armitage and Conner (2001: 485) found that, in general, the 'subjective norm × motives to comply' measure tends to show weaker predictive power towards intention than the 'multiple-item subjective norm' measure. This alleged weakness may not be so clear in the specific area of entrepreneurship research (Krueger, 2003). Nonetheless, we have used a simpler scale in the validation process, including three groups of 'reference people': family, friends and colleagues. In this manner, we also contribute to keeping the EIQ as parsimonious as possible.

In previous research, perceived behavioural control has been measured through specific self-efficacies (Chen et al., 1998; Zhao et al., 2005). More general measures of self-efficacy and perceived controllability of behaviour have also been used. In particular, Kolvereid (1996) used a general six-item scale with good results, whereas Kolvereid and Isaksen (2006) used an 18-item scale that was then grouped into four specific self-efficacies through factor analysis. This latter study showed no significant correlation between PBC and intention. In Ajzen's (1991) opinion, control beliefs would be the antecedents of an aggregate measure of perceived behavioural control. Thus, specific efficacies and control beliefs could be understood as being the antecedent of general PBC. In this sense, as aggregate measures have been used for PA and SN, we chose to keep this scheme for PBC as well.

Therefore, respondents were asked to rate their level of agreement with several general statements about the feeling of capacity regarding firm creation. In a recent work, Ajzen (2002) considers that perceived behavioural control is a concept somewhat wider than self-efficacy. It would also include a measure of controllability (the extent to which successfully performing the behaviour is up to the person). Nevertheless, Kolvereid and Isaksen (2006) used a pure 'self-efficacy' scale, because Armitage and Conner (2001) concluded that self-efficacy is more clearly defined and more strongly correlated with intention and behaviour. The EIQ includes a six-item scale: five of these items measure general self-efficacy, whereas one is a controllability statement (15c, see Appendix).

RESULTS

Fewer than half the original sample at T1 had labour experience (43.5 per cent), acquired while they were already studying. However, very few of them had been self-employed at that time (10 respondents, 2.5 per cent of the T1 sample). Three years later, things have changed notably. At T2 the great majority of respondents had labour experience (106 out of 111, 95.5 per cent). On average, it had been two years since they finished their degrees. Given the economic expansion experienced by Spain in that period, it was expected that most of them would be able to find a job. Self-employment is still rare, though, as only nine of them reported having been self-employed after 2004. Nevertheless, this figure represents a substantial improvement over T1 data (8.1 per cent of the T2 sample).

It is interesting to compare responses at both moments. Only two of the ten students having been self-employed at T1 have participated in the follow-up. And only one of them reported self-employment experience after 2004. The other eight positive responses at T2 are ex-novo entrepreneurs. This could serve as an indication that finishing the degree is a good 'strategic window' for start-up (Harvey and Evans, 1995).

To test our hypotheses, we have grouped individuals according to their labour experience at T1 and T2. As stated earlier, only five respondents had no experience at T2 and, of course, neither did they have experience at T1. We have labelled them as group C. There were 50 respondents who had already worked at T1 (group B). For this group, the career change after finishing the degree would be relatively smaller. Finally, the remaining 56 respondents had acquired their first labour experience after finishing the degree (group A). For this group, the career change from T1 to T2 would have been much larger and, correspondingly, attitudes and intentions may have been substantially altered.

Table 2.1 summarizes the main characteristics of each of those groups. Group C, without labour experience, is too small (five individuals) to reach conclusions. For this reason, it will not be considered in comparisons hereafter. Nonetheless, it is interesting to note that in 2004, these five individuals were grouped as 'no-labour experience', together with the other 56 individuals in that situation (group A). The longitudinal analysis

Table 2.1 Basic characteristics by labour experience status

	Total	Acquiring LExp after T1 (Group A)	Having LExp at T1 (Group B)	Without LExp (Group C)
N	111	56	50	5
Age (T1)	23.03	22.77	23.28	23.40
Gender (% male)	0.46	0.46	0.48	0.20
Income level (T1)	1426.80	1520.09	1394.82	725.70
Personal Attraction (T1)	4.62	4.54	4.81	3.64
Subjective Norm (T1)	5.68	5.67	5.72	5.40
Perceived Behavioural Control (T1)	3.75	3.54	4.09	2.80
Entrepreneurial Intention (T1)	3.55	3.41	3.81	2.50
PA (T2)−PA (T1)	0.05	0.10	−0.01	0.20
SN (T2)−SN (T1)	−0.05	−0.16	0.07	−0.13
PBC (T2)−PBC (T1)	0.60***	0.66***	0.48**	1.13*
EI (T2)−EI (T1)	0.08	0.05	0.11	0.00
Stability PA	0.33***	0.37***	0.31***	0.09
Stability SN	0.22**	0.29**	0.16	0.14
Stability PBC	0.19***	0.11	0.31***	0.01
Stability EI	0.14**	0.07	0.21**	0.15

Notes: Stability is measured as the average within-participant correlation between scale items at T1 and T2.
Changes in construct levels and stability measures significantly different from 0 have been marked: * $p < 0.05$; ** $p < 0.01$; *** $p < 0.001$.

has made evident that there were differences between both categories. In particular, those still without experience had the lowest level of attitudinal and intention variables even at T1. It may be argued that some of their characteristics (already shown at T1) have made them less able to find (or create) a job afterwards.

A first look at Table 2.1 offers mixed results for our hypothesis H1. The initial levels for the constructs are higher in the group already having labour experience at T1. However, these differences are not significant, except for PBC: 3.54 for individuals in group A and 4.09 for those in group B ($p < 0.05$). Therefore, final-year students with labour experience had a higher initial PBC level, which could logically be attributed to their experience. From T1 to T2, change in PA and PBC is larger for those acquiring labour experience after T1, as hypothesized. But the opposite is true for SN and Intention. However, when we use t-tests to compare those changes, only the increase in PBC is significant, and is so for both groups. For PBC, then, hypothesis H1 holds, since the increase is larger for individuals in group A. Correspondingly, the PBC group difference at T2 is smaller (4.21 for individuals in group A and 4.56 for group B) and only marginally significant (p < 0.1).

With respect to our hypothesis H2, the stability measure has been defined as the correlation of item responses from T1 to T2. Therefore, only when this measure is positive and significantly different from zero can we say the construct has remained stable. For the full sample, constructs are stable (all of them differ significantly from zero). However, this may be partly due to sample-size effect, since for the sub-groups fewer stable constructs are found. Additionally, correlation coefficients between construct averages at T1 and T2 have also been computed for the full sample, and all of them were sizeable and significant: 0.567 for the correlation between PA_{T1} and PA_{T2} (p < 0.001); 0.549 between SN_{T1} and SN_{T2} (p < 0.001); 0.559 between PBC_{T1} and PBC_{T2} (p < 0.001); and 0.700 for the correlation between EI_{T1} and EI_2 (p < 0.001). These results are comparable to those reported by Schuerger et al. (1989) or Souitaris et al. (2007), confirming the satisfactory stability of perceptions among respondents.

Hypothesis H2 implies that those in group A (acquiring labour experience after graduation) will have experienced a greater change in their perceptions since T1 and, therefore, will have less stable perceptions. PA is stable for both groups (A and B). SN is stable for the first group, but not for the second. These two results go against H2. By contrast, PBC and EI are stable for group B and not for group A, in accordance with H2. Besides, this hypothesis is partly confirmed if we use t-tests to compare mean stabilities for these two groups. In effect, the PBC stability measure is significantly higher for those in group B (p < 0.05). For the remaining constructs the difference is not significant.

To test hypothesis H3, we used a logistic regression model, with being self-employed after 2004 as the dependent variable. Entrepreneurial intention and attitudinal variables, together with age, gender and income level were included as independent variables (all measured at T1). The first column in Table 2.2 summarizes the results (control variables not shown for clarity of presentation).

Similarly, hypotheses H4 and H5 were independently and jointly tested adding the corresponding variables and interactions with intention into the logistic regression model. As may be seen from the second column, hypothesis H4 is fully supported. Respondents in group A have a much higher probability of starting a firm than those who already had labour experience (group B). The interaction term (Acquiring × Intention) is

Table 2.2 _Logistic regression of self-employment experience, B coefficients_

	H3	H4	H5	H4+H5
Constant term	-6.930^{***}	-11.496^{**}	-8.319^{**}	-12.683^{**}
Income level	0.001^{*}	0.001^{+}	0.001^{+}	0.001^{+}
Intention	0.736^{*}	1.680^{*}	0.957^{+}	1.680^{**}
Acquiring Lab. Exp		7.794^{+}		8.345^{+}
Acquiring by Intention		-1.952^{*}		-2.139^{*}
Stability of Intention			$2.680^{n.s.}$	$3.050^{n.s.}$
Stability by Intention			$-0.334^{n.s.}$	$-0.487^{n.s.}$

Note: Significance levels: n.s. not significant; $+$ $p < 0.1$; * $p < 0.05$; ** $p < 0.01$; *** $p < 0.001$.

negative. This means that after considering the positive independent effect of 'intention' and 'acquiring', there is a residual negative contribution when both variables are considered together. This may be explained by the lack of realism of their perceptions and intention at T1. In particular, there were 15 individuals without work experience and high intention levels (5.00 or above) at T1 who had not started a firm. Finding a job would have made them decrease their optimistic (and unrealistic) intention and abandon the start-up option. Alternatively, there were two individuals without work experience and low intention (3.00 or below) at T1 who had become self-employed. Finding a job would have made them realize that entrepreneurship is not such a bad option. The realism of perceptions is, once again, a relevant element to be taken into account.

Hypothesis H5 was fully rejected, as may be seen in the third column of Table 2.2. Adding stability as a regressor, either alone or in interaction with intention, has no significant effect on the start-up decision. Even when all the elements are included together in the regression function (joint hypotheses H4 and H5, fourth column in Table 2.2), stability still does not play any significant role in explaining the start-up behaviour.

DISCUSSION

Sample selection is always controversial, even though some authors have defended the suitability of student samples (Krueger, 1993). In particular, it may be plausible that students' responses differ from those of the general adult population. According to this line of reasoning, entering the labour market represents a major change for these students, and their perceptions may be substantially modified. Harvey and Evans (1995) describe this situation as a 'strategic window' of opportunity for becoming an entrepreneur. Individuals in our sample were final-year undergraduates at T1. By contrast, the great majority of them had finished their degree at T2 (92 out of 111, 82.9 per cent of the sample) and will therefore have gone through this window. Therefore, at T2 they can no longer be considered as a 'student sample'. Thus, even though the T1 survey may be accused of having some kind of bias, the T2 survey should be representative of the general young-adult population.

In this context, their attitudes and intentions towards entrepreneurship could have changed. Nevertheless, only PBC levels are substantially different from T1 to T2. In our opinion, this may be due to the effect of work experience. Individuals not having labour experience at T1, but acquiring it afterwards (group A), have increased their PBC levels more than those already having this experience at T1 (group B). Nevertheless, this latter group B has also increased its PBC levels significantly from T1 to T2. One tentative conclusion, then, is that experience is very important, but the length and breadth of this experience is also relevant. Thus, even those in group B keep on raising PBC levels as their experience grows.

With respect to labour experience, it seems to have a very relevant effect on increasing the realism of perceptions and intentions. On the one hand, this relationship between T1 intention and start-up behaviour is much weaker for those in group A (acquiring labour experience afterwards). On the other hand, this relationship is much clearer in group B (already having labour experience at T1). In this latter group, all the six individuals starting a firm after T1 had high initial intention (5.00 or above). Conversely, the proportion of individuals with high intention and not starting a firm is much lower in this group B. In this sense, Cooper and Lucas (2007) argue that 'authentic experience' is essential to increase self-efficacy perceptions and entrepreneurial intention.

Even if we assume that labour experience (nearly) always has a positive effect on PBC, this need not raise entrepreneurial intention, either because of increased realism, or because it may affect personal attitude. In our sample, even though the increase in PBC from T1 to T2 is clearly significant, no effect on intention is observed. A job position provides knowledge and helps develop skills that would make the person feel more able to start a firm. On the other hand, it may also help in the formation of a personal preference towards becoming an entrepreneur. This second effect may be weaker and, in any case, needs not always be positive. It will surely depend on the specific characteristics of the job position. It is possible, then, that work experience may decrease PA towards entrepreneurship for some individuals, compensating the increase in PBC.

In our study, the levels of PA and SN remained stable over the three years. Graduation had neither increased nor reduced the perceived attractiveness of entrepreneurship. Little is yet known about the way in which attitudes are formed. In this sense, it has been argued that social and cultural variables may have a considerable influence on the configuration of attitudes (Mitchell et al., 2000). Similarly, self-perceptions regarding personal capacities may also be relevant (Liñán, 2008). Cultural socialization processes, and the formation of the individual's self-image, would take place at an earlier age, and therefore would not be easily changed after graduation. This is especially relevant given the notable influence of PA on EI, at least in some Western societies (Liñán and Chen, 2009).

In this sense, an obvious implication may be derived for entrepreneurship education. Greater efforts should be placed on enhancing the attractiveness of entrepreneurship at earlier stages of the educational system. Developing in younger students the skills and values more closely linked to entrepreneurship (such as independence, self-realization, self-confidence and creativity) would contribute to more favourable personal attitudes towards this career option.

The stability of perceptions has been higher than initially expected. For the full longitudinal sample, the four constructs remain stable. For smaller sub-groups, this is not always so. Further analysis will surely be needed to confirm or reject this finding. Thus, graduation in itself does not seem to be a substantial change in the person's career path. At least, perceptions do not change substantially at this stage. However, the coincidence of graduation and first work experience notably alters entrepreneurial perceptions, as shown by the lower stability levels of individuals in group A compared to those in group B.

Finally, the present study suffers from a number of limitations that have to be acknowledged. First, sample size and response rates were not sufficiently large to ensure an adequate representativeness of the results. Although the initial sample was made up of 400 individuals, that of the longitudinal study was notably smaller. In particular, only nine respondents had been self-employed after T1. Deriving general conclusions from such a small sample could be risky.

A second limitation derives from the population of reference. The study has been conducted in Andalusia, a relatively backward Spanish region characterized by traditional cultural values relatively unfavourable to entrepreneurship (Maestre, 1999). As Hofstede et al. (2004) have suggested, varying national cultural patterns may result in different types of entrepreneurs. Thus, similar studies should be carried out using culturally-diverse samples to confirm these results.

CONCLUSION

As far as we are aware, this is probably the first long-term longitudinal study analysing the temporal stability of entrepreneurial intention. Similarly, research on the intention–behaviour link has long been called for, but very few attempts have been made to do it. Our sample, limited as it may be, has provided significant evidence of the existence of such a long-term relation. As a note of caution, our results should be taken as tentative until further research confirms or rejects them. If confirmed, these results may be highly relevant for the entrepreneurship research field.

It has been found that, even after a substantial time lag, entrepreneurial intention is a strong and significant predictor of the start-up decision. The relevance of understanding the intention-generation process is, therefore, confirmed. In this sense, we now know more about the specific role that labour experience plays in determining both perceived behavioural control and also intentions and start-up behaviours. Logistic regression has found that having labour experience prior to graduation is not significant to explain start-up. By contrast, acquiring it after graduation is the strongest predictor of this entrepreneurial behaviour.

When we talk about young graduates as potential entrepreneurs, several issues should be considered. First, personal attitude and subjective norm perceptions would be formed as a result of socialization processes at a younger age. Therefore, they may not be so much affected by after-graduation events (notably, finding a job) or, at least, the effect may not be easily predicted and would depend on the particular circumstances of those events. Secondly, PBC would also be partially derived from those socialization processes, but it would also derive from pre-graduation work experience. The educational system may act at the primary and secondary levels to enhance the development of favourable perceptions. Thirdly, a high entrepreneurial intention at the time of finishing studying would not be enough. Relevant experience needs to be acquired before a firm may be started. Hence, the combination of favourable perceptions developed before graduation, together with acquiring labour experience afterwards would make the potential entrepreneur act.

There is still much to be learned to really understand the mental processes leading to the start-up decision. Nevertheless, research such as the one presented in this chapter could make substantial contributions to this end. We call for further studies that may contribute to advancing our knowledge in this field.

REFERENCES

Ajzen, I. (1987), 'Attitudes, traits, and actions: dispositional prediction of behavior in personality and social-psychology', *Advances in Experimental Social Psychology*, **20**, 1–63.

Ajzen, I. (1991), 'The theory of planned behavior', *Organizational Behavior and Human Decision Processes*, **50**(2), 179–211.

Ajzen, I. (2001), 'Nature and operation of attitudes', *Annual Review of Psychology*, **52**, 27–58.

Ajzen, I. (2002), 'Perceived behavioral control, self-efficacy, locus of control, and the theory of planned behavior', *Journal of Applied Social Psychology*, **32**(4), 665–83.

Armitage, C.J. and M. Conner (2001), 'Efficacy of the theory of planned behavior: a meta-analytic review', *British Journal of Social Psychology*, **40**, 471–99.

Aspelund, A., T. Berg-Utby and R. Skjevdal (2005), 'Initial resources' influence on new venture survival: a longitudinal study of new technology-based firms', *Technovation*, **25**(11), 1337–47.

Audet, J. (2000), 'Evaluation of two approaches to entrepreneurship education using an intention-based model of venture creation', *Academy of Entrepreneurship Journal*, **6**(1), 57–63.

Audet, J. (2004), 'A longitudinal study of the entrepreneurial intentions of university students', *Academy of Entrepreneurship Journal*, **10**(1), 3–16.

Autio, E., R.H. Keeley, M. Klofsten, G.G.C. Parker and M. Hay (2001), 'Entrepreneurial intent among students in Scandinavia and in the USA', *Enterprise and Innovation Management Studies*, **2**(2), 145–60.

Bandura, A. (1997), *Self-efficacy: The Exercise of Control,* New York: Freeman.

Baron, R.A. (1998), 'Cognitive mechanisms in entrepreneurship: why and when entrepreneurs think differently than other people', *Journal of Business Venturing*, **13**(4), 275–94.

Baron, R.A. (2004), 'Potential benefits of the cognitive perspective: expanding entrepreneurship's array of conceptual tools', *Journal of Business Venturing*, **19**(2), 169–72.

Baron, R.A. and T.B. Ward (2004), 'Expanding entrepreneurial cognition's toolbox: potential contributions from the field of cognitive science', *Entrepreneurship Theory and Practice*, **28**(6), 553–73.

Bird, B. (1988), 'Implementing entrepreneurial ideas: the case for intention', *Academy of Management Review*, **13**, 442–53.

Boyd, N.G. and G.S. Vozikis (1994), 'The influence of self-efficacy on the development of entrepreneurial intentions and actions', *Entrepreneurship Theory and Practice*, **18**, 63–77.

Busenitz, L.W. and C.M. Lau (1996), 'A cross-cultural cognitive model of new venture creation', *Entrepreneurship Theory and Practice*, **20**(4), 25–39.

Bygrave, W.D. (2003), 'The entrepreneurial process', in W.D. Bygrave and A. Zacharakis (eds), *The Portable MBA in Entrepreneurship*, New York: John Wiley & Sons.

Carrier, C. (2005), 'Pedagogical challenges in entrepreneurship education', in P. Kyrö and C. Carrier (eds), *The Dynamics of Learning Entrepreneurship in a Cross-cultural University Context*, Hämmeenlinna: University of Tampere.

Chandler, G.N. and D.W. Lyon (2001), 'Issues of research design and construct measurement in entrepreneurship research: the past decade', *Entrepreneurship Theory and Practice*, **25**, 101–13.

Chen, C.C., P.G. Greene and A. Crick (1998), 'Does entrepreneurial self-efficacy distinguish entrepreneurs from managers?', *Journal of Business Venturing*, **13**(4), 295–316.

Cooper, A.C. (1985), 'The role of incubator organizations in the founding of growth-oriented firms', *Journal of Business Venturing*, **1**(1), 75–86.

Cooper, A.C. (1993), 'Challenges in predicting new firm performance', *Journal of Business Venturing*, **8**(3), 241–53.

Cooper, S.Y. and W.A. Lucas (2007), 'Developing entrepreneurial self-efficacy and intentions: lessons from two programmes', in *Proceedings of the 52nd ICSB World Conference*', TSE Entre, Turku School of Economics, Turku.

De Carolis, D.M. and P. Saparito (2006), 'Social capital, cognition, and entrepreneurial opportunities: a theoretical framework', *Entrepreneurship Theory and Practice*, **30**(1), 41–56.

De la Vega, I., A. Coduras, C. Cruz and R. Justo (2007), *Informe Ejecutivo GEM España 2006*, Madrid: Instituto de Empresa.

Dubini, P. and H. Aldrich (1991), 'Personal and extended networks are central to the entrepreneurial process', *Journal of Business Venturing*, **6**(5), 305–13.

Erikson, T. (1999), 'A study of entrepreneurial career choices among MBAs: the extended Bird model', *Journal of Enterprising Culture*, **7**(1), 1–17.

Fayolle, A., B. Gailly and N. Lassas-Clerc (2006), 'Assessing the impact of entrepreneurship education programmes: a new methodology', *Journal of European Industrial Training*, **30**(9), 701–20.

Fishbein, M. and I. Ajzen (1975), *Belief, Attitude, Intention and Behavior: An Introduction to Theory and Research*, New York: Addison-Wesley.

Gartner, W.B. (2004), *Handbook of Entrepreneurial Dynamics: The Process of Business Creation*, Thousand Oaks, CA: Sage.

Gartner, W.B., K.G. Shaver, E.J. Gatewood and J. Katz (1994), 'Finding the entrepreneur in entrepreneurship', *Entrepreneurship Theory and Practice*, **18**(3), 5–10.

Hansemark, O.C. (2003), 'Need for achievement, locus of control and the prediction of business start-ups: a longitudinal study', *Journal of Economic Psychology*, **24**(3), 301–19.

Harvey, M. and R. Evans (1995), 'Strategic windows in the entrepreneurial process', *Journal of Business Venturing*, **10**(5), 331–47.

Hofstede, G., N. Noorderhaven, A.R. Thurik, L.M. Uhlaner, A.R.M. Wennekers and R.E. Wildeman (2004), 'Culture's role in entrepreneurship: self-employment out of dissatisfaction', in T.E. Brown and J.M. Ulijn (eds), *Innovation, Entrepreneurship and Culture*, Cheltenham, UK and Northampton, MA, USA: Edward Elgar.

Jack, S.L. and A.R. Anderson (2002), 'The effects of embeddedness on the entrepreneurial process', *Journal of Business Venturing*, **17**(5), 467–87.

Kickul, J. and J.A. Zaper (2000), 'Untying the knot: do personal and organizational determinants influence entrepreneurial intentions?', *Journal of Small Business and Entrepreneurship*, **15**(3), 57–77.

Kolvereid, L. (1996), 'Prediction of employment status choice intentions', *Entrepreneurship Theory and Practice*, **21**(1), 47–57.

Kolvereid, L. and E. Isaksen (2006), 'New business start-up and subsequent entry into self-employment' *Journal of Business Venturing*, **21**(6), 866–85.

Krueger, N.F. (1993), 'The impact of prior entrepreneurial exposure on perceptions of new venture feasibility and desirability', *Entrepreneurship Theory and Practice*, **18**(1), 5–21.

Krueger, N.F. (2003), 'The cognitive psychology of entrepreneurship', in Z.J. Acs and D.B. Audretsch (eds), *Handbook of Entrepreneurship Research: An Interdisciplinary Survey and Introduction*, London: Kluwer.

Krueger, N.F. and A.L. Carsrud (1993), 'Entrepreneurial intentions: applying the theory of planned behavior' *Entrepreneurship and Regional Development*, **5**(4), 315–30.

Krueger, N.F., M.D. Reilly and A.L. Carsrud (2000), 'Competing models of entrepreneurial intentions', *Journal of Business Venturing*, **15**(5–6), 411–32.

Kyrö, P. and C. Carrier (2005), 'Entrepreneurial learning in universities: bridges across borders', in P. Kyrö and C. Carrier (eds), *The Dynamics of Learning Entrepreneurship in a Cross-cultural University Context*', Hämmeenlinna: University of Tampere.

Lee, S.H. and P.K. Wong (2004), 'An exploratory study of technopreneurial intentions: a career anchor perspective', *Journal of Business Venturing*, **19**(1), 7–28.

Liñán, F. (2004), 'Intention-based models of entrepreneurship education', *Piccola Impresa/Small Business*, **3**, 11–35.

Liñán, F. (2007), 'The role of entrepreneurship education in the entrepreneurial process', in A. Fayolle (ed.), *Handbook of Research in Entrepreneurship Education*, Cheltenham, UK and Northampton, MA, USA: Edward Elgar.

Liñán, F. (2008),' Skill and value perceptions: how do they affect entrepreneurial intentions?', *International Entrepreneurship and Management Journal*, **4**(3), 257–72.

Liñán, F. and Y.W. Chen (2009), 'Development and cross-cultural application of a specific instrument to measure entrepreneurial intentions', *Entrepreneurship Theory and Practice*, **33**(3), 593–617.

Liñán, F., J.C. Rodríguez-Cohard, J.M. Rueda and J.S. Martínez (2005), 'Effects of cognitive variables on entrepreneurial intention levels', paper presented at *Fostering Entrepreneurship Through Education*, 15th IntEnt Conference, University of Surrey, Guildford.

Liñán, F. and F.J. Santos (2007), 'Does social capital affect entrepreneurial intentions?', *International Advances in Economic Research*, **13**(4), 443–53.

Maestre, J. (1999), 'Cambio sociocultural y percepción socio-económica en Andalucia', *Boletín Económico de Andalucía*, **25**, 311–26.

Matthews, C.H. and S.B. Moser (1995), 'Family background and gender: implications for interest in small firm ownership', *Entrepreneurship and Regional Development*, **7**(4), 365–77.

Menzies, T., M. Diochon, Y. Gasse and S. Elgie (2006), 'A longitudinal study of the characteristics, business creation process and outcome differences of Canadian female vs. male nascent entrepreneurs', *International Entrepreneurship and Management Journal*, **2**(4), 441–53.

Mitchell, R.K., B. Smith, K.W. Seawright and E.A. Morse (2000), 'Cross-cultural cognitions and the venture creation decision', *Academy of Management Journal*, **43**(5), 974–93.

Peterman, N.E. and J. Kennedy (2003), 'Enterprise education: influencing students' perceptions of entrepreneurship', *Entrepreneurship Theory and Practice*, **28**(2), 129–44.

Raykov, T. (1999), 'Are simple change scores obsolete? An approach to studying correlates and predictors of change', *Applied Psychological Measurement*, **23**(2), 120–26.

Reynolds, P.D., W. Bygrave, E. Autio and M. Hay (2002), *Global Entrepreneurship Monitor: 2002 Summary Report*, Kansas City: Ewin Marion Kauffman Foundation.

Rondstadt, R. (1990), 'The educated entrepreneur: a new era of entrepreneurial education is beginning', in C.A. Kent (ed.), *Entrepreneurship Education: Current Developments, Future Directions*, Westport, CT: Quorum Books.

Scherer, R.F., J.D. Brodzinsky and F.A. Wiebe (1991), 'Examining the relationship between personality and entrepreneurial career preference', *Entrepreneurship and Regional Development*, **3**, 195–206.

Schuerger, J.M., K.L. Zarrella and A.S. Hotz (1989), 'Factors that influence the temporal stability of personality by questionnaire', *Journal of Personality and Social Psychology*, **56**(5), 777–83.

Shapero, A. and L. Sokol (1982), 'Social dimensions of entrepreneurship', in C.A. Kent, D.L. Sexton and K.H. Vesper (eds), *Encyclopedia of Entrepreneurship*, Englewood Cliffs, NJ: Prentice Hall.

Sheeran, P., S. Orbell and D. Trafimow (1999), 'Does the temporal stability of behavioral intentions moderate intention–behavior and past behavior–future behavior relations?', *Personality and Social Psychology Bulletin*, **25**(6), 724–34.

Shepherd, D.A. and A. Zacharakis (2003), 'A new venture's cognitive legitimacy: an assessment by customers', *Journal of Small Business Management*, **41**(2), 148–67.

Souitaris, V., S. Zerbinati and A. Al-Laham (2007), 'Do entrepreneurship programmes raise entrepreneurial intention of science and engineering students? The effect of learning, inspiration and resources', *Journal of Business Venturing*, **22**(4), 566–91.

Tkachev, A. and L. Kolvereid (1999), 'Self-employment intentions among Russian students', *Entrepreneurship and Regional Development*, **11**(3), 269–80.

Tubbs, M.E. and S.E. Ekeberg (1991), 'The role of intentions in work motivation: implications for goal-setting theory and research', *Academy of Management Review*, **16**(1), 180–99.

Veciana, J.M., M. Aponte and D. Urbano (2005), 'University students' attitudes towards entrepreneurship: a two countries comparison', *International Entrepreneurship and Management Journal*, **1**(2), 165–82.

Westhead, P., D. Ucbasaran and M. Wright (2005), 'Experience and cognition: do novice, serial and portfolio entrepreneurs differ?', *International Small Business Journal*, **23**(1), 72–98.

Wiklund, J., P. Davidsson and F. Delmar (2003), 'What do they think and feel about growth? An expectancy-value approach to small business managers' attitudes toward growth', *Entrepreneurship Theory and Practice*, **27**(3), 247–70.

Zhao, H., G.E. Hills and S.E. Siebert (2005), 'The mediating role of self-efficacy in the development of entrepreneurial intentions', *Journal of Applied Psychology*, **90**(6), 1265–72.

APPENDIX

Measures of Core Entrepreneurial Intention Model Elements

Personal attitude
11. Indicate your level of agreement with the following sentences from 1 (total disagreement) to 7 (total agreement).

	1	2	3	4	5	6	7
11.a Being an entrepreneur implies more advantages than disadvantages to me	□	□	□	□	□	□	□
11.b A career as entrepreneur is attractive for me	□	□	□	□	□	□	□
11.c If I had the opportunity and resources, I'd like to start a firm	□	□	□	□	□	□	□
11.d Being an entrepreneur would entail great satisfaction for me	□	□	□	□	□	□	□
11.e Among various options, I would rather be an entrepreneur	□	□	□	□	□	□	□

Subjective norm
13. If you decided to create a firm, would people in your close environment approve of that decision? Indicate from 1 (total disapproval) to 7 (total approval).

	1	2	3	4	5	6	7
13.a Your close family	□	□	□	□	□	□	□
13.b Your friends	□	□	□	□	□	□	□
13.c Your colleagues	□	□	□	□	□	□	□

Perceived behavioural control
15. To what extent do you agree with the following statements regarding your entrepreneurial capacity? Value them from 1 (total disagreement) to 7 (total agreement).

	1	2	3	4	5	6	7
15.a To start a firm and keep it working would be easy for me	□	□	□	□	□	□	□
15.b I am prepared to start a viable firm	□	□	□	□	□	□	□
15.c I can control the creation process of a new firm	□	□	□	□	□	□	□

15.d I know the necessary practical details
　　　 to start a firm   □ □ □ □ □ □ □
15.e I know how to develop an
　　　 entrepreneurial project   □ □ □ □ □ □ □
15.f If I tried to start a firm, I would have
　　　 a high probability of succeeding □ □ □ □ □ □ □

Entrepreneurial intention
18. Indicate your level of agreement with the following statements from 1
(total disagreement) to 7 (total agreement)

1	2	3	4	5	6	7

18.a I am ready to do anything to be an
　　　 entrepreneur   □ □ □ □ □ □ □
18.b My professional goal is to become an
　　　 entrepreneur   □ □ □ □ □ □ □
18.c I will make every effort to start and
　　　 run my own firm   □ □ □ □ □ □ □
18.d I am determined to create a firm in
　　　 the future   □ □ □ □ □ □ □
18.e I have very seriously thought of
　　　 starting a firm   □ □ □ □ □ □ □
18.f I have the firm intention to start a
　　　 firm some day   □ □ □ □ □ □ □

3. Meta processes of entrepreneurial and enterprising learning: the dialogue between cognitive, conative and affective constructs

Paula Kyrö, Jaana Seikkula-Leino and Jarkko Mylläri

INTRODUCTION

The question of how to learn entrepreneurial and enterprising behaviour has recently become one of the core questions in entrepreneurship education (for example Acs and Audretsch, 2003; Fayolle and Klandt, 2006; Kyrö and Carrier, 2005). According to Bosman et al. (2000) in this field the individual, competency-based approach is fast becoming the most common type of structure for training programmes and courses. It digresses from what entrepreneurs are, towards what they do, and hence towards the competencies they need in order to play their roles. Chandler and Jansen (1992), for example, found that to perform well, the entrepreneurial competencies were the most fundamental. Managerial and technical-functional competencies only become useful when the entrepreneurial competency has been activated. Recently this discussion has also introduced new elements to the conceptual development of competences by integrating the concept of competence to the learning processes (for example Cope, 2005; Hayton and Kelley, 2006). This approach argues that competencies should not be viewed as inputs, outputs or processes but as a context-dependent process of learning. However, adopting such a holistic perspective still leaves many essential concepts such as values, beliefs, motives, volition, ability, skill and knowledge undefined.

To contribute to this stream of research this chapter adopts the tripartite constructs of the personality and intelligence originally introduced by Snow et al. (1996) and further applied to entrepreneurship education by Koiranen and Ruohotie (2001). This construct helps to differentiate the cognitive, conative and affective aspects of learning and organizes such concepts as values, beliefs, motives, volition, ability, skill and knowledge for further research. Ruohotie (2000) claims that in entrepreneurial education, be it formally planned or taking place in everyday life, the key processes concern the conative aspects of motivation and volition. But as Gibb argues, the affective aspects relating to our values and attitudes should take a more explicit place in learning practices (Gibb, 2002). We suggest that to do this requires that we know far more about meta-level abilities of self-regulation and how to learn them. Self-regulation refers to an individual's active participation in his or her own learning process. It is the process through which self-generated thoughts, feelings and actions are planned and systematically adapted as necessary to affect one's learning. We argue that learning depends on the learner's ability to manage all three, cognitive, conative and affective meta-level abilities of self-regulation. Thus to know more about these and their interplay might enhance learning entrepreneurial and enterprising behaviour. This field of research, even though gaining in strength, is still rare in entrepreneurship research and thus this chapter aims to contribute to that discussion by investigating the dynamics of 'how the cognitive, conative and affective self-regulating abilities interplay in entrepreneurial and enterprising learning process'. Thus, we will focus on the learning of entrepreneurial and enterprising readiness and their meta processes by expanding knowledge of the process-oriented competence discussion in entrepreneurship education. Our contribution therefore focuses on the research stream interested in the processes of how to learn entrepreneurial and enterprising behaviour, which is a fruitful arena, for example, thinking about empowering entrepreneurship and enterprising attitude in societies.

Our context is Finnish society and its entrepreneurship education programmes. More specifically, we investigate students' experiences about and during these programmes. Finland is among those societies that first adopted entrepreneurship education by mainstreaming it throughout the education system (European Commission, 2002). It has a policy programme and implementation plan that covers all levels of education. Conceptually these documents follow the EU's broad cultural approach to entrepreneurial and enterprising learning which highlights the importance of the creation of an entrepreneurial culture by fostering the right mindset, entrepreneurship skills and awareness of its career opportunity (Commission of the European Communities, 2003, 2006.). The intensity of implementing entrepreneurship education throughout the educational system is well justified by the low degrees of entrepreneurial activity and academic start-ups. According to a Global Entrepreneurship Monitor (GEM) survey only 3.7 per cent of the population is either planning to start a business or is running a newly started business (Arenius et al.,

2005). The latest ranking statistics indicate that 2.2 per cent of those with university degrees and 2.7 per cent of those with applied science university degrees were self-employed. At the same time Finland is at the top of the PISA rating (the OECD Programme for International Student Assessment) indicating the high quality of education in Finland. This contradiction offers a fruitful arena and context for investigating the changes and dynamics of entrepreneurial and enterprising self-regulation abilities.

This chapter is organized according to our research question. After this introduction we focus on the concepts of entrepreneurial and enterprising learning and its ontological and epistemological bases. Then we proceed to the dynamics of cognitive, conative and affective constructs and meta-level self-regulating abilities. This is followed by a description of the research design and methodological approach. After that we report the results, conclusions and finally the implications of our findings.

ENTREPRENEURIAL AND ENTERPRISING LEARNING AND THEIR ONTOLOGICAL BASES

To define entrepreneurial and enterprising learning we have to lean mostly on Anglo-American terminology that focuses on the terms 'entrepreneurship', 'enterprise', 'enterprising', 'entrepreneurial' and 'entrepreneur'. Erkkilä (2000) argues that in order to avoid conceptual confusion in the USA, UK and Finland, we should use a single concept of 'entrepreneurial education'. Alain Gibb, however, claims that there is a substantial synonymity between entrepreneurial and enterprising behaviour. The only major distinction that can be made is that an entrepreneur is traditionally associated with business activity (Gibb, 1993). In his later writing Gibb (2001) uses these terms synonymously. To avoid confusion and to be exact, we use both concepts explicitly; entrepreneurial (referring to the business context) and enterprising (referring to more general readiness) learning. This reflects the expanded understanding of entrepreneurial and enterprising learning as assumed by the EU and the Finnish national policy.

Educational concepts also differ in the Anglo-American and the continental contexts. The European continental discourse on didactics is close to the Anglo-American discourse on pedagogics. Pedagogy, on the other hand, is sometimes taken as a synonym for the science of education. The Anglo-American and the continental approach to education also differ fundamentally (Kyrö, 2006). The Anglo-American approach takes as its point of departure educational practices and, as Kansanen (1995) argues, focuses on model construction, effective teaching practices and consequently concentrates on empirical research and on testing this in real situations. The point of departure in the continental approach is the ontological bases; theories are deduced from them and further applied in practice. Since gaining access to meta-level understanding requires explicating and understanding the ontological bases, in this respect we follow the continental approach. On the other hand, to study the dynamics of meta-level processes requires authentic and explorative research settings. In this respect we can learn from the Anglo-American tradition. In order to overcome the conceptual confusion of educational concepts we apply the concept of learning that also follows thematically and conceptually the recent competence discussion in entrepreneurship education research.

The very concept of entrepreneurship and consequently entrepreneurial and enterprising learning still remains a challenge to researchers; the recent discourse revolves around such concepts as creativity, opportunity recognition and a prior assumption of action as the medium between knowing and doing. This dialogue is chiefly concerned with the way that individuals and organizations create and implement new ideas and ways of doing things, respond proactively to the environment, and thus provoke change involved with uncertainty, complexity and further insecurity (Carrier, 2005; Gibb, 2005; Schumpeter, 1934). In this context it is essential to understand the dynamic and even chaotic environment, since the economy as a whole develops through experimentally organized business projects, that is new ventures, in which competencies to create entrepreneurial opportunities are a crucial element of this behaviour (Puhakka, 2006; Saks and Gaglio, 2002). However, when it comes to learning processes, Koiranen and Ruohotie argue that entrepreneurship is neither a profession nor a career, but a 'cognitive, affective and conative process intended to increase value through creation, revitalization and/or growth' (Ruohotie and Koiranen, 2000). This strives for similar aspects, which, as Gibb (2002) argues, are essential in entrepreneurial and enterprising learning; namely ways of doing, seeing, feeling, communicating, organizing and learning things. This process approach best follows the Finnish definitions and mainstreaming ideas of entrepreneurial and enterprising learning and is most appropriate for the aims of our research. It is also flexible enough to let students' experiences about the dynamics of their learning lead our research process.

At the ontological and epistemological level we lean on pragmatism-oriented phenomenology, which allows us to combine action of individual and collective experiences and further of learning processes. Thus the links between entrepreneurial and enterprising practices and educational institutions are social processes and structures that transcend an individual's life-world. Our philosophical choices lead us to emphasize a data-oriented longitudinal approach for two reasons: first to gain access to past experiences of the process of learning and second to gather data from ongoing processes.

To argue for our philosophical bases for entrepreneurial and enterprising learning according to the continental approach, we lean on two fundamental assumptions: first we view the world as it is experienced and understood, the second is the priority of an individual's action. The first leads us to phenomenology from both the ontological and epistemological perspectives. The second assumes a digression from the plain existential assumption that being in the world is a sufficient condition for entrepreneurial and enterprising learning. Instead of leaning on existential assumption we take the liberty typical of the diverse representatives of phenomenology (Audi, 1995: 578–9) and find our own approach, which represents the idea that the world is made. This we called *pragmatism-orientation to phenomenology*. Pragmatists strive to understand reality through action. For the pragmatist, truth is born through action and justified through the consequences (Dewey, 1951; James, 1913). As Mises' praxeology already assumes, economic science cannot be verified or refuted through the analysis of observable empiria, but by deriving all definitions from the fundamental proposition that human beings act (von Mises, 1966). This action takes place on the one hand as an interaction with others, and on the other hand is deeply rooted in the context in which it takes place. These assumptions lead to the fundamental role of individuals' action and interaction with others in the learning process, as, for example, Fiet (2000) and Gibb (2005) argue to be the core in entrepreneurial and enterprising learning. Also, for example, Sarasvathy's (2007) logic of effectuation explaining how expert entrepreneurs act actually represents this kind of thought.

As a reform pedagogist and as a representative of pragmatism and symbolic interactionism, Dewey's work serves well to simultaneously demonstrate our ontological commitments and also the interplay between individual and society in the pedagogy of entrepreneurial and enterprising learning. Also John Dewey (1859–1952) explicitly regards emotions as an essential factor in learning. Dewey (1951) saw man as a living being in interaction with the world. In this interaction process there is a confrontation with things. This is how meaning, emotions and interests are born. In this process, knowledge is created and tested by its consequences.

Thus affection, conation and cognition are combined into a dynamic and interactive process. Ruohotie and Koiranen (2000) highlight the meaning of conation in entrepreneurial and enterprising learning, but as Gibb argues, the affective construct is still rare in entrepreneurship research, and should take a more explicit place in learning practices.

THE DIALOGUE BETWEEN COGNITIVE, CONATIVE AND AFFECTIVE CONSTRUCTS

To research these meta processes entails understanding the differences between the affective, conative and cognitive constructs of personality and intelligence. As Snow et al. (1996: 243) argue, these three modes of mental functioning have been historically distinguished but are still regarded as interactive elements in human intelligence and personality.

Figure 3.1 indicates the interplay between constructs and meta constructs of personality and intelligence.

Personality refers to all those factors which distinguish a person as an individual human being. It includes the ability to undertake activities which are difficult, complex, abstract, demanding, goal-oriented, socially prestigious and original as well as the ability to accomplish these activities in situations which demand concentration and control of one's emotions (Ruohotie and Koiranen, 2000). Thus these two abilities deal with those qualities identified as specific to entrepreneurial and enterprising learning.

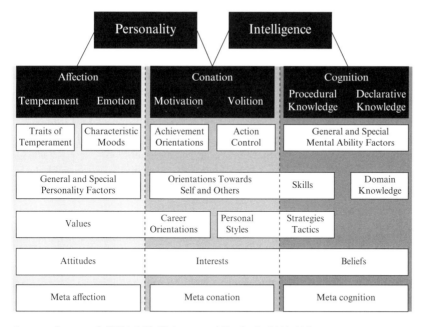

Source: Snow et al. (1996: 247); Koiranen and Ruohotie (2001: 104).

Figure 3.1   Constructs and meta constructs of personality and intelligence and complemented with meta-level construction

The cognitive construct contains declarative and procedural knowledge. The distinction between these is that the first refers to the way we link concepts together and the second to our abilities to apply this knowledge. Conation is subdivided into two parts: motivation and volition. The motivational factor includes, among other things, internal and external goal-orientation, fear of failure, need for achievement, self-esteem and belief in one's own abilities and prospects, all of which are at the core of entrepreneurial and enterprising learning. Volitional structure entails, among others, persistence, will to learn, endeavour or effort, mindfulness in learning, intrinsic regulation and evaluation processes as well as different control strategies (Ruohotie and Koiranen, 2000).

Motivation precedes volitional processes to formulate the goals, but volition guides in setting clear goals as well as in the enactment and realization of the decision. Thus both of these factors are essential in entrepreneurial and enterprising learning. From a social perspective, the conative construct contains our orientation toward self and others, which is essential in Mises' praxeology. Affection is divided into temperament and emotion. Temperament is more lasting and hardly dependent on individual situational factors, while an emotion may be strongly linked to a situation. If affection is embedded in all situations and each individual has his/her own temperament, it is hard to see that we can isolate these from a learning situation. For example, research in the field of fear of failure is deeply embedded in the concept of emotion and also temperament. A need for achievement can also be seen from an affective perspective. At a deeper level the affective construct relates to our values and attitudes. To put this simply, what we regard as valuable guides our willingness and interest to learn. Thus the affective construct is as fundamental to our learning as the conative construct. Actually the demographic perception that those whose family or significant others have been self-employed are more likely to start up their own business might exemplify this construct (Kyrö, 2008).

META PROCESSES OF ENTREPRENEURIAL AND ENTERPRISING LEARNING

To understand the individual's active participation in his or her own learning process led us to research self-regulation processes and, as Ruohotie (2003: 251) argues, to its key factors of meta-cognitive, motivational and behavioural processes and further to the concept of self-regulatory ability. This research has brought new aspects to the concepts of meta competencies that are still unexplored in the competence-oriented research of entrepreneurship. To overcome the conceptual problems and difficulties with such concepts as competencies, abilities and meta competencies and abilities as well as to bridge these debates, we employ the concept of readiness from curricula research. Although the definition of readiness varies according to the contexts, it has traditionally been defined in terms of children's skills or characteristics (La Paro and Pianta, 2000) referring to schooling and achieving the cognitive goals of the curriculum (Lewit and Schuurmann Baker, 1995). Readiness has also been regarded as a set of competencies, as a process, as a set of relationships and as a multidimensional construct involving family, peers, school and community environment (Blair, 2002). However, these traditional roots and definitions of readiness are now changing and expanding towards self-regulation processes. They also contain cognitive regulation as well as emotional and social processes regardless of the age of the learners. Besides self-regulation, intelligence is a dominant factor in readiness development (Blair, 2002). Thus readiness is a more extended concept than competence. Its current meaning is also more flexible and process-oriented than the competence concept in entrepreneurship research and helps in integrating the concept of competence to the learning processes. It also theoretically allows us to gain access to the complex conceptualization of the dynamics of meta-level learning processes.

In short, we can say that meta cognition is the concept used to describe a learner's competencies to reflect his/her learning and consequently change or improve it. Thus to cover all three constructs, besides meta cognition there are also meta conation and meta affection. Thus the competence-based approach in entrepreneurship education research is expanded to consider all these meta competencies. In formal education these should be explicitly embedded in planning, conducting and evaluating learning. As Ruohotie and Koiranen (2000: 13) argue, 'when a person learns entrepreneurship, changes take place not only in her/his knowledge constructs, but also in meta-cognitive skills, motivation, belief self-esteem etc'. Ruohotie (2003) has modelled this dynamics of meta processes between conative and cognitive constructs. The meta-cognitive component of self-regulation includes awareness of one's own knowledge structures, processes and cognitive and affective states. Limón-Lugue (2003) uses the terms 'meta motivation' and 'meta emotion' to refer to knowledge and regulation of one's motivation and emotions. Thus affective meta-aspects are interwoven into this dynamics. He argues that meta cognition consisting of meta knowledge and meta competencies is fundamental to learning to learn.

Self-regulation refers to an individual's active participation in his or her own learning process. It is the process through which self-generated thoughts, feelings and actions are planned and systematically adapted as necessary to affect one's learning and motivation. Learning depends on the learner's ability to manage all three meta-level abilities of self-regulation. Ruohotie approaches self-regulatory abilities as meta competencies and defines them through conative constructs, which intermediate between an individual's cognitive and affective attributes. However, since our perceptions highlight the importance of the affective construct as fundamental to entrepreneurial and enterprising learning, we would prefer to take affective meta abilities as an equal player in this dynamics. The affective aspect of learning processes is also stressed in some previous studies. For example, Malmivuori (2006) points out that ongoing self-appraisals and self-regulation are the key dynamic determinants in these self-system processes of students' affective experiences and cognitive learning. She also suggests that such features as high personal agency with high self-awareness, positive self-appraisals and efficient self-regulation will empower students' cognitive learning and problem/processes solving, for example to consciously act on debilitating affective responses. They may then choose to 'fine tune' the role of their affective responses in learning and problem-solving processes. As Op't Eyende et al. (2006) stress, teaching students how to solve problems then implies that we also have to teach them how to cope effectively with feelings of frustration or sometimes anger. In other words, allowing space for negative emotions might be an educational goal from a cognitive, as well as motivational, point of view. Indeed, only when experiencing negative emotions will students have the opportunity of learning how to deal with them. At the same time, experiencing negative emotions would indicate that students really care about solving the problem and are motivated. After all, only those who attach value to finding the solution are predisposed to become frustrated.

Self-reflection refers to examining and making meaning of the learning experience. Of the various meanings of reflection, we prefer Seibert's (1996) idea of regarding it as an active mental process of conscious involvement with experience that requires deliberately bringing one's thinking to the level of conscious awareness and, as Ruohotie (2003) points out, to regard it not only as retrospective action but as a continuous, ongoing process throughout the entrepreneurial and enterprising learning that facilitates and is a precondition for self-regulation process. Masui and De Corte (2005) in their intervention study found that reflection advanced both meta-cognitive and conative learning activities, which had a positive impact on academic achievements. It is notable that this process of thinking and learning could not be developed without others as assumed in symbolic interactionism. Individual thinking is developed constructively in social connections. Therefore these meta abilities have a social character. Developing entrepreneurial and enterprising readiness, referring to the entrepreneurial and enterprising competence and its learning process, involves the development of thinking and actions of both individuals and communities (Seikkula-Leino, 2007). These social experiences are crucial in learning (Seikkula-Leino, 2008).

The future challenges consist of integrating self-regulation strategy training into the everyday study context and, consequently, affective, conative and meta-cognitive competencies need to be introduced into programmes in order to enhance their self-reflection and self-regulated learning.

These propositions finalize our approach to entrepreneurial and enterprising learning and allow us to investigate 'how the cognitive, conative and affective self-regulating abilities interplay in entrepreneurial and enterprising learning process'. This approach consists of three categories of self-regulatory abilities: meta-cognitive ability referring to the cognitive construct, conative meta ability referring to the conative construct and affective meta ability referring to the affective construct. We are aware that this proposition is open to criticism, especially considering that the dynamics of these meta-level processes are drawn from and developed by cognitive psychology. However, we also argue that perhaps the role of affective self-regulatory processes is a neglected aspect in this debate and thus provides an opportunity to contribute to research in this field.

RESEARCH DESIGN AND METHODOLOGY

In order to investigate this kind of meta-level dynamics, an analysis of learners' own perceptions is required. Thus we have chosen an authentic, longitudinal and explorative research setting. It consists of the two-year follow-up reflections of 18 university students who participated in two consecutive study programmes of entrepreneurship education. These programmes were especially planned to enhance entrepreneurial and enterprising behaviour. Both programmes were available to all university students in Finland regardless of their educational disciplines and they were the largest programmes specialized in entrepreneurship education.

Figure 3.2 describes our research design from three perspectives. At the same time it defines how we understand the dynamics of the entrepreneurial and enterprising learning process, how the learning interventions were organized, how the gathered data relates to that design and finally the research and analysis methods used.

The dynamics of the entrepreneurial and enterprising learning process is the individual and social interplay between affective, conative and cognitive constructs, which should be taken into account in planning, conducting and evaluating the learning process. The continuous retrospective, on-going and future-oriented reflections are tools to learn and understand

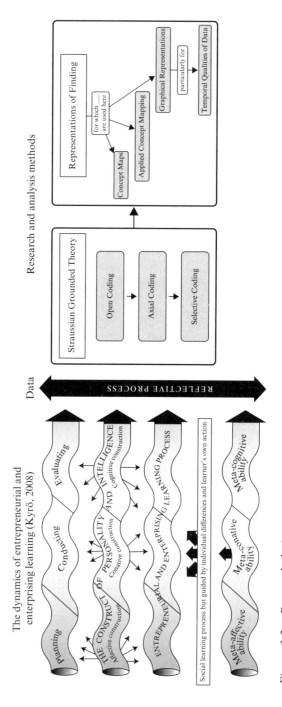

The dynamics of entrepreneurial and enterprising learning (Kyrö, 2008)

Research and analysis methods

Data

Figure 3.2   Research design

66

meta-level processes for enhancing meta-affective, meta-conative and meta-cognitive abilities. In the learning interventions the guiding principle is to respect the learner's right, freedom and (duty) to decide and act, and the way to do that is to support collaborative learning but at the same time to take account of the individual differences. The learning programmes were planned accordingly. The data consisted of students' reflections.

Research methods and data analysis follow a two-part progression. First we applied Straussian Grounded Theory with the coding proceeding through open, axial and selective phases (Strauss and Corbin, 1990), then the concept map method. The coding scheme was carried out within NVivo 7 qualitative data analysis software (QSR NVivo 7.0.281.0 SP4, 2007), while the construction and analysis of map representations expands NVivo's modelling functionalities by utilizing IHMC CmapTools concept mapping and knowledge modelling software (IHMC CmapTools 4.11., 2007; see for example Cañas et al., 2004). The resulting matrices were exported from the software to be processed further in spreadsheet and concept mapping software to summarize the results in meaningful representations.

Below we will describe in more detail the interventions, data gathering as well as the research and analysis methods.

Interventions

Entrepreneurship education courses consisted of two degree programmes and a total of seven modules and consequently reflections of each of these modules. The aims of the first 25 ECT bachelor's level programme were: (1) to learn basic competencies of entrepreneurship education and different dimensions of entrepreneurial pedagogy from the perspectives of society, individual, small business and other organizations; (2) to introduce participants to the newest international aspects of entrepreneurship concepts and theory-building; and (3) to support participants' competencies regarding applying and advancing entrepreneurial pedagogy in their own working contexts. It contained three modules: (1) orientation to entrepreneurship education and its pedagogy; (2) small business management and ownership; (3) intrapreneurship and learning organization, special themes on entrepreneurship. The second master's level 30 ECT course aimed to provide the students with an advanced study level overview of international research on entrepreneurship education, familiarize the students in scientific discussion in the entrepreneurship education field and provide them with the means to conduct research in the field. The focus was on conceptualizing entrepreneurship education, the dynamics of growing into entrepreneurship and the methodology of their research. It contained four modules: (1) orientation to entrepreneurship education; (2) international research on learning and the conceptualization of entrepreneurship; (3) methodological approach to research on entrepreneurship education and its dynamics; (4) design and analysis of an entrepreneurship education research process.

The students participated in both of these from 2003 to 2006. Both programmes were process-oriented, virtually supported with three days of face-to-face interventions per module. The students came from different fields of science. Both programmes adopted entrepreneurial and enterprising pedagogy. The responsibility for learning and freedom to do so was left to the learners. Learners were encouraged to be proactive in creating their goals, the means to achieve them, their own concepts and ideas about phenomena. Students were encouraged to start working individually and collaboratively from the beginning. The assignments actively supported students' own knowledge creation, action and interaction with surrounding firms and organizations. They contained the concept mapping examinations, group work, peer evaluations and reflections. The assignments consisted of real life cases, their peer evaluation and presentations.

Data Gathering

Textual data consisted of 400 pages of reflections from seven modules, altogether 90 documents, out of which 36 were group documents (18 students × 7 modules = 126−90 = 36). The reflection instructions to gather students' experiences were the same in all modules. The reflection format was based on action research studies. It guided towards three levels of reflection: technical, practical and critical, and focused on the learning of an individual, the group and the course as well as an organization and society.

Data Analysis

The sociologists Barney Glaser and Anselm Strauss developed Grounded Theory in the 1960s. Since then it has been applied mainly in sociology, education and only recently in new fields like nursing and information technology. Its use in entrepreneurship research is still rare and only two examples were found (Douglas, 2004 and Fernández, 2004). Both of them applied the developed Glaserian approach.

The method of Grounded Theory has been recommended for those fields with few established theories, lacking sufficient knowledge or concepts or when new perspectives are of special interest. It is suitable for this research from all these three perspectives, since we know very little about the dynamics of how the cognitive, conative and affective self-regulating abilities interplay in the entrepreneurial and enterprising learning process. Influenced by pragmatism and social interactionism, Glaser and Strauss suggested that there was a need on the one hand to respect and reveal how the actors perceive phenomena, and on the other hand to develop methodological tools for that. (Glaser and Strauss, 1967). The target of Grounded Theory has been social practices produced directly by human actors, as in this research. It can also be applied in our pragmatism-oriented phenomenology.

The question as to whether some other methodological choice would have been as useful for our purposes as Grounded Theory is always valid. For example, phenomenography might have served our purposes in some respects. However, considering the outcome of phenomenography we encounter some difficulties. Grounded Theory perceives theory as a process, that is theory as a constantly developing entity, further developed and validated in and through practice (Glaser and Strauss, 1967: 32), when the system of categories per se is the outcome of phenomenography. Instead of giving the leading role to scientific debate, it gives the leading role to the empirical data. This dynamic, data-oriented approach has remained at the core of this method regardless of its different contributors. Glaser and Strauss claimed that it is possible and even desirable to construct theories through inductive reasoning from empirical observations (Strauss and Corbin, 1990). Later, however, their opinions diverged with respect to the role of the theories and reasoning related to it. Glaser represents strictly inductive reasoning and denies the role of existing scientific theories. Strauss, together with Corbin, claims that both are needed, leading to the mixture of deductive and inductive reasoning. According to them existing theories are present in scientific research, wanted or not. Thus they lay the presumptions consciously or unconsciously to discoveries of new knowledge. Glaser criticizes that it is not Grounded Theory, but rather a method of generating a forced conceptual description based on presumptions. Siitonen (1999) suggests, however, that these two lines of thought represent different schools within Grounded Theory.

The analysis process involves, for example, making hypotheses and 'developing small theoretical frameworks, (miniframeworks) about concepts and their relationships' as in our approach and research design (Strauss and Corbin, 1990: 43).

The Coding Process

In Grounded Theory analysing includes 'operations by which data are broken down, conceptualised, and put back together in new ways' (Strauss and Corbin, 1990: 57).

In the *open coding phase* the topical content of the reflections and their related meta-level expressions were identified. In the *axial coding phase* first the references and meta references were identified and organized according to the three constructs as a mini framework. Then, by further adopting the tripartite constructs of personality and intelligence, these were organized according to different elements of each construct and presented as a concept map. Finally the transitions between these constructs were analysed (see, for example, Åhlberg, 2004). In the *selective coding phase* core categories are chosen and systematically related to other categories validating those relationships. This provides a tentative model or a theory for further development.

RESULTS

Open Coding

First 1686 expressions were coded and then categorized according to their topics. All together 25 topics were identified and out of these 72 per cent focused on seven categories. Among these 1686 references, 242 meta-level expressions were identified. From these 239 (99 per cent) were identified in seven topical categories. Thus since our research question concerns self-regulating abilities, these are most valid to us. Table 3.1 presents these frequencies.

The meta-level reflection was defined by criteria, which takes particular account of the temporally regular nature of producing the reflection texts over a lengthy period of time. This is performed in explicit order to control and/or understand the relevant factors affecting own studying action and its conditions. Expressions can also serve as a foundation for planning or anticipation of future events and action explicated in text. Thus the inherent *meta levelness* of the category refers to learning as reflected through explicating observations of how things keep changing, as different phases, activities and conditions of the path sequentially become active.

An example of each category is presented in Table 3.2.

It becomes obvious from Table 3.2 how in the respect of topical content most of the reflection focuses on collaboration and learning regarding different types of studying tasks and their practical execution. The emphasis on collaboration rather than individual work indicated how the collaborative pedagogy seems to take place in reflections. It is also noticeable in the data already examined at this level, how the emotional content of reflection seems to strongly emphasize the positive.

A notable feature of data seen in Table 3.2 is the large relative amount

Table 3.1   Topical categories and their references and meta-level expressions

Topical categories	Documents / category		Documents with meta-level expressions		References/ category		References with meta-level expressions	
	Number	%	Number	%	Number	%	Number	%
Learning and change	80	89	43	48	117	6.9	70	28.9
Collaboration, group dynamics	90	100	35	39	125	7.4	60	24.8
Studies and praxis	67	74	26	29	287	17.0	36	14.9
Individual work and processing	58	64	22	24	326	19.3	34	14.0
Time as resource	49	54	15	17	146	8.7	21	8.7
Joy, positive experiences	49	54	7	8	88	5.2	8	3.3
Teaching and pedagogy	48	53	9	10	117	6.9	10	4.1
Other 18 different categories					480	28.5	3	1.2
Documents N = 90					1686	100	242	100

of reflection related to the topical category of 'Learning and change'. A thing also worth mentioning here is that this type of reflection seems to be primarily and by nature practical. Instead of focusing on the domain knowledge of the studied academic field, the reflection mainly focuses on different actions of contributing to the problem-solving necessary to achieve the set goals of studying.

This suggests that action-oriented pedagogy is the key point in stimulating reflection. The second observation concerns the obvious emphasis on collaboration, which seems to be the key element for learning and meta learning. In our conceptual research design these were the key aspects of entrepreneurial and enterprising pedagogy (see Figure 3.2).

Axial Coding

The distributions of the 1686 references and 242 related meta-level references are presented in Table 3.3 and examples of their expressions in Table 3.4.

Table 3.2   Examples of the references and their meta-level expressions in seven main categories

Topical categories	Examples of expressions
1. Learning and change Expression	'My view on entrepreneurship and entrepreneurial education expanded. I read quite a lot of new material that was mainly interesting. Hence, learning took place . . .'
Meta-level expression	'On the other hand, the recognition of . . . this deficiency is an essential thing for my own development because for my own action as an educator of adults in the context of entrepreneurial education to evolve I must understand the diversity of the learners' starting points.'
2. Collaboration, group dynamics Expression	'Our group of people from [. . .] performed well and easy together. We even have what it takes to start an enterprise of our own'. 'The structure of the group establishes a wide content base for discussion. This makes the day even more interesting, so one has the strength to study into the evening.'
Meta-level expression	'[Therefore] we ended up dividing the work over several training periods and this section functions mainly as a lead-in and base for the next section during which we'll focus on entrepreneur hatchery and the pedagogy related to it.'
3. Studies and praxis Expression	'If this module seems in my view too theoretical and too little applicable into praxis, I'm not going to continue my studies. The needed credits I already have, I came here to begin with to learn new things necessary for my profession.'
Meta-level expression	'I've witnessed characteristics of the internal entrepreneurship in different organizations, but I've not been able to name them or justify their value. This module has opened up the internal entrepreneurship for me. I recognize the value of entrepreneurial education in different institutions, e.g. in polytechnics. The internal entrepreneurship of the teachers should be utilized in supporting the organizational development.'
4. Individual work and processing Expression	'During the first module, I've constructed a reasonable concept map on entrepreneurial education based on literature and group work. I've also dutifully participated in all the face-to-face-meetings . . .'

Table 3.2   (continued)

Topical categories	Examples of expressions
Meta-level expression	'Most of all, while there is a professorship being established in the local university, I keep wondering should I participate in the process by trying to meet the director to elaborate a dialogue of educational sciences also here in the provinces.'
5. Time as resource Expression	'Even though the studies have taken time – meetings, emails, reading, writing – studying has been in general rewarding and good for self-esteem.'
Meta-level expression	'The schedule for completing the tasks was yet again tight. First my child was ill, and after her myself. The number of face-to-face-meetings could be larger in the future; it's easier to detach from the work routine that way.'
6. Joy, positive experiences Expression	'It was a happy mental state planning the structure for the interview questions after the first face-to-face-meeting and looked for a theoretical foundation for them from the material given to us.'
Meta-level expression	'Using the terminology of Grounded Theory we started to approach the point of saturation and things started to open up. Our collaboration "waved" from [one] stage to another and our knowledge deepened by each "wave". At times it felt like we were in a "tsunami", but happily it turned out in the end that we were "just surfing"! This gave us true experiences of "empowerment" and "flow" and also the true faith that "Grounded Theory" has that certain something'.
7. Teaching and pedagogy Expression	'Three face-to-face meetings fit this type of working as such, but the face-to-face meetings in the autumn should have been further apart from each other to make among other things absorbing the literature and group work less hasty.'
Meta-level expression	'Personally I'd perceive more reasonable, if the studies were constructed less self-directed in the beginning. At least the orientation period should be more teacher-driven. During the latter modules the self-directed action is naturally better grounded.' 'How should we design teaching to have it include all the constructs [in the table]? This requires a great deal of flexibility already at the planning stage. One must also take care of aiming the planning particularly towards the learner's right and freedom to act.'

Table 3.3 References and meta-level references according to the tripartite constructs of personality and intelligence

Construct	References		Meta-level references		Meta-level as % of total references
	Number	%	Number	%	
Cognition	698	41.4	169	69.7	24.2
Conation	561	33.3	57	23.6	10.2
Affection	427	25.3	16	6.7	3.7
Total	1686	100	242	100	

Both the references and meta references are cognition dominated. Almost 70 per cent of all meta-level reflection of the constructs is focused on the cognitive content, whose reflection is fairly evenly distributed over the path of seven consecutive modules. Also, it is obvious that all three constructs are represented in the references. In the meta level, however, it is notable that the affection-related references seem to disappear and also conative references are proportionally less represented than the actual proportion of references assumes.

To look into these in more detail we constructed a concept map describing the relationships inside each construct (see Figure 3.3).

Within the cognitive category's sub-categories the reflection focuses on the areas of strategy and domain knowledge. This is largely due to the students' tendency to reflect on the decisions made in order to solve different kinds of problems mainly related to coordinating collaboration and organizing their own action accordingly. The understanding of the strategic reflection being connected with collaborative operations gets support even at this level of representation, while viewed in context with the results from the open coding stage and especially when observing stress being received by the 'Orientation towards self and others' sub-category within the conative content.

The second large sub-category within cognition, labelled 'Domain knowledge', should also be investigated in close connection with the previous two. At the same time it is instructive to view it alongside with the understanding of the prominent weight that comparative reflection on studies and praxis represents within the results of open coding (see Tables 3.1 and 3.2). Here, looking at the open coding category, 'Studies' are seen as both the content and materials used in teaching, and also the pedagogically grounded action of task-setting. 'Praxis' in turn is the professional

Table 3.4   *Examples of the references and their meta-level expressions in three constructs*

Construct	Examples of expressions/references
Cognition Expression	Domain knowledge: 'I received theoretical substance among other things about the parameters related to computation and economics in the starting phase of an enterprise. I learned that from the parameters it is quite [easy] to deduct the viability and economical stability of an enterprise. The process of constructing a business plan from a give[n] model took form through the good material and the instruction from the entrepreneuship center.'
Example of meta-level expression	Domain knowledge: 'I need concrete help and training for my own business plan. The correct address for receiving that could possibly be [Pirkanmaan TE-keskus]. My knowledge on countryside travelling business is also too shallow. For this there is literature available, but a training session by an institute would be in order.'
Conation Expression	Action control: 'Nobody has to be dragged along with the group but everyone strives to do one's best and invest in the effort.'
Example of meta-level expression	Action control: 'I felt myself receiving something else in exchange. I was the first to announce that "I'm allowed to do what I want". This was the element of freedom that also the research indicates entrepreneurhip to bring.'
Affection Expression	* 'I felt truly happy. [The beginning of the 15 credits unit suited me well timing wise.]'* 'After meeting the people of the group for the first time I felt like I'd rubbed [shoulders] with them for a long time already.'
Example of meta-level expression	'[. . .] Another praiseworthy thing is that all the group members were enthusiastic about our effort, [de]spite their other obligations and hurries in work and studies. This enthusiasm is contagious and has made studying extremely fun and rewarding. [. . .] Also it was obvious from observing the peer-group activity, how it had evolved. Most of the groups had truly examined their peer-group's work and considered the possible improvements to be implemented. In this sense, the peer-group activity should be first and foremost consoling, seeking for the positive and good qualities and aimed at improving the products, sustaining not that much focus on the negative or failed things.'

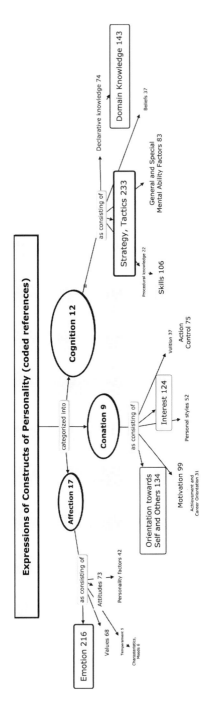

Expressions of Constructs of Personality (coded references)

categorized into

Affection 17

as consisting of

Emotion 216
Values 68
Attitudes 73
Temperament 5
Characteristics, Moods 6
Personality factors 42

Conation 9

as consisting of

Orientation towards Self and Others 134
Achievement and Career Orientation 31
Motivation 99
Interest 124
Personal styles 52
Volition 37
Action Control 75

Cognition 12

as consisting of

Declarative knowledge 74

Strategy, Tactics 233

Procedural knowledge 22
Skills 106
General and Special Mental Ability Factors 83
Domain Knowledge 143
Beliefs 37

Note: Size of a sub-category relates to the frequency of coded references, size of the main construct to the relative size summed from the frequency of references in the sub-categories.

Figure 3.3 Expressions of constructs of personality with their associated sub-categories

and everyday experience of the student related to the subject of teaching and studying.

In addition to the interplay between cognitive and conative constructs within the reflected content, the main finding at this point of analysis is the dominant quality of the processes accessed through reflection. The strong presence of the elements of 'Procedural knowledge' presented by the reflection on *how to act* gets even stronger when taking into account the amount of reflection on skills. Skills can be reflected as either being learned as a result of studying or as operating as resource or limitation for the variety of strategies being available for application.

Secondly the aforementioned generally positive nature of the reflection reveals itself here, too. The content related to the construct of affection holds within the second largest, single theoretical category of 'Emotion'. This is due to students' notable tendency to eagerly name and point out positive feelings and emotion throughout and across the reflection on different themes – to say, events, activities and stages of the study path.

At this stage we can say that all three constructs are present, that action and positive emotions are extremely visible within these constructs and also that the reflections are written as interplay between these three constructs. However, to look more deeply into their interplay we still identified the transitions between different constructs. Transition is defined as a distinct, sequential passage within text from reflecting one construct to reflecting another, throughout which the narrative and thematic focus remains unbroken (see examples in Table 3.5). The analysis of such transitions was done to understand the dynamics of reflecting constructs of personality in more detail, for example to see in which kinds of sequences constructs get reflected in context with one another. Among 1686 references, 238 transitions were identified. Their relationships are presented as a concept map in Figure 3.4. Now looking at the relationships between three constructs, it becomes obvious that all of them are important in learning interventions. Cognitive related relationships cover 74 per cent of transitions, conative related 61.3 per cent and affective related 64.7 per cent. The transitions between the three constructs take place in all directions. The most coded transition is from reflecting cognitive to conative content and the second-most coded transition is from affective to cognitive construct. It is a very common pattern within the data for the reflective writing sequences to initiate from recollection of having distinct emotions connected to different stages of the studying path and the related actions. This can be seen as an indication of how the catalyst nature of affective construct also manifests itself within reflection.

Table 3.5   Examples of expressions of transitions

Transitions	Examples of expressions
From cognitive to conative	'Will the assignment fail, if the references aren't the "correct ones"? When searching for the idea of [. . .] entrepreurship education, from the perspective of the subject, this is in turn an "academic" conflict which is the evaluation criteria used for not ending up "murdering souls" once again? On the other hand, there emerged an idea, that we definitely won't be content with ourselves receiving "less than two" [for a grade]. . . . . .this to notify [teacher], even though we're not promoting rivalry for its own sake.'
From conative to affective	'[. . .] On the other hand, there emerged an idea, that we definitely won't be content with ourselves receiving "less than two" [for a grade] . . . this to notify [teacher], even though we're not promoting rivalry for it's own sake. We are in that sense "typical female entrepreneurs, for whom [. . .] entrepreneurship is a way of life". This perspective of female entrepreneurship has come up also, when [. . .]'
From affective to conative	'I've managed to form a distinct feeling about things that motivate me and to which I'm committed to invest my time and resources. I'm not even going to collect the necessary credits from courses that are not interesting or useful concerning my future.'
From cognitive to affective	'During the 15 credits at hand, I've aimed at extracting as much as possible out of the subject. Even though the studies have taken time – meetings, emails, reading, writing – studying has been in general rewarding and good for self-esteem.' 'We aim to read up on the theory widely and variedly. Surely our work must meet the requirements of the assignment and be contentually relevant. Therefore our products tend to swell to relatively large dimensions and in particular with this period the tightness of the schedule caused slight anxiety.'
From affective to cognitive	'I experienced a sensation of insight each time I started to work on a new paper; yet again I'd learned to think about things from another perspective.' 'We also felt positively about the relatively similar world of ideas. Questioning took place too, which produced contemplation and conceptual clarification.'
From conative to cognitive	'I anticipated especially Iris Aaltio's lectures with great interest, for earlier I'd gotten acquainted with her articles about female entrepreneurship. Ulla Suojanen's lecture on sustainable development in turn provided new learning, for she highlighted such perspectives I wasn't familiar with before.'

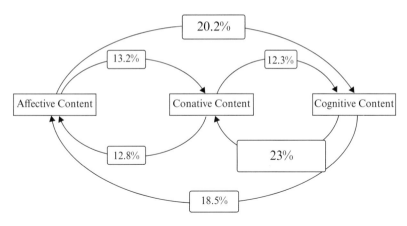

Note: N = 238.

Figure 3.4   Transitions between the constructs

Selective Coding

Now, as the selective coding assumes, we can select the core categories and relate them to other categories, thus compiling a tentative model for further development. As Strauss and Corbin (1990: 116–42) express it, 'put the data back in new ways'.

The open coding indicates that action-orientated pedagogy stimulates reflections and meta abilities. Collaboration seems to be the key element of the learning and meta learning of entrepreneurial and enterprising readiness. The research design of this study enhanced the entrepreneurial and enterprising learning process.

Axial coding shows how all three constructs, affective, conative and cognitive, are present and involved in the three construct dynamics, although meta-level affective reflections are missing. Conation orientation towards others and self are reflected the most, which is presumably grounded on the fact that courses designed were based on the collaborative pedagogy.

All the results point to the fact that affection seems to stimulate action in the cognitive construct, and collaborative learning stimulates action and affection. Conative construct is stimulated by action. The meaningful element of learning is interaction with others, which enhances reflection processes and the emergence of meta abilities. The results highlight that affection is under-reflected, which as a consequence will give us an idea that the conative process for this reason is not present enough in learning entrepreneurial and enterprising readiness.

As a conclusion to the selective coding phase we can answer the research question of 'how the dynamics of cognitive, conative and affective self-regulating abilities interplay in the entrepreneurial and enterprising learning process' as follows: the interplay between the dynamics of affective, conative and cognitive meta abilities is present in the entrepreneurial and enterprising learning process, especially if it is designed from the basis of collaborative learning. Moreover, meta abilities are reflected but the differences between the reflections of these constructs indicate that for some reason we can not advance the reflection of meta affection which would empower the reflection of conation and which as a consequence would enhance entrepreneurial and enterprising behaviour.

Thus our tentative model as a suggestion for further studies to be developed towards the theory is that: affection stimulates action in the cognitive construct and collaborative learning stimulates action and affection. Conative construct is stimulated by action (about the theory see Strauss and Corbin, 1990: 57).

Thus getting deeper access to meta-affective processes seems to be the key towards influencing the conative construct which is the key to stimulating intentions and, as Ajzen (1991) suggests, intentions best anticipate performance.

CONTRIBUTION AND IMPLICATIONS

These results indicate that all constructs emerged in these entrepreneurship education learning interventions as well as transitions between them. The study indicates how affective meta abilities and affective, conative and cognitive constructs determine our learning processes. Thus if this interplay is taken into account more, it might help to enhance entrepreneurship in general.

However, the disappearance of affective construct in meta-level reflections might reflect our poor ability to enhance entrepreneurial attitudes and values which are both found important, for example, in research of intentions. The low total entrepreneurial activity (TEA) index, but high PISA rating in Finland might reflect these shortcomings in our education and thus these findings might also provide some ideas for renewing the pedagogy and mainstreaming activities of entrepreneurship education. Strengthening these underrepresented elements might enhance students' reflection and self-regulation processes and as a consequence empower entrepreneurial and enterprising learning. Such ideas encourage us to suggest that this stream of research should receive more emphasis in entrepreneurship education research.

Snow et al.'s (1996: 243) frame of the affective, conative and cognitive constructs of personality and intelligence seems to work well in our research and the contribution of our findings adds to this discussion the importance of the affective construct previously underestimated. Also, the dynamics between these three constructs has a more precise tentative form than before. Moreover, the pragmatist orientation to phenomenology was a valid choice here and thus confirms Mises' and Dewey's ideas of action and interaction in the learning process. The practical implications of these findings are that in enterprising and entrepreneurial learning processes the impact could be enhanced by possibly taking learners' action, interaction and affective factors as an integrated aspect of this process. How to do this is both a theoretical and practical challenge for every teacher and it is also crucial to the understanding of the process-oriented competence discussion.

However, it should be noted that even though the key concepts and their relationship have been defined, this research is still decidedly tentative and thus needs a great deal of effort to reach the state of theory. First of all, to follow individual learning paths and their differences and similarities might add to our knowledge about entrepreneurial and enterprising learning processes and perhaps even question these more general findings. Then to achieve more learning interventions, both formal and informal in different contexts, might indicate that perhaps our interventions have culture-bound specifics that might affect the findings and change the model. Finally to find a way to gain a more profound understanding about meta processes and to learn how to enhance them could be among the most interesting and important topics for further research.

ACKNOWLEDGEMENTS

We would like to thank the INNOLA/INLAB Project funded by European Social fund (ESF) and the State provincial Office of Southern Finland, for their contribution to this chapter.

REFERENCES

Acs, Z. and D. Audretsch (eds) (2003), *Handbook of Entrepreneurship Research*, Dordrecht: Kluwer Academic Publishers.
Åhlberg, M. (2004), 'Varieties of concept mapping', proceedings of the First International Conference on Concept Mapping, Vol. 2, pp. 25–8.
Ajzen, I. (1991), 'The theory of planned behaviour', *Organizational Behavior and Human Decision Processes*, **50**(2), 179–211.

Arenius, P., E. Autio and A. Kovalainen (2005), *Finnish Entrepreneurial Activity in Regional, National and Global Context*, Technology Review 176/2005, Helslnki: TEKES.

Audi, R. (ed.) (1995), *The Cambridge Dictionary of Philosophy*, Cambridge: Cambridge University Press.

Blair, C. (2002), 'School readiness: integrating cognition and emotion in a neurobiological conceptualization of children's functioning at schools entry', *American Psychologist*, **57**(2) 111–27.

Bosman, C., F.-M. Gérard and R. Roegiers (2000), *Quel Avenir pour les Compétences?*, Brussels: De Boeck.

Cañas, A.J., G. Hill, R. Carff, N. Suri, J. Lott, T. Eskridge, G. Gómez, M. Arroyo and R. Carvajal (2004), 'Cmap tools: a knowledge modeling and sharing environment', in A.J. Cañas, J.D. Novak and F.M. González (eds), *Concept Maps: Theory, Methodology, Technology*, Proceedings of the First International Conference on Concept Mapping, Universidad Pública de Navarra, Pamplona, Spain, pp. 125–33.

Carrier, C. (2005), 'Pedagogical challenges in entrepreneurship education', in P. Kyrö and C. Carrier (eds), *The Dynamics of Learning Entrepreneurship in a Cross-cultural University Context*, Entrepreneurship Education Series 2/2005, Hämeenlinna: University of Tampere, Research Centre for Vocational and Professional Education.

Chandler, G.N. and E. Jansen (1992), 'The founder's self-assessed competence and venture performance', *Journal of Business Venturing*, **7**(3), 223–36.

Commission of the European Communities (2003), 'Summary report: the public debate following the Green Paper, Entrepreneurship in Europe', Brussels.

Commission of the European Communities (2006), 'Communication from the Commission to the Council, the European Parliament, The European Economic and Social Committee and the Committee of the Regions: Putting Knowledge into Practice: A broad-based innovation strategy for the EU', Brussels.

Cope, Jason (2005), 'Toward a dynamic learning perspective of entrepreneurship', *Entrepreneurship Theory and Practice*, **29**(4), 373–98.

Dewey, J. (1951), *Experience and Education*, 13th edn, New York: MacMillan Company.

Douglas, D. (2004), 'Grounded theory and the "and" in entrepreneurship research', Business School, Staffordshire University, UK, *Electronic Journal of Business Research Methods*, **2**(2), available at http://www.ejbrm.com, accessed 1 March 2005.

Erkkilä, K. (2000), *Entrepreneurial Education*, New York: Carland Publishing.

European Commission (2002), 'Final report of the expert group "best procedure" project on education and training for entrepreneurship', November, Brussels.

Fayolle, A. and H. Klandt (eds) (2006), *International Entrepreneurship Education*, Cheltenham, UK and Northampton, MA, USA: Edward Elgar.

Fernández, W.D. (2004), 'Using the Glaserian approach in grounded studies of emerging business practices', *The Electronic Journal of Business Research Methods*, **2**(2), available at http://www.ejbrm.com/, accessed 24 February 2005.

Fiet, J.O. (2000), 'The pedagogical side of entrepreneurship theory', *Journal of Business Venturing*, **16**(2), 101–17.

Gibb, A. (1993), 'The enterprise culture and education: understanding enterprise education and its links with small business, entreprenurship and wider educational goals', *International Small Business Journal*, **11**(3), 11–24.

Gibb, A. (2001), 'Creating conducive environments for learning and entrepreneurship: living with, dealing with, creating and enjoying uncertainty and complexity', paper presented at first conference on International Entrepreneurship Forum, Naples, 21–24 June

Gibb, A. (2002), 'In pursuit of a new "enterprise" and "entrepreneurship" paradigm for learning: creative destruction, new values, new ways of doing things and new combinations of knowledge', *International Journal of Management Review*, **4**(3), 233–69.

Gibb, A. (2005), 'The future of entrepreneurship education: determining the basis for coherent policy and practice?', in P. Kyrö and C. Carrier (eds), *The Dynamics of Learning Entrepreneurship in a Cross-cultural University Context*, Entrepreneurship Education Series 2/2005, Hämeenlinna: University of Tampere, Research Centre for Vocational and Professional Education.

Glaser, B. and A. Strauss (1967), *The Discovery of Grounded Theory*, Chicago: Aldine.

Hayton, James and Donna Kelley (2006), 'A competency-based framework for promoting corporate entrepreneurship', *Human Resource Management*, **45**(3), 407–27.

James, W. (1913), *Pragmatismi*, Helsinki: Otava.

Kansanen, P. (1995), 'Discussion on some educational issues', Research report 145, Department of Teacher Education, University of Helsinki, available at http://www.helsinki.fi/~pkansane/deutsche.html, accessed 22 February 2005.

Koiranen, M. and P. Ruohotie (2001), 'Yrittäjyyskasvatus: analyyseja, synteesejä ja sovelluksia' ('Enterprise education: analyses, syntheses and applications'), *Aikuiskasvatus*, **2**(2001), 102–11.

Kyrö, P. (2006), 'Action research and networking benchmarking in developing Nordic statistics on woman entrepreneurship', *Benchmarking: An International Journal*, **13**(1/2).

Kyrö, P. (2008), 'A theoretical framework for teaching and learning entrepreneurship', *International Journal of Business and Globalisation*, **2**(1), 39–55.

Kyrö, P. and C. Carrier (2005), *The Dynamics of Learning Entrepreneurship in a Cross-cultural University Context*, Entrepreneurship Education Series 2/2005, Hämeenlinna: University of Tampere, Research Centre for Vocational and Professional Education.

La Paro, K.M. and R.C. Pianta (2000), 'Predicting children's competence in the early school years: a meta-analytic review', *Review of Educational Research*, **70**(4), 443–84.

Lewit, E.M. and L. Schuurmann Baker (1995), 'School readiness', *The Future of Children: Critical Issues for Children and Youths*, **5**(2), 128–39.

Limón-Lugue, M. (2003), 'The role of domain-specific knowledge in intentional conceptual change', in G.M. Sinatra and P.R. Pintrich (eds) *Intentional Conceptual Change*, Mahwah, NJ: Lawrence Erlbaum Associates, pp. 134–36.

Malmivuori, M. (2006), 'Affect and self-regulation', *Educational Studies in Mathematics*, **63**, 149–64.

Masui, C. and E. De Corte (2005), 'Learning to reflect and to attribute constructively as basic components of self-regulated learning', *British Journal of Educational Psychology*, **75**, 351–72.

Op't Eyende, P., E. De Corte and L. Verschaffel (2006), '"Accepting emotional complexity": a socio-constructivist perspective on the role of emotions in the mathematics classroom', *Educational Studies in Mathematics*, **63**, 193–207.

Puhakka, V. (2006), 'Effects of social capital on the opportunity recognition process', *Journal of Enterprising Culture*, **14**(2), 107–26.

Ruohotie, P. (2000), 'Conative constructs in learning', in P.R. Pintrich and P. Ruohotie (eds), *Conative Constructs and Self-regulated Learning*, Hämeenlinna, Finland: RCVE.

Ruohotie, P. (2003), 'Self-regulatory abilities of professional learning', in B. Beairsto, M. Klein and P. Ruohotie (eds), *Professional Learning and Leadership*, University of Tampere: Research Centre for Vocational Education.

Ruohotie, P. and M. Koiranen (2000), 'In the pursuit of conative constructs into entrepreneurship education', *Journal of Entrepreneurship Education*, **3**, 9–22.

Saks, N.T. and C.M. Gaglio (2002), 'Can opportunity identification be taught?', *Journal of Enterprising Culture*, **10**(4), 313–47.

Sarasvathy, S. (2007), '*Effectuation: Elements of Entrepreneurial Expertise*, Cheltenham, UK and Northampton, MA, USA: Edward Elgar Publishers.

Schumpeter, J.A. (1934), *Theory of Economic Development*, Cambridge, MA: Harvard University Press.

Seibert, K.W. (1996), 'Experience is the best teacher, if you can learn from it: real-time reflection and development', in D.T. Hall & associates (eds), *The Career is Dead – Long Live the Career*, San Francisco: Jossey-Bass Publishers, pp. 246–64.

Seikkula-Leino, J. (2007), 'The process of entrepreneurship education development through curriculum reform', proceedings of the Internationalizing Entrepreneurship Education & Training Conference, 8–11 July, Gdansk, Poland, pp. 1–16.

Seikkula-Leino, J. (2008), 'Advancing entrepreneurship education in Finnish basic education: the prospect for developing local curricula', in A. Fayolle and P. Kyrö (eds), *The Dynamics between Entrepreneurship, Environment and Education*, Cheltenham, UK and Northampton, MA, USA: Edward Elgar.

Siitonen, J. (1999), *Voimaantumisteorian Perusteiden Hahmottelua*, Acta Univ. Oul. E37, Oulu: Oulu University Press.

Snow, R.E., L. Corno and D. Jackson (1996), 'Individual differences in affective and conative functions', in D.C. Berliner and R.C. Calfee (eds), *Handbook of Educational Psychology*, New York: Simon & Schuster Macmillan, pp. 243–310.

Strauss, A. and J. Corbin (1990), *Basics of Qualitative Research: Grounded Theory Procedures and Techniques*, Newbury Park, CA: Sage.

von Mises, L. (1966), *Human Action: A Treatise on Economics*, Chicago: Henry Regnery Company.

4. Entrepreneurial opportunity identification: the case of Skype Technologies

Rok Stritar and Mateja Drnovšek

INTRODUCTION

The ability of entrepreneurs to identify opportunities and develop new ventures intrigues researchers from the very beginning of entrepreneurship as a scientific discipline (Kirzner, 1979; Schumpeter, 1934). The rapid technological development during the late 1990s triggered an especially intriguing period in entrepreneurial history as prevailing investor optimism fuelled the growth of internet ventures at an unprecedented pace. The bursting of the Internet stock market bubble in March 2000 grounded the high-flying dreams of new economy ventures based on Internet technologies. However, the following period of prevailing investor pessimism and maturing technologies was the breeding ground for some of the fastest-growing entrepreneurial ventures in history.

One of such companies was Skype, founded in 2002 by Niklas Zennström and Janus Friis. The company offered an alternative to traditional telephones by offering a free service that enabled Internet users to use their computers for voice communication. The first version of the software was released in August 2003. Up until October 2005 the service attracted 54 million users and it was sold to EBay for $2.6 billion. By the time it was sold the total amount of money invested in the company was $20 million, making it one of the fastest growing start-ups in history (Gruber, 2006).

Such rapid entrepreneurial growth opens several 'Why?' and 'How?' questions connected to the opportunity, the entrepreneurs and the venture itself, and offers a unique and interesting research case for the study of the entrepreneurial process. We focus the study on the opportunity identification and development of the venture.

The chapter proceeds as follows: first we review the existing literature on entrepreneurial opportunities, focusing on the opportunity identification and creation. This is followed by a case study of Skype Technologies. We focus mostly on the period before the venture was created, analysing the development of technologies that enabled the creation of the venture and the role the entrepreneurs played in the identification and creation of the opportunity. The case data is used to develop a grounded model of opportunity identification for the venture. In the final part we apply the theory on opportunity identification and development on the model to propose a more general model for further testing and analysis.

ENTREPRENEURIAL OPPORTUNITIES

The study of entrepreneurial opportunities is in the nexus of entrepreneurship research (Ardichvili et al., 2003; Busenitz et al., 2003; Eckhardt and Shane, 2003; Shane, 2000; Shane and Venkataraman, 2000). The study of favourable junctures of circumstances[1] that enable the emergence of new ventures, products and services and their role in the entrepreneurial process are among the traditional and still current topics in entrepreneurship research (for example Kirzner, 1979; Shane and Venkataraman, 2000; Ardichvili et al., 2003; McMullen et al., 2007; Ucbasaran et al., 2009). Without opportunities there is no entrepreneurship, yet there is an ongoing debate within the entrepreneurship literature on issues such as the source, scope and objectivity of entrepreneurial opportunities (Shane and Venkataraman, 2000; Ardichvili et al., 2003; McMullen et al., 2007; Dimov, 2007a; Sarasvathy, 2001; Nicolaou and Shane, 2009; Davidsson, 2008).

The vast body of research on entrepreneurial opportunities can be roughly divided into two distinct ontological streams. The traditional positivist view assumes that opportunities exist in the environment independently of the entrepreneur. They are objective phenomena in the environment, yet the process of opportunity discovery is a subjective process (Shane and Venkataraman, 2000). Different people will discover different opportunities based mostly on their previous experience and beliefs. Given that an asymmetry of beliefs is a precondition for the existence of entrepreneurial opportunities, all opportunities must not be obvious to everyone all of the time. People must not agree on the value of resources at a given point in time. Entrepreneurs find new ways of using available resources to produce more valuable outcomes (Eckhardt and Shane, 2003). The approach assumes that market imperfections exist in the environment and that the entrepreneurs play a passive and responsive role (Alvarez and Barney, 2005). Entrepreneurs are only proactive when they exploit the opportunity (Eckhardt and Shane, 2003). The process of the discovery of objective opportunities is normally treated as the process of opportunity recognition and is the prevailing view in the entrepreneurship literature.

Alternatively a more recent stream of research (for example Ardichvili et al., 2003; Dimov, 2007b; Dutta and Crossan, 2005; Sarasvathy, 2004; Vaghely and Julien, 2010) argues that the entrepreneurs play a central role in the creation of an entrepreneurial opportunity. Entrepreneurs do not discover opportunities; rather, they create them by taking advantage of technological change or innovation occurring in the economy. The opportunities arise as an outcome of the new conditions on the market created by the innovating 'entrepreneur-hero' (Dutta and Crossan, 2005).

Also the mere discovery of opportunities is not enough to ensure a viable venture, and the entrepreneurs play a key role in the development of the opportunity (Ardichvili et al., 2003 Dimov, 2007b; Sarasvathy, 2004).

Sarasvathy (2004) proposes that what are discovered are not opportunities yet merely possibilities that have to be developed to become opportunities. In a similar manner Ardichvili et al. (2003) suggest that the process of opportunity recognition should be studied in two phases: (1) identification and (2) development. The way an opportunity is developed is strongly connected to the individual which means that two different entrepreneurs would not develop the same opportunity in the same way (Dimov, 2007a).

However, not only does the individual play an important role in the development phase, but also their role is very important in the identification phase. According to the positivist view, which assumes that opportunities exist independently of the entrepreneurs, the question concerning whether an entrepreneur will discover and pursue an opportunity is the question of entrepreneurial alertness to specific ideas, which is a result of previous experience, an interpretative framework and past knowledge (Yu, 2001; Kirzner, 1997). Constructionists emphasize the role of the individual even more by treating the entrepreneur and his/her actions as a necessary condition for the creation of an opportunity (Dimov, 2007a). Some elements of opportunities may be recognized; opportunities in general are made, not found.

What both approaches have in common is the moment (or process) of recognition or identification of the opportunity.[2] Following the positivistic ontology, the opportunities recognized also consist of scripts and actions that need to be taken in order to develop the opportunities into successful ventures, while the identification approach treats the identified opportunities as subjective perceptions of what the entrepreneurs believe (Dimov, 2007a) could be possibilities (Sarasvathy, 2004) for the development of successful ventures. The moment when an entrepreneur becomes aware of an opportunity is treated as 'insight'. During insight, the individual has a breakthrough, 'Aha!' moment. Corbett (2005) suggests that during insight a cognitive shift takes place as the individual begins to consciously realize that he/she may have identified an opportunity to break an existing means–end relationship. In broadest terms, a person's business idea constitutes a mental image of a particular group of customers benefiting from using a particular product or service (Sarasvathy, 2004). It can be either convergent, by making sense of apparently disconnected facts, or divergent, by generating possibilities that others would not consider (Dimov, 2007a). The insights can happen as a result of a causation process or an effectuation process (Sarasvathy, 2001); however, in most cases entrepreneurs employ both at different times (Vaghely and Julien, 2010).

Opportunity identification and development is a process through which the entrepreneurs massage, develop and alter the opportunity. The opportunity takes many forms, from a mere identified possibility through business concepts and business models until it is developed and tested enough to be ready for commercial exploitation (Ardichvili et al., 2003). The literature makes a notable distinction between the identification and development phase of the entrepreneurship process; however, less is clear when it comes to the questions regarding what the result of both phases is and where the process of identification ends and development starts.

METHODOLOGY

To study the opportunity identification phase of the entrepreneurial process further we turn to the studied phenomenon itself. We embrace a grounded theory building approach to study with the purpose of exploratory richness (Bygrave, 2006). We ground our research in rich data gathered on Skype Technologies.

Grounded theory methods consist of systematic, yet flexible guidelines for collecting and analysing qualitative data to construct theories grounded in the data themselves (Charmaz, 2006). The method was conceived by Glaser and Strauss (1967) who conveyed a discontent with the dominant logico-deductive approach to research practices of their time. They introduced a grounded systematic approach to data analysis that leads to inductive discovery of theory. We define grounded theory as theory derived from data that has been systematically collected and analysed using an iterative process of considering and comparing earlier literature, its data and the emerging theory (Mäkelä and Turcan, 2006).

The study uses secondary data in forms of written interviews, video interviews, presentations and Internet news feeds. The ample media attention received by the studied company made it possible to build a reliable chain of events supported by rich data. A qualitative data analysis software, Atlas.ti, is used to organize and code the studied data. The software is also used to organize codes and form categories and concepts keeping the links to the raw data to enable double checks. Data triangulation (as suggested by Yin, 2003) is used to verify key events and concepts.

Identified categories are organized in a network to build a grounded case-specific model of opportunity identification. We attempt to generalize the categories in the model by testing the discovered relationships and concepts with established theory and identifying potential building blocks of a more general theory.

As always with inductive research designs based on single case studies, the question of applying the finding to a more general level of theory is questionable, as the nature of the method demands subjective inferences and interpretations not present with quantitative methods. Those negative aspects of the methodology employed can be improved by employing the same level of rigidity as with quantitative methodologies when collecting and analysing the data; however, complete objectivity can never be achieved. While being fully aware of the limitations, we followed the call of several established scholars in entrepreneurship research (for example Davidsson, 2008; Bygrave, 2006 and Hindle, 2004) to employ more exploratory qualitative research designs in entrepreneurship aimed at the collection of rich data and a deeper understanding of the intriguing entrepreneurship process and development of new grounded theoretical concepts.

Having said that, we are fully aware of the limitations for generalization of the findings of the study. The identified concepts should be further tested and explored to become building blocks of a more general theory.

OPPORTUNITY IDENTIFICATION: THE CASE OF SKYPE TECHNOLOGIES

When asked about the key factors that made the rise of Skype possible, Niklas Zennström responds: 'a lot of things are of course timing and luck' (Q1, Q2).[3] We start by first studying the favourable developments of technologies and markets that made the timing right for the start of the venture.

Voice over the Internet Protocol: VoIP

The entrepreneurs chose to start their venture in the telephony market that was 'characterized both by what we think is rip-off pricing and a reliance on heavily centralized infrastructure' (Q3). The heavily centralized infrastructure resulted in high levels of needed capital investments with high economies of scale leading to natural monopolies, which resulted in strict government regulation of the telecommunications market. The entrepreneurs saw a possible alternative in the Internet infrastructure 'any digital content should be delivered over the Internet because it's so much more efficient' (Q4). In addition to bringing a lower cost of telecommunication by using the Internet infrastructure, the technology makes it possible to add advanced digital features to telephony as well as device and location independence (Wikipedia, 2008a).

However, the idea of using the Internet for voice communication was not one first discovered by the entrepreneurs. The first successful VoIP transmission was tested in 1974 on ARPAnet, which was the basis for the modern Internet. Rapid development and commercialization of the technology started in 1996 when visionary companies such as Vocaltec, Netspeak and Net2Phone (Aguilar, 1996) were trying to tackle the technological barriers and develop viable business models. VoIP received ample attention during the late 1990s with several companies, even such as Yahoo (in 1998), Netscape (in 1999) and Microsoft (in 2001), trying to benefit from the huge potential of the technology with little success. By 2000 VoIP was to some extent commercialized with services offering cheaper international calls (IBT, 2000) and slowly DSL (digital subscriber line) and cable television providers were starting to offer telephony as an addition to their regular services (Bygrave, 2006). While slowly attracting new users, companies failed to lower the cost of services significantly, with cost savings of merely 10 per cent as a lot of expensive equipment still had to be purchased with every new user (Aguilar, 1996).

After years of over-promising and underperforming, in 2002 the technology seemed mature enough; however, a clear market leader could not easily be identified and no major disruption happened on the telecommunications market. Viable business models were built around selling calling cards that made it possible to make cheaper telephone calls, and cable and broadband operators were offering flat rate VoIP telephone calls as a part of their service. There were still few cost advantages as they had to invest in the infrastructure and connected equipment. Several instant messaging services (such as MSN, Yahoo Messenger) also had voice chat, but failed to leverage it to be a profitable business and to technologically solve the problem of high server loads connected with the service. The existing software also had problems with firewalls that made the installation of VoIP software complicated, and the existing solutions were user unfriendly, demanding advanced computer knowledge. Also institutional black clouds were gathering to block the development of the technology as it presented a serious risk to the lucrative telecommunication business.

This was seen by the entrepreneurs: 'I remember us saying (around 2002) that Internet telephony should work by now. We certainly didn't invent Internet telephony, but it wasn't very good and was too hard to use' (Q6). 'The time is right to take on Internet telephony. Broadband penetration is high enough, and people are ready for it; it's been an unfulfilled promise for years' (Q7).

Broadband Internet

In the early years of the Internet most people accessed it using a modem on a traditional telephone line. This was slow, with speeds hardly fast enough to deliver text messages and basic pictures; it was also inconvenient as it blocked the whole telephone line. Also the payment was based on a pay-per-minute system, which made the use of the Internet very costly.

Broadband access has many advantages over dial-up, the most notable being a fixed fee for accessing the Internet regardless of the time spent on-line. In addition to that, high transfer speeds enable users to exchange types of data that are bigger, such as images, video and audio. In 2006 the OECD treated an Internet connection as broadband if its speed exceeded 256 kbit/s (OECD, 2006); in 2008 the US FCC increased that speed to 768 kbit/s (Wikipedia, 2008b). The term 'broadband' does not define the technology used to achieve the above-mentioned speeds. Most common are: ISDN, DSL, cable internet, fibre optics to the end user and so on. In this research we focus on the development of broadband access up to the year 2003 when Skype Technologies was founded.

An analog modem that converted digital signals was developed to the point where it could transfer up to 56kbit/s in the late 1990s (Wikipedia, 2008c). Using a modem to access the Internet was costly, slow, unreliable and time-consuming. After some tries with the ISDN technology, ADSL, Asymmetric Digital Subscriber Line, was developed to provide faster access. The technology was first designed to make it possible to provide video on demand, yet when these high-flying dreams faded away it was repacked to provide high-speed Internet access (Marples, 2004). The main benefit of the technology was that it used the existing copper wire cables used by telephones to transmit a much greater volume of data to the end user and at the same time enabled the use of telephones while surfing the Internet (Wikipedia, 2008g). Another boost came with the passage of the Telecommunications Reform Act of 1996, which allows local phone companies, long-distance carriers, cable companies, radio/ television broadcasters, Internet/online service providers, and telecommunications equipment manufacturers in the United States to compete in one another's markets. The race to provide broadband bandwidth was on.

The start of commercial ADSL was in late 1997 with a more aggressive market entry in 1998 (Emory, 2008). By the end of 2001 the penetration of broadband Internet access was fairly small. According to OECD (2008) the broadband penetration in the USA was 4.3 per cent, just 2.2 per cent in Japan and a mere 1.6 per cent in the EU. The figure grew sharply until at the end of 2003 there was a penetration of 10.9 per cent in the USA, 5.9 per cent in the EU and 10.7 per cent in Japan. The majority of the penetration growth can be attributed to the DSL technology, as in 2007 it accounted for 62 per cent of broadband Internet access (OECD, 2008). The volume of data transmitted over the Internet in the period has grown more than 100 times in the period from 1996 to 2003 (Minnesota Internet Traffic Studies, 2008).

The rapid increase in Internet connection capabilities and the flat rate billing system that enabled Internet users to stay connected and transfer data from the Internet even when they were not using the computer made a strong impact on the way people were using the Internet. The era of using the Internet to transmit mostly text messages was over. 'With our work at Kazaa, we began seeing growing broadband connections and more powerful computers and more streaming multimedia, and we saw that the traditional way of communicating by phone no longer made a lot of sense' (Q5).

The first data format to flourish with Internet exchange was audio. MP3 codec, used to compress audio files, was developed in 1991 by the Fraunhofer Institute; this greatly decreased the size of audio files while maintaining the quality at a high level. It became highly popular with the launch of the Winamp software in 1997 (Wikipedia, 2008h). With the growing popularity of the MP3 format, the need to exchange large files easily over the Internet was greater than ever. Yet the traditional server–client infrastructure Internet couldn't be applied for the needs of file exchange as it presented great hardware server requirements as well as presenting severe legal issues. The answer to the challenge was the development of peer-to-peer networks.

Peer-to-Peer Networks

A peer-to-peer (or 'P2P') computer network uses diverse connectivity between participants in a network and the cumulative bandwidth of network participants rather than conventional centralized resources where a relatively low number of servers provide the core value to a service or application (Wikipedia, 2008i).

P2P is a widely used and abused term. Software is not peer-to-peer just because it establishes direct connections between two users; most Internet software does this to some extent. True P2P software creates a network through which all clients join together dynamically to help each other route traffic and store information. The power of the network grows with the number of users (Q8).

The core concept of the Internet is designed in a peer-to-peer architecture, yet bandwidth problems and the processing power of personal computers dictated a more server-based structure in the early years. Yet with the increased availability of broadband Internet, the capabilities of the limited servers became the one of the key problem for exchanging files between Internet users. One of the first major companies to tackle the problem was Napster, which operated between June 1999 and July 2001 (BusinessWeek, 2000). The software enabled Internet users to share music files, using a combination of server and peer-to-peer technology. It was an instant hit, peaking at 26.4 million global users in early 2001 (Wikipedia, 2008f). The service was heavily sued for its role in the illegal distribution of copyrighted material (Lefevre, 2000). As a result it was finally shut down in July 2001 (Wikipedia, 2008f).

The legal problems Napster had and the limitations on the transfers left millions of Internet users wanting to continue to download free music from the Internet, looking for a substitute service. The lack of a way to share files through the Internet was seen by Niklas Zennström and Janus Friis.

Niklas Zennström and Janus Friis

Niklas was born in Sweden in 1966. He has a dual degree in Business Administration (BSc) and Engineering Physics (MSc) from Uppsala University in Sweden. He spent his final year at the University of Michigan, Ann Arbor, USA (Wikipedia, 2008d). He started his professional career in one of the biggest European telecommunication operators, Tele2. There he worked on a project for launching a Danish ISP provider, get2net, and managed a web portal called www.everyday.com. At Tele2 he met Janus Friis (Gruber, 2006). Janus was born in 1976 and has no formal education. He left school during his 10th grade to work at a helpdesk at a Danish ISP provider called CyberCity. In 1996 he was hired by Niklas Zennström to run the customer support of Tele2 in Denmark (Gruber, 2006; Wikipedia, 2008e). In 1999 they left Tele2 to start a company that developed a protocol called FastTrack that enabled cheap peer-to-peer transaction over the Internet. The main advantage of the protocol was that it needed no server to run the network as the index of users and files on the network was distributed among the users, which made it the perfect platform for file exchange systems (Gruber, 2006).

Kazaa

In 2000 Janus and Niklas hired a group of three Estonian programmers to develop software that enabled file search and exchange between computers without any central server infrastructure. The development took a mere four months and in July 2000 Kazaa was launched (Tarm, 2003). The platform was perfect for people wanting to exchange music, software and video files after the fall of Napster. The software was an instant hit, with more than 34 million downloads up to October 2001 (Borland, 2001a). This started to attract attention from the big music companies, who started legal action against the company (Borland, 2001b). As a result the company was sold to Sharman Networks, established in Vanuatu in the beginning of 2002 (Yang, 2002). The company was under severe legal pressure; also the business model was based on including adware to the software pack, which made the user's computer work slower, and also other security issues occurred (Borland and Konrad, 2002). After the sale of Kazaa, Niklas and Janus stopped working for the company.

They started a new company called Joltid, which was focused on the development of a technology that made the peer-to-peer networks faster (Olsen, 2003). With a superior knowledge of the new network protocols that enabled an efficient transfer of large files over the Internet without a server infrastructure and extensive entrepreneurial experience from Kazaa, the entrepreneurs searched for new opportunities to put their experience into action. Their time with Kazaa made Janus and Niklas experienced web entrepreneurs with a specific knowledge of peer-to-peer networks and designing and managing viral Internet products.

Opportunity to Start Skype

After Kazaa the entrepreneurs were looking for another field where they could put their specific knowledge on P2P technologies into action. 'After Niklas Zennstrom and I did Kazaa, we looked at other areas where we could use our experience and where P2P technology could have a major disruptive impact.' (Q3). When asked about how they identified the opportunity, Zennstrom replies, 'It is about trying to see what are the technical capabilities and what are the consumer trends and try to connect the dots' (Q10) and 'First it is not about crushing industries. It is about creating opportunities. Usually it is like: Why is somebody not doing that? It is not a method. There are discussions. . . the most important thing is the ability to question things' (Q11).

'The telephone is a 100-year-old technology. It's time for a change. Charging for phone calls is something you did last century.' (Q9). The basis for such a claim from the founder of Skype was grounded in several developments in the telecommunications market in the 1990s. The introduction of the commercial Internet has significantly changed the way in which people live, communicate and do business. One of the most visible changes the Internet brought to the global marketplace was the possibility for the ventures to reach global markets easily. While services like online retail were still limited to certain geographical areas because of the costs of sending goods, companies offering pure online services could access the global market almost without barriers. Marginal costs per each new user added to Internet services were very low, making it possible for entrepreneurs to reach millions and to gain from economies of scale on a completely new level. Despite the Internet bubble burst in 2000 the number of Internet users nearly doubled in the period between 2000 and 2002 (Global Village Online, 2008).

In 1996 the USA deregulated its telecommunications market, making it possible for smaller players to compete in the market and to introduce new technologies and services. As described above, the unlimited time broadband Internet was also on the rise, greatly altering the way people used the Internet. With fast and unlimited time access, users spent more time on the Internet, using additional functionalities and new services.

Seeing the market trends and the emerging technologies and infrastructure collide, the entrepreneurs identified the opportunity to start an Internet telephony company 'The time is right to take on Internet telephony. Broadband penetration is high enough, and people are ready for it; it's been an unfulfilled promise for years. P2P technology is really very well suited for Internet telephony, so it is a natural next phase' (Q7). 'People were having more and more broadband connections. If we would have launched Skype three years earlier we wouldn't have taken off as people were using much more dial up connections' (Q2).

The growing broadband Internet penetration was one of the key factors that made the start of the venture possible. However, several others have tried to introduce VoIP services even at the time of the rise of Skype but failed to achieve success: 'all this things have been made but haven't been made good' (Q1). 'We certainly didn't invent Internet telephony, but it wasn't very good and was too hard to use' (Q6). According to the entrepreneurs, Skype addressed the core problems with existing VoIP services, 'bad sound quality, difficult to set up and configure, and the need for expensive, centralized infrastructure. No one has seriously addressed these problems before, and this is why VoIP has never really taken off.' (Q14)

When designing a business model the entrepreneurs followed a 'freeconomics' (Anderson, 2008) design, offering their core service free of charge to the users, therefore attracting users to adopt the service and invite new users to it. By offering added-value services the entrepreneurs managed to develop a highly profitable business model. 'What we are doing is taking advantage of the broadband Internet to provide basically unlimited free calls to anyone at a higher voice quality than they can with the phone lines' (Q14). 'We want to make as little money as possible per user. We don't have any cost per user, but we want a lot of them.' (Q15) Adoption of such a model was possible primarily due to the fact that by using peer-to-peer technology, the company used the infrastructure of their users to act like servers for the network, thus having no cost per user when growing the network.

GROUNDED MODEL OF OPPORTUNITY IDENTIFICATION FOR SKYPE TECHNOLOGIES

During the analysis of the gathered secondary data we did extensive coding of different segments of the text. After analysis we reviewed the codes and merged where the segments coded were similar in meaning. We then identified links between different codes to form a network view on the data as shown in Figure 4.1. During the process the quotations underlying the codes were reread and reorganized. Finally the nodes were grouped using different colours to identify different phases in the opportunity identification process.

Based on the organized codes we further explored and developed the notion proposed by the entrepreneurs that 'it is not about crushing industries. It is about creating opportunities' (Q11) and 'it is about trying to see what are the technical capabilities and what are the consumer trends and try to connect the dots' (Q10). As shown in Figure 4.2, opportunities are created to connect the technological development with market trends.

The evolving markets and technologies can be treated as objective external developments that are more or less equally available to all entrepreneurs at a certain given point of time.

However, while technological and market trends represent the 'dots', the design of the connection of the dots was strongly influenced by the entrepreneurs. Previous knowledge and experience strongly influenced the way the dots were connected. What is more, the process of looking for an opportunity was to some extent directed by the use of a certain technology and consequently a business model the entrepreneurs wanted to pursue 'after Niklas Zennstrom and I did Kazaa, we looked at other areas where we could use our experience and where P2P technology could have a major disruptive impact' (Q3). The entrepreneurs were looking for an opportunity where a certain service and business design that they have already

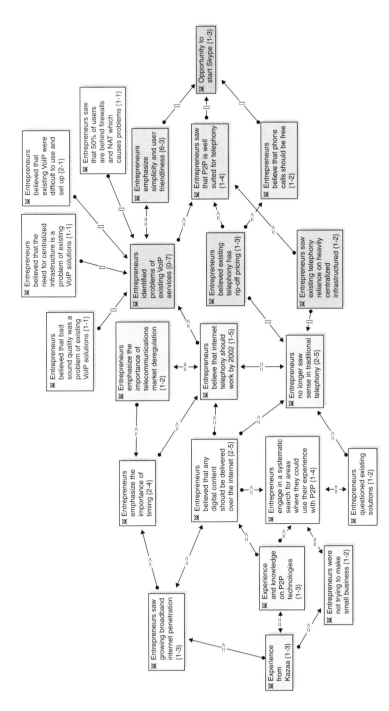

Figure 4.1 Network view on the opportunity identification process for Skype Technologies

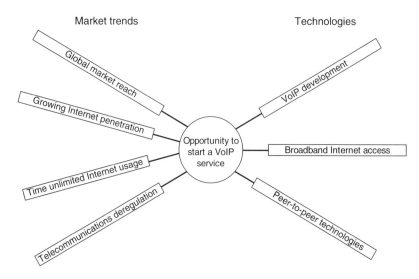

Market trends   Technologies

Figure 4.2   Opportunity for Skype as a combination of market trends and emerging technologies

tested with Kazaa could be implemented. The success and the mistakes they made with their previous venture gave them self-confidence and big plans for the new venture, best seen in the claim that 'we're not here to try to make some small business' (Q16). The process of opportunity development was simultaneous with the process of opportunity identification as the way the entrepreneurs wanted to develop the opportunity was one of the key criteria when looking for a suitable opportunity to pursue. Figure 4.3 includes the entrepreneurs in the model as well as a separate dimension for entrepreneurial opportunity development.

MODEL GENERALIZATION AND THEORETICAL DISCUSSION

Kirzner (1979) defines an entrepreneurial opportunity as an imprecisely defined market need or underemployed resource that is present at a specific moment in time, while Shane and Venkataraman (2000) propose that entrepreneurial opportunities are those situations in which new goods, services, raw materials and organizing methods can be introduced and sold at greater than their cost of production. The second, more adopted definition was later criticized because it inevitably contains the final result

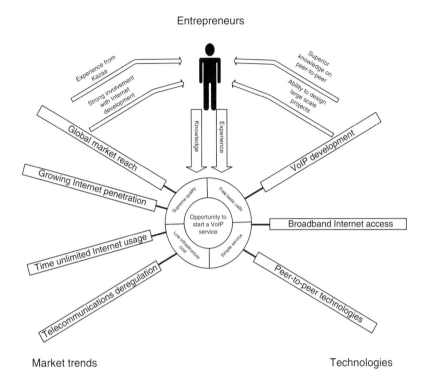

Figure 4.3   Opportunity for Skype as a combination of market trends, emerging technologies influenced by knowledge and experience of the entrepreneurs

of their realization (the creation of future goods and services). Such a view is time-neutral – it pertains to opportunities now, yet deems them as such only after knowing future outcomes. As uncertainty cannot be removed from our world it is impossible to perceive an opportunity *ex-ante*, therefore opportunities could only be claimed as such retrospectively. Therefore in order to avoid foreknowledge the opportunities should be looked at through the 'worldviews' of individuals (Dimov, 2007a).

In the studied case the entrepreneurs offered an alternative view on what entrepreneurs do when they look for opportunities 'it is about trying to see what are the technical capabilities and what are the consumer trends and try to connect the dots' (Q10).

The idea of opportunities being perceived possibilities of junctures of favourable circumstances as seen by the entrepreneurs fits to the two-phase view of opportunity identification and development. In the

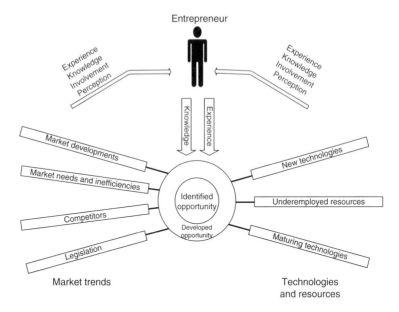

Figure 4.4   Proposed model of opportunity identification and development

opportunity identification phase, the entrepreneurs process the different signals from the market, strongly influenced by their involvement, knowledge and experience, and try to fit them with their perception, knowledge and experience on technological development and available resources. The insight happens when the different signals collide in what entrepreneurs perceive could be a possible juncture of market needs, available resources and technologies. We propose that the result of the opportunity identification in the entrepreneurship process is the perceived possibility to create a juncture of circumstances that is the identification of the dots and the perceived belief that it is possible to connect them.

Instantly, together with the realization that a possible juncture of circumstances could exist, the entrepreneurs begin the process of opportunity development or firm design (as proposed by Sarasvathy, 2004), which is the design of how the dots should be connected. The art and craft of connecting the dots seems a promising field for future research as it is a scarcely studied, yet extremely important phase in the entrepreneurial process.

The grounded model in Figure 4.3 is case-specific and is more applicable for technological entrepreneurship as it strongly emphasizes the role of technology. Therefore in our attempt to propose a more general model, we build on Kirzner's (1979) definition of entrepreneurial opportunities further enhancing both sides of the model as shown in Figure 4.4.

Case-specific technologies and market trends are replaced by more case-general categories, and resources are added to the model.

The studied case shows that the way the entrepreneurs want to develop an opportunity can also strongly influence the opportunity identification itself, as entrepreneurs could see more potential in certain business models thus influencing their perception of which trends and developments are potentially interesting.

Our research also further emphasized the role of an individual in the identification and development of opportunities. Experience, knowledge and the involvement of entrepreneurs with specific markets and technologies proved to be crucial parts of both opportunity identification and development.

NOTES

1. As opportunities are defined by Websters online dictionary.
2. The terminology used depends on the ontological view followed.
3. The complete list of quotations can be found in one Appendix.

REFERENCES

Aguilar, R. (1996), 'CompuServe licenses Net phone', *Cnet News*, available at http://www.news.com, accessed 6 May 2008.

Alvarez, S.A. and J.B. Barney (2005), 'How do entrepreneurs organize firms under conditions of uncertainty?', *Journal of Management*, **31**(5), 776–93.

Anderson, C. (2008), 'Free! Why $0.00 is the future of business', *Wired*, available at http://www.wired.com, accessed 19 April 2008.

Ardichvili, A., R. Cardozo and S. Ray (2003), 'A theory of entrepreneurial opportunity identification and development', *Journal of Business Venturing*, **18**(1), 105–23.

Borland, J. (2001a), 'Rocky financial road awaits file swappers', *Cnet News*, available at http://news.cnet.com, accessed 10 June 2008.

Borland, J. (2001b), 'Suit hits popular post-Napster network', *Cnet News*, available at http://news.cnet.com, accessed 10 June 2008.

Borland, J. and R. Konrad (2002), 'They're camping out in your hard drive – with your express consent', *Cnet News*, available at http://news.cnet.com, accessed 10 June 2008.

Busenitz, L.W., G.P. West III, D. Shepherd, T. Nelson, G.N. Chandler and A. Zacharakis (2003), 'Entrepreneurship research in emergence: past trends and future directions', *Journal of Management*, **29**(3), 285–308.

BusinessWeek (2000), 'Napster's high and low notes', *BusinessWeek*, available at http://www.businessweek.com, accessed 15 May 2008.

Bygrave, W.D. (2006), 'The entrepreneurship paradigm (I) revisited', in H. Neergaard and J. Parm Ulhoi (eds), *Handbook of Qualitative Research Methods in Entrepreneurship*, Cheltenham, UK and Northampton, MA, USA: Edward Elgar, pp. 17–45.

Charmaz, K. (2006), *Constructing Grounded Theory*, London: Sage Publications.

Charny, B. (2003), 'Is VoIP ready for the Prime Time?', *Cnet News*, available at http://news.cnet.com, accessed 8 June 2008.

Corbett, A.C. (2005), 'Experiential learning within the process of opportunity identification and exploitation', *Entrepreneurship Theory and Practice*, **29**(4), 474–91.

Davidsson, P. (2008), *The Domain of Entreprenurship Research*, Cheltenham, UK and Northampton, MA, USA: Edward Elgar.

Dimov, D. (2007a), 'From opportunity insight to opportunity intention: the importance of person–situation learning match', *Entrepreneurship Theory and Practice*, **31**(4), 561–83.

Dimov, D. (2007b), 'Beyond the single-person, single-insight attribution in understanding entrepreneurial opportunities', *Entrepreneurship Theory and Practice*, **31**(5), 713–31.

Dutta, D.K. and M.M. Crossan (2005), 'The nature of entrepreneurial opportunities: understanding the process using the 4I organizational learning framework', *Entrepreneurship Theory and Practice*, **29**(4), 425–49.

Eckhardt, J.T. and S.A. Shane (2003), 'Opportunities and entrepreneurship', *Journal of Management*, **29**(3), 333–49.

Emory (2008), *The History of DSL*, available at http://www.emory.edu/BUSINESS/et/p98/dsl/history. htm.

Glaser, B. and A. Strauss (1967), *The Discovery of Grounded Theory: Strategies for Qualitative Research*, London: Weidenfeld and Nicolson.

Global Village Online (2008), 'Internet growth statistics', available at http://www.internetworldstats.com, accessed 7 October 2008.

Gruber, J. (2006), 'Disrupter man goes after TV this time', *USA Today*, available at http://www.usatoday.com, accessed 24 May 2008.

Hindle, K. (2004), 'Choosing qualitative methods for entrepreneurial cognition research: a canonical development approach', *Entrepreneurship Theory and Practice*, **28**(6), 575–607.

IBT (2000), 'VocalTec reports record results for the fourth quarter and year 2000', *Business Wire*, available at http://www.accessmylibrary.com, accessed 12 May 2008.

Kirzner, I. (1979), *Perception, Opportunity, and Profit*, Chicago: University of Chicago Press.

Kirzner, I. (1997), 'Entrepreneurial discovery and the competitive market process: an Austrian approach', *Journal of Economic Literature*, **35**(1), 60–82.

Lefevre, G. (2000), 'Napster shutdown seen as potential boon for competitors', CNN, available at http://edition.cnn.com, accessed 16 May 2008.

Mäkelä, M.M. and R.V. Turcan (2006), 'Building grounded theory in entrepreneurship research', in H. Neergaard and J.P. Ulhři (eds), *Handbook of Qualitative Research Methods in Entrepreneurship*, Cheltenham, UK and Northampton, MA, USA: Edward Elgar pp. 122–43.

Marples, G. (2004), 'The history of DSL Internet access', speedguide.net, available at http://www.speedguide.net, accessed 8 June 2008.

McMullen, J., L. Plummer and Z. Acs (2007), 'What is an entrepreneurial opportunity?', *Small Business Economics*, **28**(4), 273–83.

Minnesota Internet Traffic Studies (MINTS) (2008), 'Internet growth trends & Moore's Law', available at http://www.dtc.umn.edu/mints/igrowth.html, accessed 10 June 2008.

Nicolaou, N. and S. Shane (2009), 'Can genetic factors influence the likelihood of engaging in entrepreneurial activity?', *Journal of Business Venturing*, **24**(1), 1–22.

OECD (2006), 'OECD broadband statistics to December 2006', OECD Directorate for Science, Technology and Innovation, available at http://www.oecd.org, accessed 8 June 2008.

OECD (2008), 'Historical broadband penetration rates', available at http://www.oecd.org, accessed 9 June 2008.

Olsen, S. (2003), 'P2P caching: unsafe at any speed?', *Cnet News*, available at http://news.cnet.com, accessed 12 June 2008.

Sarasvathy, S. (2001), 'Causation and effectuation: toward a theoretical shift from economic inevitability to entrepreneurial contingency', *Academy of Management Review*, **26**, 243–63.

Sarasvathy, S.D. (2004), 'Making it happen: beyond theories of the firm to theories of firm design', *Entrepreneurship Theory and Practice*, **28**(6), 519–31.

Schumpeter, J.A. (1934), *The Theory of Economic Development: An Inquiry into Profits, Capital Credit, Interest, and the Business Cycle*, Cambridge: Harvard University Press.

Shane, S. (2000), 'Prior knowledge and the discovery of entrepreneurial opportunities', *Organization Science,* **11**(4), 448–69.

Shane, S. and S. Venkataraman (2000), 'The promise of entrepreneurship as a field of research', *Academy of Management Review*, **25**(1), 217–26.

Tarm, M. (2003), 'Youths from cyber-savvy Estonia write the new Napster, delivering a blow to the global entertainment industry', *City Paper, The Baltic States*, March/April.

Ucbasaran, D., P. Westhead and M. Wright (2009), 'The extent and nature of opportunity identification by experienced entrepreneurs', *Journal of Business Venturing*, **24**(2), 99–115.

Vaghely, I.P. and P.-A. Julien (2010), 'Are opportunities recognized or constructed? An information perspective on entrepreneurial opportunity identification', *Journal of Business Venturing*, **25**(1), 73–86.

Wikipedia (2008a), 'Voice Over the Internet Protocol', available at http://en.wikipedia.org, accessed 8 June 2008.

Wikipedia (2008b), 'Broadband Internet access', available at http://en.wikipedia.org, accessed 8 June 2008.

Wikipedia (2008c), 'Modem', available at http://en.wikipedia.org, accessed 8 June 2008.

Wikipedia (2008d), 'Niklas Zennström', available at http://en.wikipedia.org, accessed 12 June 2008.

Wikipedia (2008e), 'Janus Friis', available at http://en.wikipedia.org, accessed 24 May 2008.

Wikipedia (2008f), 'Napster', available at http://en.wikipedia.org, accessed 10 June 2008.

Wikipedia (2008g), 'ADSL', available at http://en.wikipedia.org, accessed 8 June 2008.

Wikipedia (2008h), 'MP3', available at http://en.wikipedia.org, accessed 10 June 2008.
Wikipedia (2008i), 'Peer-to-peer', available at http://en.wikipedia.org, accessed 10 June 2008.
Yang, P. (2002), 'KaZaA sold to Sharman Networks', *ars technica*, available at http://arstechnica.com, accessed 10 June 2008.
Yin, R.K. (2003), *Case Study Research: Design and Methods*, Applied Social Research Methods Series, London: Sage Publications.
Yu, T.F.-L. (2001), 'Entrepreneurial alertness and discovery', *The Review of Austrian Economics*, **14**(1), 47–63.

APPENDIX

Table 4A.1   List of quotations

Q1	A lot of things are of course timing and luck. But you always hear someone say. . . we hear it so many times: it has already been done before, there is a product out there. If you are entrepreneurial you have to say fine. . . all this things have been made but haven't been made good.	**Niklas Zennström: interview at SIME 2007 conference**
Q2	The other thing is I think also timing. We launched Skype. . . There was good timing I think. . . People were having more and more broadband connections. If we would have launched Skype three years earlier we wouldn't have taken off as people were using much more dial up connections.	**Niklas Zennström: SevenLoad interview, 22 January 2007**
Q3	After Niklas Zennström and I did Kazaa, we looked at other areas where we could use our experience and where P2P technology could have a major disruptive impact. The telephony market is characterized both by what we think is rip-off pricing and a reliance on heavily centralized infrastructure. We just couldn't resist the opportunity to help shake this up a bit.	**Janus Friis: 'Why VoIP is music to Kazaa's ear', 23 November 2003**
Q4	Kazaa set the stage for Skype. While considering what to do after Kazaa, Zennström says he and Friis thought about how 'any digital content should be delivered over the Internet because it's so much more efficient.'	**Niklas Zennström: 'Disrupter man goes after TV this time', *USA Today*, 12 June 2006**
Q5	With our work at Kazaa, we began seeing growing broadband connections and more powerful computers and more streaming multimedia, and we saw that the traditional way of communicating by phone no longer made a lot of sense.	**Niklas Zennström: Engadget interview, 8 November 2004**
Q6	I remember us saying (around 2002) that Internet telephony should work by now. We certainly didn't invent Internet telephony, but it wasn't very good and was too hard to use.	**Niklas Zennström: 'Disrupter man goes after TV this time', *USA Today*, 12 June 2006**

Table 4A.1   (continued)

Q7	The time is right to take on Internet telephony. Broadband penetration is high enough, and people are ready for it; it's been an unfulfilled promise for years. P2P technology is really very well suited for Internet telephony, so it is a natural next phase	**Janus Friis: 'Why VoIP is music to Kazaa's ear', 23 November 2003**
Q8	P2P is a widely used and abused term. Software is not peer-to-peer just because it establishes direct connections between two users; most Internet software does this to some extent. True P2P software creates a network through which all clients join together dynamically to help each other route traffic and store information. The power of the network grows with the number of users.	**Janus Friis: 'Why VoIP is music to Kazaa's ear', 23 November 2003**
Q9	The telephone is a 100-year-old-technology. It's time for a change. Charging for phone calls is something you did last century.	**Niklas Zennström: Engadget interview, 8 November 2004**
Q10	It is about trying to see what are the technical capabilities and what are the consumer trends and try to connect the dots. But it is also a lot about gut instinct and just go for it.	**Niklas Zennström: interview at SIME 2007 conference**
Q11	First it is not about crushing industries. It is about creating opportunites. Usually it is like: Why is somebody not doing that? It is not a method. There are discussions. . . the most important thing is the ability to question things.	**Niklas Zennström: interview at SIME 2007 conference**
Q12	Those calling for Skype to further increase revenues from users fail to understand the balance that must be struck between seeking profits and supporting expectations built around free phone calls. Some people may want to monetize faster but the key is to figure out what is the right speed of monetization. If you act too aggressively there is a real risk you will lose the huge active user base.	**Niklas Zennström: interview for thomascrampton.com, 1 October 2007**

Table 4A.1 (continued)

Q13	Skype is addressing all the problems of legacy VoIP solutions: bad sound quality, difficult to set up and configure, and the need for expensive, centralized infrastructure. No one has seriously addressed these problems before, and this is why VoIP has never really taken off.	**Janus Friis: 'Why VoIP is music to Kazaa's ear', 23 November 2003**
Q14	Vonage is much more similar to Verizon and AT&T than to us. With Vonage, you're using a regular telephone, dialling a number, and its services have rates similar to the telecoms. What we are doing is taking advantage of the broadband Internet to provide basically unlimited free calls to anyone at a higher voice quality than they can with the phone lines.	**Niklas Zennström: Engadget interview, 8 November 2004**
Q15	We want to make as little money as possible per user. We don't have any cost per user, but we want a lot of them.	**Niklas Zennström: 'The meaning of free speech', *Economist*, 2005**
Q16	There is multibillion dollars in potential in Skype. We're not here to try to make some small business.	**Niklas Zennström: 'Disrupter man goes after TV this time', *USA Today*, 12 June 2006**

PART II

Entrepreneurship as a Social Process of
Becoming Entrepreneurial

5. Heuristic method: insights into a conceptual understanding of women's entrepreneurship and social capital

Iiris Aaltio, Paula Kyrö and Elisabeth Sundin

1. INTRODUCTION

In this chapter we examine how conceptual thinking progresses through heuristic method and enriches the conceptual understanding of the dialogue between women's entrepreneurship and social capital. The positivistic era believed that we end up with pyramids of knowledge, but does the contribution mean some kind of accumulation of knowledge and conceptual deepening of the phenomenon that is studied as well? As we find it, the qualitative approach in particular needs a lot of conceptual pondering in order to relate to other knowledge concerning the subject (Kyrö and Kansikas, 2005). Since the contribution of the study is the main purpose of academic work, on the one hand we need to understand and investigate what is meant by a contribution, and on the other hand find a way of increasing innovativeness in providing this contribution (Aaltio, 2006: 451–4). New fields like women's entrepreneurship benefit from 'going to the roots of existence'.

Academic research is published in special issues of journals, in conference proceedings with certain themes and as edited collections of articles in book form. The unifying element in these arenas is often loose and barely shows a relation between the approaches. Moreover, like calls for conference papers, they are meant to stimulate thought and insights around the themes presented. There is a search for progress and development in the field. It is not rare that new concepts arise and soon supersede established ones. Sometimes they are cynically called fads and fashions or consultant-driven knowledge production in managerial sciences and entrepreneurship especially. One reason for this may be the lack of innovative conceptual work when new knowledge is presented even if it is a result of a new empirical reality. In complex social settings there are also difficulties in communicating this innovativeness that after all is the core of contribution. The results might show the heuristic nature of the material, giving us insights, but using a heuristic method in analysing its impact is still rare. Good, if slightly older articles are those by Black (1951), dealing with a heuristic statement of race relations, and Emery (1986), developing a heuristic theory of diffusion. Both of them use the term 'heuristic' in their titles, but do not explain why and how it is used in their work.

Conceptual work that combines and investigates the multiple results of the study is still rare in the jungle of academic publishing. We need tools that enable conceptual development in this field to enhance our conceptual analysis and understanding.

Gender research and the feminist approach are more often classified to be change orientated and radical in that sense. As stated by Albert Mills (2002: 127–8), a key problem in reading any cultural history is the overwhelming modernist tendency to present history as a progressive unfolding of events. He adds that feminist researchers are not immune to the problem. For instance, when we study gender systems, the studies do not follow a linear development because systems are changing and flexible themselves. Mills states that 'the feminist researcher may be better served avoiding a search for cues that support a notion of progress over time, instead examining events to see what they tell us'. Thus change is more important than progress. Processes and eradication of specific forms, for instance in gender discrimination, are of importance. One reason for that might be found from Abbott's criticisms of the questions we pose. He claims that often our questions of gender might represent 'comfortable one-sidedness', with women representing gender in a reductionist way. He further argues that this could be avoided by adopting a heuristic method, which opens more holistic and versatile views to the phenomena and aspects that might change the understanding about them (Abbott, 2003: 85–6). How the debate on entrepreneurship is progressing, what its heuristics are and which kind of new insights we get into social and economic life through its lens, are thus crucial questions for research and its contribution.

Women's entrepreneurship can be studied from multiple angles. One of them is discrimination. Do the practices of entrepreneurship make women invisible and potentially hinder their participation on establishing and running small businesses? Or, what is their special role; do they contribute to entrepreneurship in a special way? We find gender here as a metaphor to understand entrepreneurship better and to bridge our understanding from body-counting, which means seeing women only in a statistical and quantitative way, to asking what their special connection is to social capital accumulation. We further study if a heuristic method can be used as a tool to new understanding. A similar example of this can be found in leadership. Morrell and Hartley (2006) developed a model of political leadership serving, as they say, a heuristic purpose, as a summary of the ways in which contexts for political leadership differ and as a representation of the complex way in which political leaders' authority is configured. However, the difference here is that we explain how and why we have used a heuristic method and what led to the new understanding. Thus the method itself can help others to adopt it in their multiple and complex contexts.

2. SEARCH AND ARGUMENT HEURISTICS FOR NEW UNDERSTANDING

Social capital can be seen as a metaphor through which we try to understand some other societal phenomena. It has been even criticized as not easily rendering itself to quantitative analysis. We see that its metaphorical use can, however, be stimulating and can be shown to be otherwise. Overall, interpretative and analytical methods differ from each other in terms of how we understand the phenomenon that is studied. Lämsä and Takala (2001) argue that contextuality and a theoretical thematization distinguish the interpretative method of concepts from the traditional, analytical approach to conceptualization. Interpretative concept research aims at describing and interpreting the meanings of concepts holistically. The interpretation is linked to the contextual factors and perceived as ever-changing, dynamic processes. Thus the concepts are ambiguous, changing, as well as socially and culturally constructed. Referring to Wittgenstein, Lämsä and Takala argue that if we wish to learn the meaning of concepts, we have to examine how they are used, and then the use and situation of words – contextuality – determines the meaning. They divide the interpretative study of concepts into categories and one of them they name heuristic, which emphasizes constructing and specifying new concepts by producing them intuitively through reflective thinking. The process of reflective thinking is a dynamic way of examining the experiences, as well as thinking intuitively and rationally (Mezirow, 1995). This opens up further possibilities for creating new concepts (Leontjev, 1977). The dialogue between social capital and women's entrepreneurship provides an excellent arena for this process.

Problems of Connecting Social Capital and Gender Approach

In studying social capital Lin (2001: 24–7) criticizes this approach to conceptualization by highlighting how the theoretical and measurement problems should be separated. According to him, to identify social capital through its outcome is not valid, since the causal outcome cannot be defined by the effectual factor. However, for us this criticism offers an opportunity to apply the heuristic approach. The heuristic approach captures both the concepts and their conceptualization. Thus it serves as a means and end in the reflective conceptualizing process.

Another criticism comes from Helene Ahl (2008: 167–93). She thinks that there is a risk of seeing social capital as a collective phenomenon and assuming that women entrepreneurs have a social capital distinctly different from that of men. This actually essentializes what women are. If social capital is that which is enacted in interactions, how can one possibly talk about it as an entity at a collective level? How does one meaningfully measure it? And how does one distinguish social capital from its manifestations (this is the same critique Lin presented in other words). Saying that women are different from men probably tends to reinforce their subordination.

> Example would be arguments that women's social capital is especially successful in labor intensive sectors such as care and services (as these are businesses with many women owners) and that their experience and expertise should be used fruitfully to further develop these sectors and make a valuable contribution to the economy.

Just as such an argument might encourage women, it may also hold women, back from entering other, more lucrative sectors. As gender studies underline, the reason that women are concentrated in certain businesses is not to be found in their being as women, but in gendering processes that have cultural, historical and political origins. A version of the same problem is the assumption of women's social capital as inherently good, the extension of an idea of 'the good mother' on a collective level, argues Ahl. She suggests that we should use gender as an analytical concept instead of an explanatory variable, use constructivism, and study gendering processes.

Essence of Heuristics

The history and traditions of the heuristic approach go back a few decades. The etymology of the word 'heuristics' comes from the Ancient Greek '*heuriskein*', 'to find', and '*heuretikos*', 'inventive'. In its modern adaptations Frank (1997) traces heuristic traditions in two directions: first to the traditional idealistic approach to science in Central Europe followed, for example, by Michael Polonyi, and to the American origins of problem-solving starting from Thorndike, but furthered especially by the Hungarian George Polya. These two traditions can also be identified in the current use of heuristic research and evaluation.

The latter tradition emerges in particular in usability studies in computer sciences since the 1990s. It emphasizes the effectiveness of using heuristics in identifying the problems and shortcomings of on-line activities and interfaces or, based on cognitive psychology, emphasizes the problems of heuristics in decision-making (Chen and Macredie, 2005; Levit, 2006). Abbott (2003: 82–3) claims that the work of Polya is difficult to apply in the social sciences since both the problem and its solution are hard to anticipate as probabilistic thinking assumes. The former, idealistic approach is more concerned with the creative aspects of heuristics as a process of discovery and self-reflection. It is, for example, used in educational studies as a reflective action-oriented research method often referring to Polanyi's concept of a heuristic act (for example Vickie, 1997). The heuristic act of achieving innovation is an act of invention and discovery (Polanyi, 1958). Another example of this direction is the Hamburg approach, which aims to overcome the problems of hermeneutics as they formulate it by replacing hermeneutic and/or interpretative research by heuristic research aiming at exploration and discoveries in the study of explorative experience in everyday life (Kleining and Witt, 2001).

The aim of this chapter is to find a way to achieve innovation as an act of invention and discovery as Polanyi defines it, but now in the field of conceptual research, thereby expanding the research methods of discovery. Actually heuristics is often used to develop conceptual understanding and modelling, but is not methodologically articulated (for example Black, 1951; Emery, 1986; Morrell and Hartley, 2006; Ofori-Dankwa and Julian, 2002).

Polanyi talks about personal revisions of guiding assumptions that change the rules of interpreting our experiences. He describes the adaptation of a framework to fit new experiences and the discovery of movement from one framework to another as 'heuristic vision'. Clandinin (1986) interprets Polanyi's descriptions of heuristic acts as 'acts achieving innovation'. Abbott's book *Methods of Discovery: Heuristics for the Social Sciences* (2003), combines and analyses all these aspects and introduces different kind of methods to proceed in this process. Thus borrowing this method from him is a natural choice for us.

In the field of entrepreneurship research, however, we were not able to find examples of usage of heuristics (for example Hine and Carson, 2007; Neergaard and Uthoi, 2007). Thus we might meet the problems anticipated by Wiklund et al. (2006). By using the metaphor of explorer they anticipate that if this metaphor holds true, these modern explorers will still face perils in the process of discovery and in the process of repatriating their findings in their home cultures. To take a recent example of articles during 2007–2009 in *Entrepreneurship Theory and Practice* (114 articles) and in the *Journal of Business Venturing* (82 articles), none of these applied the heuristic method (Kyrö et al., 2009). This does not necessarily mean that it has not been used, but rather its use has not been explicated. Thus we have to take hints from different directions in order to find a way to implement it in our research. This kind of methodological borrowing process is typical of search heuristics. As Abbott describes it, it is often 'subterranean force driving analogy' (Abbott, 2003: 114–20). In many fields of research this kind of borrowing is ordinary nowadays. For instance organizational studies started to borrow culture concept from anthropology in the 1980s.

Abbott introduces different heuristics as a method of discovery. Overall, general heuristics are used as self-conscious devices for producing new ideas by manipulating arguments, descriptions and narratives in particular ways. Search and argument heuristics differ from each other: when search heuristics get new ideas from elsewhere the argument heuristics concern ways of turning old and familiar arguments into new and creative ones (Abbott, 2003: 120). However, we think these two can be combined based on Abbott's ideas.

3.   THE PROCESS AND RESULTS OF DISCOVERY

Heuristics Applied

In this chapter we explicate this combination and use as data the book edition of *The Dialogue between Women's Entrepreneurship and Social Capital* we edited together (Aaltio et al., 2008). Its ideas originated in the EIASM Institute workshop held in 2004 in Brussels, on 'Female managers, entrepreneurs and the social capital of the firm'. This workshop for the first time evinced the idea of making a dialogue between women's entrepreneurship and social capital theory and research. In the Nordic Academy of Management Conference in Aarhus 2005 this dialogue continued and expanded with new participants from the group of researchers that convenes annually on the initiative of the government of France at the Dauphin University, in Paris. The shared understanding of these women's entrepreneurship researchers from different countries and continents was that both the concept of entrepreneurship and social capital are multiple and complex, but interrelated. The book described the landscape of social capital and women's entrepreneurship as we argue heuristically, using social capital as a metaphor against which we reflect research conducted on female entrepreneurs.

According to Polanyi and Prosch (1975), when one sees a problem and undertakes its pursuit, one sees a range of potentialities for meaning which one thinks are accessible. The interplay between social capital and women's entrepreneurship contains these potentialities.

We believe that conceptualizing the heuristic dialogue between social capital and women's entrepreneurship provides a helpful approach in expanding our understanding of women's entrepreneurship. Lämsä and Takala (2001) argue that although the creation of new concepts can be seen as a creative dialectical process which combines intuition and rational thinking, there may also be political objectives behind the creation of concepts. This is understandable because these kinds of objectives give vision and direction to the process. Hardy and Phillips (1999: 20) maintain that the lack of suitable concepts decreases the chances of some groups to wield power. Women's entrepreneurship is typically marginalized through its lack of concepts of its own.

As Yeager (1999: xxi) argues, 'women's influence in economy has been modest or almost invisible and their voices faint and cacophonous, despite the collectivity of sounds'. The interplay between social capital and women's entrepreneurship might provide some collectivity for this voice and thus delineate this phenomenon. This encourages us to apply the heuristic approach in exploring this interplay between women entrepreneurs and social capital. Among different heuristics, more specifically we integrate search and argument heuristics as two forms of general heuristics. For this purpose we lean heavily on Andrew Abbott's (2003) work in sociology. After employing search heuristics, that is finding analogy and borrowing method, we cultivate the analogy by adopting argument heuristics. We describe what we mean by heuristics as a method of discovery and how we use this integration in order to understand the explorations present in the book. We aim to find tools to progress conceptually the studies that share a similar conceptual background.

The central point in search heuristics is analogy, for example analogy of the problem. Adopting ecology models to organizations is a good example of this; biological concepts are used in understanding organizations. In fact, a lot of cross-disciplinarity between branches of science can be explained through analogies. To cultivate analogy assumes that we are willing to make rough connections, but are also able to find the means to do it. For us, finding Abbott's ideas opened a new avenue to the methodological problems of discovery. Thus the methodology leads us to analogy. 'Borrowing methods often involves analogy, but goes beyond it to invoke not only some ideas, but also whole apparatus of analysis. Analogy is usually well concealed and often only a starting point for an argument. It must be carefully elaborated and critically worked out on its own.' Many influential papers have their roots in a fairly simple analogy that is carefully worked out (Abbott, 2003: 114–20). This working out process can benefit from argument heuristics, which focus on ways of turning old and familiar arguments into new and creative ones. Once the analogy is found it can be elaborated by argument heuristics. 'Argument heuristics works with the ideas one already has, trying to make them look unfamiliar and strange' (Abbott, 2003: 120). This kind of combination can be found, for example, in Ofori-Dankwa and Julian's (2002) work, a heuristic model of diversity and similarity curves based on the basic supply and demand curves from the field of economics. They argue that heuristics serves an important function in creating useful insights and new ways of thinking when an established approach or method in one field is successfully applied to another discipline. They argue their case well but they do not explain it methodologically. For example Abbott differentiates four different categories of argument heuristics: (1) problematizing the obvious; (2) making a reversal; (3) making an assumption and seeing what it gets you; and finally (4) reconceptualizing.

We suggest here that the analogy can be elaborated by these forms of heuristics and we have chosen to use two of them; problematizing the obvious and then making a reversal. Next we will explicate what we mean by these and how they are used in revisiting the conceptualization of the dialogue between women's entrepreneurship and social capital in the compilation of articles, all around the theme of women, entrepreneurship and social capital.

Starting with an Analogy

We further study the possibilities of heuristic discovery to create new understanding on phenomena, like the one of women's entrepreneurship and social capital. Moustakas (1990: 15) defines heuristic inquiry as 'a process that begins with a question or problem which the researcher seeks to illuminate or answer. The question is one that has been a personal challenge and puzzlement in the search to understand one's self and the world in which one lives'. Women's entrepreneurship is for us such a challenge that the interplay with social capital might elucidate. Our editing process can be seen as Polanyi's vision to fit new experiences and the discovery of movement from one framework to another based on heuristic vision, and this is followed by a heuristic act. Abbott describes this kind of a problem as a base for the analogy.

Abbott highlights that analogy first and foremost should have the ability to break out of the standard frames put around the phenomenon. The analogy we take from him concerns education. He illuminates argument heuristics with an example of college education. What if its purpose is not to educate, but something else, for example to store unemployed youngsters? This problematizing results from the division of college education in to educational and non-educational purposes.

Keeping in mind the critics about progress in gender studies and Abbott's critics of one-sidedness in posing questions, perhaps we should reconsider the questions of research and focus on its purpose as Abbott exemplifies. This leads to problematizing the obvious: what if the social capital for women entrepreneurs represents something other than social capital as it is usually defined? Going further leads to making a reversal: what if women entrepreneurs are not only constructed by social capital but are constructing it for some purpose? These two argument heuristics lead to two different dialogues, one drawn from social capital and one drawn from women's entrepreneurship. Even if both are the dialogue between social capital and women's entrepreneurship, their meaning and conceptualizing might be quite different. Thus to cultivate the analogy assumes that these two argument heuristics can be explicated.

Originally when the book was edited social capital was used heuristically as a metaphor against which the landscape of the research on social capital and women's entrepreneurship was reflected. Now, taking a conceptual approach, we further progress this dialogue. Our analogy that leads to question this approach gives the leading role to women's entrepreneurship and asks if it can add something to the conceptualizing of the social capital or if it can bring some specifics that cannot been drawn from the social capital discussion alone. The data, consisting of the ten chapters in the book, were originally divided into three parts. These chapters are presented in the appendix. Here we restrict ourselves to what we find are the most important statements and questions as formulated in the texts. The first part discusses the specifics of women's entrepreneurship and social capital discourse, having in mind theoretical reflection and transformation in particular. The second part deals with the gendered nature of social capital in entrepreneurship, the crucial element of business life. The third part focuses on the cross-cultural context of woman entrepreneurship. As a metaphorical approach this division of parts worked well. However, in the conceptual analyses with argument heuristics it takes on a slightly different form. In problematizing the obvious, our first question, 'what if the social capital for women entrepreneurs represents something other than social capital as it is usually defined?' is approached through the theoretical chapters of the book (Chapters 2, 3, 4 and 8). The other, making a reversal, 'what if women entrepreneurs are not only constructed by social capital but are constructing it for some purpose?', is based on the empirical chapters of the book (Chapters 5, 6, 7, 9, 10 and 11).

Problematizing the Obvious: Social Capital for Women Entrepreneurs Represents Something Other than Social Capital as Usually Defined

Even if social capital is a concept creating images of stability and boundaries, it is flexible, leading to many alterations. Research on both social capital and women's entrepreneurship has aroused interest within a relatively short time as a tool to explain social and economic phenomena (Aaltio, 2008a: 83–99). The growth of society's wealth depends on its total capital, which consists of physical capital, natural resources, human capital and social capital. In the knowledge society the share of physical capital constitutes only a minor part of a society's total capital and a growing role is being played by the human and social capital in economic development and processes. As Fukuyama (1995) claims, social capital creates prosperity in societies.

As stated by Kovalainen (2004: 156–7), the elasticity of the term 'social capital' has led to a situation where it is used very differently, depending on the context and research purpose in question. Usually political science and sociology refer to a set of norms, networks, institutions and organizations through which access to some actions or power is gained. Coleman argues that social capital is embodied in relations among individuals (2000: 37), which in many ways are interlinked to trust. Keeping things together and saving society from disintegration are popular themes of social capital and trust. The accumulation of people's knowledge and their emotional work in creating trust is needed in the accumulation of social capital. Social capital developing through economic infrastructures can also be underlined (Bourdieu, 1986).

Women's entrepreneurship is a field, and not a marginalist approach in entrepreneurship studies (Moore, 1999). Women and men hold occupations, professions and managerial positions differently and likewise also differ as entrepreneurs. The segregation of female and male entrepreneurship resembles the division of the workforce in general. Their areas of entrepreneurship are along the lines of gendered work segregation. Women work more in areas where females are the majority, like in education and training fields, and in work close to the home, such as caring for children and the elderly, restaurants and family businesses in services. The nature of the managerial jobs of women and men is different: human-resource management attracts more female managers to top organizational positions than other managerial areas. Findings from women's entrepreneurship also indicate that there are gender differences between men and women that pave the way to starting and running the business (Holmquist and Sundin, 2002). By studying businesses as sites and women's entrepreneurship as a context in which gender attributes are assumed and reproduced, we can make visible their gendered nature, but also easily marginalize women entrepreneurs as gendered actors and overshadow their individual roles as human capitalists. On the other hand gender lenses can make visible the position of women entrepreneurs and women managers in industries and fields of activities where the social capital is created and maintained by human capitalists. Moreover, gender lenses can indicate that perhaps women entrepreneurs are key actors in these processes, which represent a major asset of societies and economies as well as those new innovative fields and processes that societies and economies have found essential for their renewal and competitiveness.

When female entrepreneurs initiate change they tend to base their innovations on social ideas. In technical fields as well as in general as small business owner-managers they constitute the minority worldwide (GEM, 2007). It was not until the 1990s that women entrepreneurs began to embark on business ventures in all types of markets and industry sectors, and today we are witnessing a rapid increase of women-owned businesses on a global scale. In many countries their numbers are growing faster than men. Their position as minority and the fact that their firms are smaller than those run by men has led to stereotypes according to which 'women' are less risk-taking, 'women' are carers, and 'women' are not innovative as entrepreneurs. Thus women are easily rendered as 'the Other' in the analysis of entrepreneurship, which emphasizes the universality of the concept. We can ask if social capital represents the means to break and access to breaking the boundaries of 'otherness' (Ahl, 2004).

Gender needs cultural lenses and awareness of social processes. Gender is present when social relations actualize and indicate how women and men are 'done' in and by these processes. The concept of social capital and the cultural approach to organizations, being collective concepts with relational aspects, both promote understanding of organizations with shades of gender. Innovations and innovative organizational behaviour are among the key factors in social capital, but it is not obvious why and how women entrepreneurs participate in these processes (Aaltio, 2008b: 23–38). *To know what gender means is to understand its cultural dimensions in the context explored.*

As Gartner and Baker (2008) claim, the definitions scholars use for characterizing the phenomenon of entrepreneurship matter in that these definitions tend to direct scholars towards a focus on certain questions about entrepreneurship while ignoring others. For example, looking at Stevenson and Jarillo's definition (1990: 23), 'entrepreneurship is a process by which individuals – either on their own or inside organizations – pursue opportunities without regard to the resources they currently control', leaves us with many questions about its interpretation in entrepreneurship research. Men's access to visible innovative industries and their resources, marginalize women from opportunity recognition and do not recognize the arenas where women dominate. This tends to exclude them from the core of entrepreneurship research. While today innovations are in many ways based on social capital and collectivity, in many studies on women's entrepreneurship their less important role in innovative industries and growth orientated business is emphasized. Perhaps social capital could be a means and an opportunity for women entrepreneurs to pursue opportunities and get access to those resources they don't currently control but need in the development of their businesses.

Summarizing the opportunities social capital can represent to women entrepreneurs and small business owner-managers seems to open up quite a different avenue from its usual definitions.

- Social capital seems to be the field of innovation for women entrepreneurs – actually the content and means of their businesses, which is a highly valued and needed asset in society, the economy and organizations.
- It seems to give access to pursue opportunities and to get access to resources needed for these activities.
- Finally it seems to offer an opportunity to break the boundaries of 'otherness', which has paved the way of women's entrepreneurship so far.

However, all of these assume the adoption of gender lenses to explicate and to make visible on one hand the intangible asset of social capital and its processes, and on the other hand women's diverse contribution to its creation and maintenance. Thus it finally explicates how it could enhance breaking the rules and norms leading to the marginalization of women entrepreneurs and not only break the otherness, but create the sameness. In this meaning social capital represents innovation and innovativeness to women entrepreneurs, neither boundaries and stability, nor structures, networks, norms or arenas for action as such. Women's entrepreneurship and social capital are socially constructed concepts, because both women and men construct social structures and reproduce gender differences. Also the future analogies for advancing the research on the dialogue between women's entrepreneurship and social capital should rather be addressed to the innovations, innovativeness and opportunity development and exploitation, than to the aspects of social cohesion, processes and stability.

Looking now at the chapters of Aaltio et al.'s (2008) book with the ideas of this problematizing, part of argument heuristics broadens the previous view provided by heuristically using social capital as a metaphor against which these chapters were reflected.

Chapter 2 discusses the gendered nature of social capital in entrepreneurship. The reasons behind the attraction of the social capital metaphor are discussed in a critical perspective as the inclusive element also has an exclusive potential. Social capital is embedded in positive labels like trust, often with a positive female stereotype. Even though social capital is not something that easily puts women in a strong position, rather social capital can be segregated by gender as both entrepreneurship and organizational positions are segregated by gender. It is essential that women become organizational entrepreneurs and break the marginality often given to them. Organizations create social capital and are created by social capital, and this moulding process is always gendered.

All the elements of the previous argumentation are present in this chapter, but we now add heuristics to provide new understanding of the area.

Chapter 3 examines the scope of women's entrepreneurship research in recent decades and ends up by recommending that rather than continuing to debate on the differences between male and female entrepreneurs, it would perhaps be more useful to examine the experiences, values, meanings and choices preferred by women entrepreneurs in order to find ways of supporting their progress without cutting them off from entrepreneurship in general.

This chapter actually provides the means to break the otherness in research and thus facilitates the process of getting access to pursue opportunities and to get access in order to resources needed for these activities.

Chapter 4 argues that the problems of equality with respect to women entrepreneurs are far more complex than is assumed by the policy makers. It indicates how giving up the gender neutrality in policymaking might provide equality.

Thus this chapter describes the role and concrete political means regarding how to break the otherness through gender lenses, by identifying the specifics of women's entrepreneurship.

Chapter 8 argues that social factors are crucial in understanding women's entrepreneurship, but the social capital theory has limitations regarding its content, its courses and outcomes, and in addition to its lack of clarity there is a danger of restricting women's role to the private sector.

Thus this chapter summarizes the central message of the results of the argument heuristics. All these more or less theoretical chapters tell us the same message that women's entrepreneurship and social capital discussion is gendered, but do not as such serve as an explanation for the interplay between women's entrepreneurship and social capital. Thus the starting point for understanding the interplay between women's entrepreneurship and social capital is women's gendered position. That is globally shared and paves the way to women's entrepreneurship. However, it does not explain why and how women participate in and create social capital. That might be quite different in different contexts. It also leaves open the question regarding the relationship between constructing and being constructed when it comes to women's entrepreneurship.

Making a Reversal

What if women entrepreneurs are not only constructed by social capital but are constructing it for some purpose? Making a reversal is one of Abbott's four categories of argument heuristics. Some of the contributions in the anthology give clear examples along that line.

The use of gendered lenses in the study of entrepreneurship has added to our perspectives of the social capital aspects of society. Entrepreneurs appear to have a special position in forming, developing and reorganizing the social capital in the business world, and women can probably contribute to this process differently compared to men. But why and how they do so is not so obvious in the current stream of research in this field. Rather it has been taken for granted that somehow there is a strong relationship between women's entrepreneurship and social capital, and this relationship is different compared to their counterpart. We now look at these perceptions in the empirical chapters of the book in the light of the results of argument heuristics.

Chapter 5 investigates empirically female organizational entrepreneurs in Swedish public healthcare and elderly care. Innovative ways to save municipal funds as well as horizontal and local networks improved the results and demonstrated these women's abilities to take social risks. All these findings challenge traditional thinking on female abilities as entrepreneurs and also show how women-occupied areas such as healthcare and elderly care can be improved by using social capital and risk-taking if we understand them in new ways.

The results of this example indicate how women entrepreneurs in the organization context intentionally choose the strategy of creating social capital for creating and exploiting opportunities.

Chapter 6 introduces us to the power of the network-credit system in different societies, in poor countries and in one of the Nordic countries, Norway. By analysing social networking through different forms of trust, the chapter indicates how, by joining the network, women entrepreneurs overcome gender-related obstacles in financing, regardless of culture.

This chapter gives full 'credit' to the Nobel prizewinner Yunus Mohammed's invention of the micro credit system. It also shows how abilities to build social capital in organizational settings are an essential and innovative way to exploit opportunities and entrepreneurship.

Chapter 7 deals with organizational entrepreneurship, and the specifics of women's opportunities to gather social capital in organizational settings. Social capital has a role in building one's reputation, and in particular the strength of women's relationships with others and the extent of their connections to reach other contacts are crucial in women's ways to the top. This chapter shows how abilities to build social capital in organizational settings are an essential and innovative way to exploit opportunities and enhance entrepreneurial behaviour in organizations.

Also this chapter highlights the way in which creating social capital represents both an innovation that is the content of opportunity as well as access to entrepreneurial behaviour that is to exploit opportunities in organizational settings.

Chapter 9 elaborates the concepts of identity, entrepreneur/entrepreneurship, profession and gender. Narratives of six women who have started private schools in Sweden describe how the women handle the complexity of the partly conflicting bases for identity construction in different ways. This chapter is a sociological window that shows the evolutionary character of the identity of the entrepreneur. Women take different positions at every stage of their life cycles. Initially a teacher in the public sector, the woman becomes the creator of a business, a pioneer of new pedagogical methods, a manager of relations with parents, and so on. From a professional situation where they had little decision-making power, they have become resourceful, entrepreneurial and dynamic. Thus, they feel able to do what they want to do. Entrepreneurship helps women to achieve, as teachers, power over the way they decide to do their job.

This example exemplifies how women innovate by creating social capital, which becomes an essential asset and a success factor for achieving and fulfilling their personal and professional needs and desires.

Chapter 10 explores the paradox between entrepreneurial competences and Islamic patriarchal, subordinating traditions that influence women's spatial mobility and occupational opportunities. It exemplifies how women-only training helped to overcome some of the problems faced with this paradox. Empirical findings from Pakistan indicate that the training programme based on women's specific needs plays an important role in the improvement of their ventures' performance and also provides an opportunity to build self-esteem and confidence for creating and exploiting opportunities. The authors recommend that the right support, proper capacity-building, and conducive environment will help women to improve their entrepreneurial competences and thus exert influence on equality in Islamic societies.

Also this example indicates how women entrepreneurs and potential entrepreneurs intentionally overcome the obstacles of otherness and join the network for building social capital. For their cultural context it is also a social innovation for fulfilling women's needs and desires.

Chapter 11 introduces the results of a comparative study in Argentina, Brazil, Canada, the United States and Mexico. The findings from large surveys indicate that, by and large, female small business owners are more similar to one another than one would expect from the host of studies on cultural differences among managers. The relations between success and the two personal variables, self-efficacy and need for achievement, are particularly notable. The authors highlight the potential value of education and mentoring which would help budding female small business owners, regardless of national context.

This chapter summarizes the findings of entrepreneurship in general, which highlight the meaning of self-efficacy and need for achievement in entrepreneurial processes. The results indicate that, regardless of culture, the same issues are of importance to women as have been found to be essential for male entrepreneurs. The question it poses is whether social capital for women entrepreneurs also represents an innovative way to increase self-efficacy and increase their competencies for entrepreneurial behaviour, which otherwise is not possible given women's marginal position in whatever culture it takes place.

Summarizing our reversal, 'what if women entrepreneurs are not only constructed by social capital but are constructing it for some purpose' seems to be quite a valid suggestion. Actually for women entrepreneurs, either creating social capital or joining social capital networks seems to be an essential strategic decision for creating and exploiting opportunities, for increasing their human capital and fulfilling their needs and desires. The reason for creating social capital and joining existing networks seems to be due to their gender position and otherness, which creates obstacles that their counterparts do not encounter. Thus social capital breaks down the boundaries of otherness despite the culture and context.

4. CONCLUSIONS

We argued that conceptual work that combines and investigates the multiple results of the studies is needed for explicating the contribution of special issues and book editions. As a tool to enable conceptual development in this field we introduced two forms of heuristic method, that of search and argument heuristics, and explicated how they provided new angles to the understanding of the dialogue between social capital and women's entrepreneurship. By reflecting, we made explicit what was implicit in the edition. The lack of suitable concepts typically marginalizes women's entrepreneurship, and thus finding a way to enhance conceptualizing in this field is valid for advancing the research and practices of women's entrepreneurship. Instead of 'marginalizing' we promote 'innovating' as an intrinsic line of women's entrepreneurship and social capital concepts.

After employing search heuristics, that is finding analogy and borrowing heuristic method from sociology, we cultivated the analogy by adopting argument heuristics. Finding the analogy from the field of education led us to argument heuristics first by problematizing the obvious with the question 'what if the social capital for women entrepreneurs represents something other than social capital as it is usually defined?', then by making a reversal, 'what if women entrepreneurs are not only constructed by social capital but are constructing it for some purpose?' Social capital seems to be the field of innovations for women entrepreneurs – actually the content and means of their businesses, which is a highly valued and needed asset in society, the economy and organizations. It seems to give access to the pursuit of opportunities and to resources needed for these activities. Thus it offers an opportunity to break down the boundaries of 'otherness', which has paved the way for women's entrepreneurship so far. Adopting these to the book chapters indicated that the starting point for understanding the interplay between women's entrepreneurship and social capital is women's gendered position. The reason for creating social capital and joining existing networks seems to be due to their gender position and otherness, which creates obstacles that their counterparts do not encounter. Thus social capital breaks down the boundaries of otherness despite the culture and context. Thus the heuristic method has indicated the essential role of innovativeness in conceptualizing the interplay between social capital and women's entrepreneurship which, through gender lenses, can cross the borders of otherness and deepen our understanding more than using social capital as a metaphor against which we reflect research conducted on female entrepreneurs.

Research on women's entrepreneurship has evolved in recent decades with multiple results. For instance, women and men entrepreneurs have different backgrounds and the world of enterprise is gendered many ways (Calás and Smircich, 2007). Women are still a minority as entrepreneurs, even if their number is somewhat bigger nowadays than it used to be (Davidson and Burke, 2004). Previous work in psychology and sociology theorizes that women are situated in a different reality from men, who are rooted in their situation and experiences (Brush, 1992: 24). According to some studies, their motivation, performances, networking, financing, work–family balance and even management style are somewhat different from those of men entrepreneurs (Carrier et al., 2008). Entrepreneurs identify themselves within societal and structural contexts, too. Even if broad and rich, research on women's entrepreneurship is scattered, and the results of this research indicate that conceptual methods like heuristics may show the implicit argumentation and the innovative nature of this research to entrepreneurship theory; how women's entrepreneurship research is not only a part of entrepreneurship theory, but how it renews the whole approach, like in the area of social capital.

The expansion of research, seen in the growing numbers of journals and textbooks, needs analytical tools to understand and search the essence of study findings that they present. As a method, it invites the search for other methodological solutions to increase the rigorous elaboration of academic publishing in special issues and compilations. It turns out that the heuristic method is also a conceptual tool that enlightens the learning process of the researcher and supports reflexivity in work.

We believe that these kinds of tools, individual and shared, will be needed more and more in the future.

To perceive these advantages there is a need to take more examples and employ other forms of heuristics to develop this method further. However, even this small study has indicated that it might be useful in contexts other than entrepreneurship where new ideas and concepts are needed in complex relationships. Thus, rather than repatriating these findings in our home culture of entrepreneurship, as Wiklund et al. (2006) suggest, we hope they can be used in other cultures as well. Moreover, this combination of search and argument heuristics as used here could be further elaborated by using larger data on women's entrepreneurship publications and different contexts to identify its opportunities in making implicit dialogues explicit to us.

REFERENCES

Aaltio, I. (2006), 'Editorial', *Liiketaloudellinen Aikakauskirja (The Finnish Journal of Business Economics)*, **2**, 451–4.
Aaltio, I. (2008a), 'Management education as an identity construction: the case of Estonia and its transition economy background', *International Journal of Entrepreneurship and Small Business*, **5**, 83–99.
Aaltio, I. (2008b), 'Entrepreneurship in organization: gender and social capital', in I. Aaltio, P. Kyrö and E. Sundin (eds), *The Dialogue between Women's Entrepreneurship and Social Capital*, Denmark: Copenhagen Business School Press, pp. 23–38.
Aaltio, I, P. Kyrö and E. Sundin (eds) (2008), *The Dialogue between Women's*

Entrepreneurship and Social Capital, Denmark: Copenhagen Business School.

Abbott, A. (2003) *Methods of Discovery: Heuristics for the Social Sciences*, New York: Norton.

Ahl, H. (2004), *The Scientific Reproduction of Gender Inequality: A Discourse Analysis of Research Texts on Women's Entrepreneurship*, Malmö: Liber.

Ahl, H. (2008), 'The problematic relationship between social capital theory and gender research', in I. Aaltio, P. Kyrö and E. Sundin (eds), *The Dialogue between Women's Entrepreneurship and Social Capital*, Denmark: Copenhagen Business School Press, pp. 167–93.

Black, P. (1951), 'Toward a systematic field of race relations: a heuristic statement of objectives', *Human Relations*, **4**, 95–102.

Bourdieu, P. (1986), 'The forms of capital', in J.G. Richardson (ed.), *Handbook of Theory and Research for the Sociology of Education*, Westport, CT: Greenwood Press, pp. 241–58.

Brush, C.G. (1992), 'Research on women business owners: past trends, a new perspective and future directions', *Entrepreneurship Theory and Practice*, **16**, 5–30.

Calás, M.B. and L. Smircich (2007), 'Knowing Lisa? Feminist analyses of "Gender and Entrepreneurship"', in D. Bilimoria and S. K. Piderit (eds), *The Handbook of Women in Business and Management*, Cheltenham, UK and Northampton, MA, USA: Edward Elgar Publishing.

Carrier, C., P.-A. Julien and W. Menville (2008), 'Gender in entrepreneurship research: a critical look at the literature', in I. Aaltio, P. Kyrö and E. Sundin (eds), *The Dialogue between Women's Entrepreneurship and Social Capital*, Denmark: Copenhagen Business School Press, pp. 39–66.

Chen, S.Y. and R.D. Macredie (2005), 'The assessment of usability of electronic shopping: a heuristic evaluation', *International Journal of Information Management*, **25**, 516–32.

Clandinin, D.J. (1986), *Classroom Practice*, Philadelphia, PA: The Falmer Press.

Coleman, S. (2000), 'Access to capital and terms of credit: a comparison of men- and women-owned small businesses', *Journal of Small Business Management*, **38**, 37–52.

Davidson, M. and R. Burke (eds) (2004), *Women in Management Worldwide: Facts, Figures and Analysis*, Aldershot: Ashgate.

Emery, M. (1986), 'Toward an heuristic theory of diffusion', *Human Relations*, **39**, 411–32.

Frank, T. (1997), 'George Polya and the heuristic tradition fascination with genius in central Europe', *The periodical of the Michale Polanyi liberal philosophical association. Polanyiana, 6.* www.kfki.hu/chemonet/polanyi/

Fukuyama, F. (1995), *The Social Virtues and the Creation of Prosperity*, London: Penguin.

Gartner, W.B. and T. Baker (2008), '"No cash no fear:" Just So stories for an entrepreneurial age', paper presented at the 15th Nordic Conference on Small Business Research, Tallinn University of Technology, August 2008.

GEM (2007), 'Global Entrepreneurship Monitoring Report 2007', Babson College, USA.

Hardy, C. and N. Phillips (1999), 'No joking matter: discursive struggle in the Canadian refugee system', *Organization Studies*, **20**, 1–24.

Hine, D. and D. Carson (eds) (2007), *Innovative Methodologies in Enterprise Research*, Cheltenham, UK and Northampton, MA, USA: Edward Elgar.

Holmquist, C. and E. Sundin (eds) (2002), *Företagerskan: Om Kvinnor och Entreprenörskap*, Stockholm: SNS Förlag.

Kleining, G. and H. Witt (2001), 'Discovery as basic methodology of qualitative and quantitative research', *Forum: Qualitative Social Research*, **2**, Art. 16.

Kovalainen, A. (2004), 'Rethinking the revival of social capital and trust in social theory: possibilities for feminist analysis', in B.L. Marshall and A. Witz (eds) *Engendering the Social: Feminist Encounters with Sociological Theory*, Maidenhead: Open University Press, pp. 155–70.

Kyrö, P., O. Hägg and K. Peltonen (2009), 'Experiential explorative research: an unexploited opportunity for entrepreneurship education research', paper to be published in RENT XXIII: Research in Entrepreneurship and Small Business Proceedings, Budapest, Hungary, 19–20 November.

Kyrö, P. and J. Kansikas (2005), 'Current state of methodology in entrepreneurship research and some expectations for the future', in A. Fayolle, P. Kyrö and J. Uljin (eds), *Entrepreneurship Research in Europe: Perspectives and Outcomes*, Cheltenham, UK and Northampton, MA, USA: Edward Elgar.

Lämsä, A.-M. and T. Takala (2001), 'Tulkitseva käsitetutkimus organisaatio- ja johtamistutkimuksen tutkimusmetodologisena vaihtoehtona', *Liiketaloudellinen Aikakauskirja*, **3**, 371–90.

Leontjev, A.N. (1977), *Toiminta, Tietoisuus ja Persoonallisuus*, Helsinki: Kansankulttuuri.

Levit, N. (2006), 'Confronting conventional thinking: the heuristics problem in feminist legal theory', *Cardozo Law Review*, **28**.

Lin, N. (2001), *Social Capital: A Theory of Social Structure and Action*, Cambridge: Cambridge University Press.

Mezirow, J. (1995), 'Kriittinen reflektio uudistavan oppimisen käynnistäjänä', in J. Mezirow (ed.), *Uudistava Oppiminen*, Helsinki: Miktor.

Mills, A. (2002), 'History/herstory: an introduction to the problems of studying the gendering of organizational culture over time', in I. Aaltio and A. Mills (eds), *Gender, Identity and the Culture of Organizations*, London: Routledge, pp. 127–8.

Moore, D.P. (1999), 'Women entrepreneurs: approaching a new millennium', in G.N. Powell (ed.), *Gender & Work*, USA: Sage Publications, pp. 371–91.

Morrell, K. and J. Hartley (2006), 'A model of political leadership', *Human Relations*, **59**, 483–504.

Moustakas, C. (1990), *Heuristic Research: Design, Methodology, and Applications*, Newbury Park, CA: Sage Publications.

Neergaard H. and J.P. Uthoi (2007), *Handbook of Qualitative Research Methods in Entrepreneurship*, Cheltenham, UK and Northampton, MA, USA: Edward Elgar.

Ofori-Dankwa, J.C. and S.D. Julian (2002), 'Toward diversity and similarity curves: implications for theory, research and practice', *Human Relations*, **55**, 199–224.

Polanyi, M. (1958), *Personal Knowledge*, Chicago, IL: University of Chicago Press.

Polanyi, M. and H. Prosch (1975), *Meaning*, Chicago, IL: University of Chicago Press.

Stevenson, H.H. and J.C. Jarillo (1990), 'A paradigm of entrepreneurship: entrepreneurial management', *Strategic Management Journal*, **11**, 17–27.

Vickie D.H. (1997), 'Volitional change in elementary teachers' conceptions of science pedagogy via a generative learning model of teaching', 1997 AETS

Conference Papers and Summaries of Presentations, available online at: http://
www.ed.psu.edu/ci/Journals/97pap24.htm, date accessed November 12, 1997.
Wiklund, J., D. Dimov, J.A. Katz and D.A. Shepherd (2006), 'Entrepreneurship:
framework and empirical investigations from forthcoming leaders of European
research', *Advances in Entrepreneurship firm Emergence and Growth*, **9**.
Yeager, M.A. (ed.) (1999), *Women in Business*, Cheltenham, UK and
Northampton, MA, USA: Edward Elgar.

APPENDIX

BOX 5A.1   THE CONTENT OF THE BOOK
CHAPTERS

Part I: Specifics of Women's Entrepreneurship Theory
Chapter 1:   Introduction
            Iiris Aaltio, Paula Kyrö and Elisabeth Sundin
            Argues for how social capital is used heuristically as
            a metaphor against which the landscape of the
            research on social capital and women's entrepre-
            neurship was reflected.
Chapter 2:   Entrepreneurship in organization, gender and social
            capital
            Iiris Aaltio
Chapter 3:   Gender in entrepreneurship research: a critical look
            at the literature
            *Camille Carrier, Pierre-André Julien and William
            Menvielle*
Chapter 4:   From marginality to centre: women's entrepreneur-
            ship policy challenges government's gender neutral-
            ity in Finland
            Paula Kyrö and Kaisa Hyrsky

Part II: Gendered Nature of the Social Capital in
            Entrepreneurship
Chapter 5:   Organisational entrepreneurs in the public sectors:
            social capital and gender
            Elisabeth Sundin and Malin Tillmar
Chapter 6:   Network credit: the magic of trust
            May-Britt Ellingsen and Ann Therese Lotherington
Chapter 7:   Examining the role of social capital in female
            professionals' reputation building and opportunities
            gathering: a network approach
            Yuliani Suseno
Chapter 8:   The problematic relationship between social capital
            theory and gender research
            Helene Ahl

6. Entrepreneurs' social capital enhancing performance and venture advancement

Hannes Ottósson and Thomas Schøtt

INTRODUCTION

Many studies in the field of entrepreneurship, borrowing from sociology and economics, have investigated the effects of social capital on entrepreneurial performance, such as growth in sales, employees or profit (Lee et al., 2001; Westhead et al., 2001; Baum and Locke, 2004). Some of this line of research has been criticized for the performance measures used (Robinson, 1999; Witt, 2004) and recommendations made for increased integration of outcome and process-oriented research (Hoang and Antoncic, 2003).

Hoang and Antoncic (2003) call for increased integration between process and outcome-oriented research by exploring how concepts from one research stream can usefully extend theoretical models in the other. They argue that outcome-oriented research can become richer when combined with theoretical insights arising from research on network dynamics. With a dynamic panel research design that covers the whole entrepreneurial process scholars can stop asking 'whether' questions and start asking 'when' and 'how' questions. Furthermore, by using a panel design it is possible to limit the 'success' bias, where potential entrepreneurs who abandon their intentions are often excluded from sampling.

Gartner (1985) describes the process of new venture creation in a framework of four perspectives. The perspectives include the characteristics of the individuals, the process, the environment and the organization. The individual perspective covers background of entrepreneurs, such as age and entrepreneurial parents, human capital such as education and experience, and personality or psychological characteristics, such as need for achievement and propensity for risk-taking. The social capital is important in the first steps of the process perspective as it includes location of business opportunity and accumulation of resources. This study will be limited to the process perspective based on social capital. The individual perspective will somewhat be taken into account by including human capital measures.

This study is positioned along entrepreneur network literature (reviews: O'Donnell et al., 2001; Hoang and Antoncic, 2003) at the crossroads of entrepreneurship theory and social network theory. Much of the research done in entrepreneur network literature has focused on the outcome of the venture emerging process (reviews: Chakravarthy, 1986; Murphy et al., 1996). This study focuses on ego-networks (Greve and Salaff, 2003) of entrepreneurs in three phases of venture emergence – gestation, emerging and newly established – as defined by the Global Entrepreneurship Monitor (Reynolds et al., 2005; Levie and Autio, 2008) and effects of the network on entrepreneurial performance and advancement.

Previous entrepreneurship research is expanded, by viewing venture emergence as a dynamic process, which is captured using a panel design with a random sample of entrepreneurs operating in all phases of the process. Social capital is a broad concept, encompassing several dimensions, and is here operationalized as network size and network content. Network size denotes the volume of the network, and network content refers to the qualitative substance of the network. Performance is also a broad concept comprising several dimensions, and is here operationalized as effectiveness and as advancement in the entrepreneurial process, as two major dimensions of performance. Effectiveness refers to the entrepreneurs' effectiveness in their entrepreneurial efforts. Advancement denotes the entrepreneurs' stepwise process through their venture formation.

Next we review previous literature in order to develop our hypotheses. The literature review is followed by a methodology section before the empirical results are presented. The chapter ends with an interpretation and a conclusion including practical implications and implication for future research.

ENTREPRENEURS' SOCIAL CAPITAL AND THEIR PERFORMANCE

Social Capital in an Entrepreneur's Network

Studies on social capital typically consider aspects of social capital such as trust, shared values or norms, and social resources gained within a social environment. Nahapiet and Ghoshal (1998), inspired by Bourdieu (1986) and Burt (1992), propose a more narrow definition of social capital: 'The sum of the actual and potential resources embedded within, available through, and derived from the network of relationship possessed by an individual or a social unit. Social capital thus comprises both the network and the assets that may be mobilized through that network' (Nahapiet and Ghoshal, 1998: 243). Such a conception of social capital has been imported to entrepreneurship theory through the literature on entrepreneurial networks. The literature on entrepreneurial networking suggests that entrepreneurs obtain resources from their social networks which facilitate their performance. Properties of the network have been argued to influence entrepreneurship, notably density, diversity, range, size and centrality. Here, we focus on two network properties: size and content.

Size of an entrepreneur's network
Network size here denotes the number of direct links between the entrepreneur (ego) and his/her contacts in the *activated* network. The activated network is different from the entrepreneurs' total network, as it only contains the contact they have received advice from during the venture emergence process. A general proposition is that the number of contacts has a positive impact on resource flows and hence on entrepreneur outcome (Hoang and Antoncic, 2003).

Network size is among the most investigated network concepts. It is argued that network size increases entrepreneurs' performance. A larger network is expected to provide entrepreneurs with more information and also more non-redundant information than a smaller network. The proposition that network size increases entrepreneurs' performance has received empirical support (Greve, 1995; Hansen, 1995; Greve and Salaff, 2003), although some studies report insignificant findings (Aldrich and Reese, 1993). Schøtt (2009) has found that network size also increases performance in terms of innovativeness, exporting and growth-orientation. While it thus seems that network size increases entrepreneurial performance, it is also acknowledged that the relationship may not be linear (Watson, 2007). If the network becomes very large, the amount of time spent on maintaining the network exceeds the value of adding to the network. Thus, a large network could prove counter-productive (Watson, 2007).

Content of an entrepreneur's network
Research is limited on network content of entrepreneurs (O'Donnell et al., 2001; Hoang and Antoncic, 2003), and even more so on how it affects the venture emergence process. Scholars differ in conceptualizations and ideas, and the concept has been described in terms such as expectations, trust, values, identity (Podolny and Baron, 1997) and quality of network (Burt, 1997).

The more time and effort spent on the network, the more affluent and encompassing the content will be and thus the opportunities to mobilize a variety of assets through the network. Ostgaard and Birley (1994) found that content of network exchanges, which they argued gave a crude measure of its quality, was positively associated with firms' competitive strategy. A diverse discussion within the network might relate to the quality of the contacts. The quality of a contact can be approached from its uniqueness compared to other contacts (Burt, 1983). Similarly, the quality of the network can be understood as the variation of the substance.

As we shall see in the data, the size and content of the network are highly correlated (0.47). Thus, they will be combined in one network indicator as network size and content.

Performance in Entrepreneurship

Entrepreneurial performance as an outcome with several dimensions has been measured in various ways. Some considerations include what measures suit the different phases of the venture emerging process and whether to use objective or subjective measures (Cooper, 1993). Furthermore, when including all phases of venture emergence it becomes difficult to choose indicators that are suitable for all phases.

In a review covering literature published between 1987 and 1993, Murphy et al. (1996) classified 51 articles based on the performance measures used. They found that growth (used in 23 articles), efficiency (13), sales (13) and profit (11) were very common measures, but failure (4) and subjective assessment (used in 4 articles) were rarely used. Growth and efficiency have been and still are common performance measures but process-oriented measures (Davidsson and Honig, 2003; Elfring and Hulsink, 2003), and perception measures (Erikson, 2002; Paige and Littrell, 2002) have become more common in recent years.

In our own review of performance measures covering the years 1994 to 2006 and limited to five major entrepreneurship journals we discover that the use of process-oriented measures has become the second most used measure after growth, and the use of subjective and survival measures has increased from earlier reviews. Thus, the development seems to be for more process-oriented research and subjective measures. Here we focus on entrepreneur advancement and entrepreneur effectiveness, so as to cover two different dimensions of performance measures that might be suitable for all phases of venture emergence.

Advancement in the entrepreneurial process
In this study we are interested in advancement of the entrepreneur through venture emergence. The entrepreneur can exit from the process, remain in

the same phase or advance to another phase in the process. It is accepted that not all transitions are completely comparable between phases. The concept of advancement encompasses previously used measures such as survival or rather *non-survival* to indicate exit, *start-up activities* to indicate the start-up phase and actual *self-employment* to indicate the young business venture phase.

Survival can be seen as a minimum criterion of success (Bruderl and Preisendorfer, 1998). The criterion for survival is usually defined as staying in business for the first few years of operation and sometimes stands alone as an outcome measure (Littunen, 2000). More often it is accompanied by other outcome measures, such as growth (Cooper et al., 1994) and then non-survival represents the lowest level of performance.

Before the venture has been founded, the most commonly defined outcome indicator is start-up activity. Carter et al. (1996) have identified certain start-up activities as representative of a successful start-up and suggest that those activities can be viewed as milestones towards founding a venture. The frequency and pace by which these activities are completed move the nascent entrepreneur forward in the process toward founding a venture and moving into self-employment (Davidsson and Honig, 2003).

Many studies have used reported self-employment as a major indicator for entrepreneurial behaviour (Bates, 1995; Reynolds, 1997; Henley, 2007). Founding the venture and entering self-employment is a primary goal of most entrepreneurs, just as stopping the process is not a goal of many.

Effectiveness in the entrepreneurial process

Entrepreneurs' behaviour and performance have increasingly become examined by using subjective measures based on their own perceptions (Forbes, 1999; Erikson, 2002; Baum and Locke, 2004). It has been claimed that individuals' perceptual values, including variables such as alertness, autonomy, self-efficacy and self-confidence, are important in explaining entrepreneurship (Krueger et al., 2000; Arenius and De Clercq, 2005).

Chandler and Hanks (1994) found a positive association between self-perceived competence or effectiveness of entrepreneurs and performance; the conclusion was that their ventures enjoyed a higher level of growth and earnings. Arenius and De Clerc (2005) and Arenius and Minniti (2005) suggest that perception of one's own skills to start a business is the single most important factor influencing the decision to start a business. Koellinger et al. (2007) came to a similar conclusion using data from 18 countries. On the basis of this literature it seems reasonable to view entrepreneurs' self-perceived effectiveness as an aspect of performance.

Advancement and effectiveness are expectedly positively associated, as they are two dimensions of performance. But, as we shall see in the data, they are not so highly correlated (0.21) that they should be considered as one combined indicator of the concept of performance.

Hypotheses

The hypothesis, in its broadest formulation, is that entrepreneurs' social capital enhances their performance. More specifically, the following two hypotheses are put forward:

Hypothesis 1: Social capital measured as network size and network content, has a positive influence on performance measured as advancement in the entrepreneurial process of venture formation.

Hypothesis 2: Social capital measured as network size and network content, has a positive influence on performance measured as perceived effectiveness in the entrepreneurial process.

These two hypotheses are tested in the following.

METHODS

Data

The original data for this study was collected in 2006 in connection with the Danish participation in the international research project Global Entrepreneurship Monitor (GEM). Randomly, 10 000 adults (between 18 and 64 years old) were contacted and telephone interviewed about their entrepreneurial activities (Schøtt, 2007). The survey identified three kinds of entrepreneurs, namely potential entrepreneurs, nascent entrepreneurs and new-business owner-managers. Up toward a thousand such entrepreneurs were identified and a follow-up interview was successfully completed with 714 entrepreneurs. They are classified as potential entrepreneurs, who intend to start a business within the next three years (N = 395), as nascent entrepreneurs, who are active in the process of starting a business (N = 101), or as new-business owner-managers, who are running a newly established business younger than 42 months (N = 218). This definition of kinds of entrepreneurs is based on well-tested GEM survey methodology (Reynolds et al., 2005). The three kinds of entrepreneurs also form our measurement of the three stages, namely gestation, emergence and newly established.

The position-generator (Lin, 2001) was used to capture the respondents' *activated* networks. Two methodologies are frequently used to measure social networks: the name generator and the position generator. The use of the name generator, where respondents report names of contacts, is most frequently applied (Campbell et al., 1986; Burt, 1992); however, the position generator methodology has also been used extensively (Lin and Dumin, 1986; Lin, 2001; Watson, 2007). The advantages of the position generator are that it measures access to structural positions, it captures occupational or positional characteristics of the network, and it enables researchers to collect data on strong and weak ties simultaneously (Lin and Dumin, 1986). Further it is content-free and role/location-neutral, and does not promote personal ties as the name generator tends to (Campbell and Lee, 1991).

Respondents were specifically asked whether they had received advice regarding the start-up from individuals presented as a list of 18 distinct roles. The roles range from family members to various kinds of business relations. The following questions are used to construct the network size variable: 'Have you asked for advice from . . . (repeat for every option) your family? friends? a bank adviser? a lawyer? an accountant? another kind of adviser in the private sector? a public sector adviser at your local business support office? another kind of adviser in the public sector? a person with much business experience? a person who is currently starting a business? a researcher or an inventor? an expert in your field? your current supervisor? a former supervisor? current colleagues? former colleagues? a possible investor? an international contact?' The respondents could answer each of the 18 questions with a yes or no.

To construct the network content variable, the following question was used: 'What have you discussed with others about the start-up? Have you discussed . . . (repeat for every option) a plan for how the start-up shall be operated, how the start-up shall be financed, how the operations shall be organized, innovation and entrepreneurship, possible exports of the new venture, if the new venture shall grow large, over ten employees, the business idea of the new venture?' Again the respondents could answer each question with a yes or a no.

Measures of Social Capital and Performance

Advancement in the entrepreneurial process of venture formation
Our measure of advancement thus takes advantage of the longitudinal design of our study as a panel survey, with repeated measurement of phase of the entrepreneur, namely as follows. Entrepreneurs at any phase in 2006 who in 2007 reported to have exited the process are coded 0.

Entrepreneurs at any phase, who reported to remain in the same phase in 2007 as in 2006, are coded 1, and entrepreneurs at any phase, who report a transition between phases from 2006 to 2007, are coded 2. Transition between phases is measured as 2 when a person, who in 2006 was a potential entrepreneur, became a nascent entrepreneur or an owner-manager by 2007. Furthermore, a person, who was a nascent entrepreneur in 2006 but became an owner-manager by 2007, is also coded 2. Our dependent advance variable, in the first two hypotheses, is thus measured on a three-point scale, which in our analyses will be treated as numerical.

Perceived effectiveness in the entrepreneurial process
The following question is used to measure the respondent's effectiveness: 'Compared to other entrepreneurs, do you think that you are equally effective, more effective, or less effective?' Here respondents can choose one of these options and are coded 1 for less effective, 2 for equally effective, and 3 for more effective. The face-validity of this measurement makes it a reasonable operationalization of performance.

Size and content of network
The number of direct ties between the respondent (ego) and his/her contacts constructs the network size variable. The size is measured on a numerical scale and can vary from 0 to 18 based on the number of direct ties. To construct the ratio of size the number of ties are divided by 18, with values from 0 to 1. The number of issues discussed in the network constructs the network content variable. The content is measured on a numerical scale and varies from 0 to 4 for potential entrepreneurs and 0 to 7 for the other kinds of entrepreneurs. To measure network content on the same scale for all entrepreneurs, a new network content ratio variable is constructed, with values from 0 to 1. The social capital indicator size and content of network is constructed by adding the size and content variables together and dividing by 2, resulting in values from 0 to 1.

Control Variables and Descriptive Statistics

Descriptive statistics are used together with multiple linear regressions. Furthermore, the regressions control for the respondent's age, gender and one of three venture stages: gestation, emerging and newly established.

Possible response bias was checked using t-tests and chi-square comparing the sample with non-respondents. All variables were compared across the two groups, and no differences were detected at the 0.05 level of statistical significance, except that minor differences were seen in phase and effectiveness. The similarity between respondents and non-respondents, together with randomness in sampling, suggests that the sample is representative of entrepreneurs in Denmark.

Education
A dichotomous scale is used to measure the respondents' higher education: less than 3 years of higher education is coded as 1, and 3 years or more higher education is coded as 2.

Start-up skills
Respondents' start-up skills are measured with the following question: 'Do you have the knowledge or skills needed to start a new venture?' Perceived start-up skills are coded 1 and lack of start-up skills is coded 0.

Start-up experience
The respondents are given two options regarding their start-up experience, with the following question: 'Have you ever been involved in starting up a business before?' Start-up experience is coded 1, while lack of start-up experience is coded 0.

Other control variables
The age of the respondent is coded as the number of years of age. Gender is coded 1 for men and 2 for women. The phase in the first year, 2006, is coded 1 for gestation, 2 for emerging and 3 for newly established, and in the same way in the second year, 2007, except that respondents who report they have abandoned the process are coded 0.

Table 6.1 shows the mean, frequency and percentage distributions of the variables.

There is considerable variation in the variables, which makes it feasible to test the hypotheses by multiple regressions.

RESULTS

Correlations between variables are presented in Table 6.2. Advancement and effectiveness are positively and moderately correlated, as two dimensions of performance, and are not so highly correlated that they should be combined into an index of performance. Since size and content of network are highly correlated (0.47), they are combined into a combined index of social capital. No correlation between independent variables is so high as to be a problem of multicollinearity. All correlations between the independent variables and the dependent variable are positive and most are quite significant. All the human capital variables are significantly

Table 6.1   Descriptive statistics

Network size and content – mean (and st. dev.)	0.31 (0.20)
Advancement – mean (and standard deviation)	0.92 (0.67)
Transition	103 (19%)
Status quo	293 (54%)
Exit	144 (27%)
Effectiveness – mean (and standard deviation)	0.92 (0.76)
High	189 (28%)
Medium	285 (43%)
Low	195 (29%)
Education – mean (and standard deviation)	1.47 (0.50)
High	329 (46%)
Low	378 (54%)
Start-up skills – mean (and standard deviation)	0.78 (0.41)
Yes	537 (78%)
No	150 (22%)
Start-up experience – mean (and standard deviation)	0.35 (0.48)
Yes	251 (35%)
No	457 (65%)
Age – mean (and standard deviation)	39 years (10.46)
Gender – mean (and standard deviation)	1.39 (0.49)
Men	439 (62%)
Women	275 (38%)
Phase in 2006 – mean (and standard deviation)	1.75 (0.89)
Gestation	395 (55%)
Emergence	101 (14%)
Newly established	218 (31%)

Note: N = 714.

positively correlated with the dependent variables advancement and effectiveness, except for higher education which surprisingly has no significant association with effectiveness. The gender variable has a significantly negative association with both dependent variables, which indicates that women have lower perceived effectiveness and are less likely to advance through the venture emergence process. Unsurprisingly, phase has a significantly negative association with advancement and effectiveness, since the control group for phase is the potential entrepreneurs positioned early in the process. The other correlations are insignificant.

Table 6.2   Correlations

Variables	1	2	3	4	5	6	7	8	9
1 Advancement	1	0.21**	0.11*	0.10*	0.14**	0.13**	0.05	−0.12**	−0.16**
2 Effectiveness		1	0.09*	−0.04	0.16**	0.12**	0.02	−0.08*	−0.14**
3 Network size and content			1	0.05	−0.02	0.02	−0.24**	0.04	0.23**
4 Higher education				1	0.02	0.04	0.18**	0.08*	−0.05
5 Start-up skills					1	0.15**	0.18**	−0.11**	−0.12**
6 Start-up experience						1	0.22**	−0.02	0.05
7 Age							1	0.0	−0.16**
8 Gender								1	−0.07*
9 Phase									1

Notes: Level of statistical significance: * indicates $p < 0.05$; ** indicates $p < 0.01$.

Table 6.3   Advancement and effectiveness regressed on content and size of network

	Advancement	Effectiveness
Network size and content	0.15**	0.14**
Education	0.10*	−0.05
Start-up skills	0.10*	0.12**
Start-up experience	0.10*	0.10*
Age	0.00	−0.02
Gender	−0.14**	−0.05
Phase	−0.15**	−0.16**
R^2	0.099**	0.073**
Adjusted R^2	0.086**	0.063**
N respondents	508	635

Notes: Standardized regression coefficients (betas) are displayed in the table. The reference phase is 1. Level of statistical significance: * indicates $p < 0.05$; ** indicates $p < 0.01$.

Multiple linear regression models will now be used for testing the hypotheses. Hypothesis 1, stating that advancement is enhanced by size and content of the network, is tested by the linear regression of advancement upon network size and content and the control variables in Table 6.3. Network size and content has a significant influence on entrepreneurial advancement ($p < 0.01$). The human capital variables, education (p < 0.05), start-up skills (p < 0.05) and start-up experience (p < 0.05), have a significant positive influence on entrepreneur advancement. Phase (p < 0.01) and gender (p < 0.01) have a significant negative influence on advancement. Hypothesis 1 is supported.

Hypothesis 2, stating that effectiveness is enhanced by size and content of the network, is tested by the linear regression of effectiveness upon network size and content and the control variables in Table 6.3. Network size and content has a significantly positive influence on effectiveness (p < 0.01). This is also the case for start-up skills (p < 0.01) and start-up experience (p < 0.05). Surprisingly, higher education has no significant influence on effectiveness, as is the case with age and gender. Phase (p < 0.01) shows a negative significant relation with effectiveness. Network size and content remains to have a positive influence on effectiveness after the control variables are introduced, thus Hypothesis 2 is corroborated.

Correlation analysis was completed to further delineate the kind of contacts and content and their relationship with advancement and effectiveness. A significant positive correlation was found between advancement and lawyers, accountants, experts, investors and foreigners, while a significant negative correlation was found between advancement and current colleagues. A significant positive correlation was found between effectiveness and bank contacts, lawyers, accountants, contacts with much business experience and current colleagues, while a significant negative correlation was found between effectiveness and a contact that is currently starting a business. In the case of content and advancement, a significant positive correlation was found with discussing planning, innovation and export. Effectiveness was found significantly positively related to the discussion of innovation and growth.

DISCUSSION

Most previous research shows a positive influence between the size of social networks and entrepreneurial performance measures (Greve, 1995; Hansen, 1995; Greve and Salaff, 2003), although some findings are inconclusive (Aldrich and Reese, 1993). This study supports former results and extends them in the ways that it uses novel and improved measures of social capital and performance.

In this study the concept of network size and content is related to diversity and quality of information, since every new tie in the network adds information available to the entrepreneur. The larger the network, the more the likelihood of a higher diversity of information is increased. Access to non-redundant information permits entrepreneurs to perform better. Therefore, it is important to have access to people in different positions in society. Information from two people in different positions in society is more likely to be non-redundant than information from two people in similar positions (Neergaard and Madsen, 2004). Thus, entrepreneurs need a network consisting of people in different positions in society in order to access the information they need. The results of this study can further be extended to support former network diversity research.

Former research on network content, as described here, is very limited. The results here are in line with the conceptual discussions that diverse content increases quality of contacts and the network (Burt, 1983) and the empirical findings of Ostgaard and Birley (1994) that diverse content improves firm competitive strategy. The results on network content further strengthen former research on the positive relation social capital has with outcome.

The positive influence of the human capital variables on entrepreneur advancement does not come as a surprise and supports former research (Gimeno et al., 1997; Arenius and Minniti, 2005). Given the general result of human capital on outcome, the insignificant association of education with effectiveness was unexpected. This suggests that start-up experience and perceived skills make people feel more effective than higher education does. This calls for attention since education has a similar association with advancement as the other human capital variables. Another notable result is a significantly negative effect of women entrepreneurs on the advancement of the venture emergence process. This has been suggested in entrepreneur literature (Rotefoss and Kolvereid, 2005), but based on the advancement measure this extends former research.

The association between the social capital variables and the performance variables may be affected by different factors. Factors that might explain the difference in these findings and previous research include the methodology used.

Potential entrepreneurs, who represent a large proportion of the total sample, might make the finding here different from previous research. Actually, although it is outside the realm of this study, the association between social capital and performance is weakest among the potential entrepreneurs.

Another methodological factor that might affect the findings is the modelling of a linear association that the network measures have with performance measures. It has been suggested that this might not be the case (Watson, 2007). If the network becomes very large, the amount of time spent on maintaining the last relationship exceeds the value of that last contact. Thus, a large network might influence the performance measures in a negative way (Watson, 2007).

The interaction effects between human and social capital might influence their association with the outcome measure. It has been suggested that human capital and social capital might be co-productive and complement each other while individuals are getting an education. They increase their human capital through increase in knowledge and skills and at the same time they might create a long-lasting social network that generates social capital (Fedderke et al., 1999). Furthermore, individuals are likely to form social networks as they gain start-up experience. Greve et al. (2006) argue that human capital supports and strengthens social capital as people with high human capital more easily utilize their social capital. Here the social capital and human capital generally have a positive relation with the outcome measure, but there is no significant association between them. This suggests that social capital and human capital neither complement nor substitute each other under conditions where entrepreneurs are utilizing resources from an activated network.

Although not a main part of this study, investigating the kinds of contacts and content in the network provides an opportunity for a deeper understanding of the process. Granovetter (1973) was among the first to discuss how different types of relations provide different value for people. He distinguishes between strong and weak ties and discusses how people access different information from strong and weak ties. Ostgaard and Birley (1996) define personal ties as relations with family, friends and acquaintances to whom the entrepreneur relates primarily on a social level, and professional ties as primarily concerned with business, such as professional consultants.

Examining the contacts in this study reveals a more significant relationship between the formal or professional contacts and the performance measures. Thus, entrepreneurs that receive advice from lawyers and accountants are more likely to advance and feel effective. On the other hand receiving advice from contacts that could be categorized as informal or personal, such as contacts currently starting a business or current colleagues, can have a negative relation with advancement and perception of effectiveness. Regarding the content of the network, we suggest that discussing innovation, planning and growth increases the likelihood of advancement and perception of effectiveness.

CONCLUSION

In this study we investigated effects of entrepreneurs' social capital on their performance. The investigation was based on a survey of 714 randomly selected entrepreneurs originally carried out in 2006 and a follow-up survey in 2007. Two hypotheses were tested and both were supported. Network size and content was found to positively affect the advancement of entrepreneurs through the venture emergence process and to positively influence the effectiveness of entrepreneurs during the venture emergence process. Regarding the control variables, human capital generally had a positive impact on advancement and effectiveness, with the exception of the effect of higher education on effectiveness. The results also suggest that women are less likely to advance through the venture emergence process.

Limitations of the study are mostly associated with the operationalization of social capital, the concept of advancement and causality.

First, due to the position-generator approach, the network size and content variable might be imprecise since each respondent was offered a predetermined selection of contacts or discussions to choose from. This list is, of course, not exhaustive, and some entrepreneurs might have more contacts within one single position or spend more time on a specific topic. However, this study actually deals with more positions than most previous research using the position-generator approach (Watson, 2007) and is more detailed than previously used measures. Also, this methodology does not allow tie strength to be measured in detail, but a simple correlation analysis of kinds of advice and content in the network aims at providing some understanding of the weak and strong tie dimensions of the network.

Secondly, the advancement concept allows for three different types of advances. The entrepreneur can exit from the process, remain in the same phase or transit to the next phase in the process. The concept of advancement is more complex than operationalized in this study. Although not taken into account here, exit, status quo or transit from one of the phases are not the same processes, although they are all treated the same here. Also, it is accepted that not all exits should be understood as failures. More sophisticated statistical methods and a longer period of investigation might assist in decreasing this limitation.

Thirdly, it is accepted that causality might be a problem, especially with the dependent effectiveness variable, measured in the first year, 2006. To improve causality it might have been better to measure effectiveness in the following year, 2007, but that would have introduced an even larger problem of success bias, since such a later measurement is only available for the respondents that were still defined as entrepreneurs in the second year.

This study is different from most others through its focus on the whole venture emergence process and the use of social capital and performance measures. This might prove fruitful in theory-building as well as in practice, in that it might increase our theoretical understanding of venture emergence and identify efficient policies and measures to lower exit rates of entrepreneurs. This study suggests that opportunities for further research may be found in using similar longitudinal research designs with widely defined concepts within social capital and outcome. Secondly, further developing the concepts of network content and entrepreneurial advance will contribute to entrepreneurial social network literature. Thirdly, the interaction between social and human capital might render rewarding results. Fourthly, the results that women tend to advance through the venture emergence process to a lesser degree than men and that higher education does not significantly affect performance as other human capital measures do, call for further research.

These results have essential implications for entrepreneurs intending to found a new venture. They should pay attention to the importance of social capital and seek situations and try to act in ways where the benefits can be maximized. Entrepreneurs should also be aware that social capital might prove important for them in order to utilize their possessed human capital (Coleman, 1988; Greve et al., 2006).

There is a universal acceptance of the importance of entrepreneurship for the economy, but high exit rates of entrepreneurs are costly. This study stresses the importance of a large social network and a wide scope of content in that network.

ACKNOWLEDGEMENT

We gratefully acknowledge funding for the GEM and the follow-up interviews by grants from the International Danish Entrepreneurship Academy, IDEA.

REFERENCES

Aldrich, H. and P.R. Reese (1993), 'Does networking pay off? A panel study of entrepreneurs in the research triangle', in N.C. Churchill, S. Birley, J. Doutriaux, E.J. Gatewood, F.S. Hoy and W.E. Wetzel Jr (eds), *Frontiers of Entrepreneurship Research*, Wellesley, MA: Babson College, pp. 325–39.
Arenius, P. and D. De Clercq (2005), 'A network-based approach on opportunity recognition' *Small Business Economics*, **24**(3), 249–65.
Arenius, P. and M. Minniti (2005), 'Perceptual variables and nascent entrepreneurship' *Small Business Economics*, **24**(3), 233–47.
Bates, T. (1995), 'Self-employment entry across industry groups', *Journal of Business Venturing*, **10**(2), 143–56.
Baum, J.R. and E.A. Locke (2004), 'The relationship of entrepreneurial traits, skill, and motivation to subsequent venture growth' *Journal of Applied Psychology*, **89**(4), 587–98.

Bourdieu, P. (1986), 'The forms of capital', in J.G. Richardson (ed.), *Handbook of Theory and Research for the Sociology of Education*, New York: Greenwood, pp. 241–58.

Bruderl, J. and P. Preisendorfer (1998), 'Network support and the success of newly founded businesses' *Small Business Economics*, **10**(3), 213–25.

Burt, R.S. (1983), *Applied Network Analysis*, Beverly Hills: Sage Publications.

Burt, R.S. (1992), *Structural Holes: The Social Structure of Competition*, Cambridge, MA: Harvard University Press.

Burt, R.S. (1997), 'A note on social capital and network content' *Social Networks*, **19**(4), 355–73.

Campbell, K.E. and B.A. Lee (1991), 'Name generators in surveys of personal networks', *Social Networks*, **13**, 203–21.

Campbell, K.E., P.V. Marsden, and J.S. Hurlbert (1986), 'Social resources and socioeconomic status', *Social Networks*, **8**(1), 97–117.

Carter, N.M., W.B. Gartner and P.D. Reynolds (1996), 'Exploring start-up event sequences', *Journal of Business Venturing*, **11**(3), 151–66.

Chakravarthy, B.S. (1986), 'Measuring strategic performance', *Strategic Management Journal*, **7**(5), 437–58.

Chandler, G.N. and S.H. Hanks (1994), 'Founder competence, the environment, and venture performance', *Entrepreneurship Theory and Practice*, **18**(3), 77–89.

Coleman, J.S. (1988), 'Social capital in the creation of human-capital', *American Journal of Sociology*, **94**, 95–120.

Cooper, A.C. (1993), 'Challenges in predicting new firm performance', *Journal of Business Venturing*, **8**(3), 241–53.

Cooper, A.C., F.J. Gimeno-Gascon and C.Y. Woo (1994), 'Initial human and financial capital as predictors of new venture performance', *Journal of Business Venturing*, **9**(5), 371–95.

Davidsson, P. and B. Honig (2003), 'The role of social and human capital among nascent entrepreneurs', *Journal of Business Venturing*, **18**(3), 301–31.

Elfring, T. and W. Hulsink (2003), 'Networks in entrepreneurship: the case of high-technology firms', *Small Business Economics*, **21**(4), 409–22.

Erikson, T. (2002), 'Entrepreneurial capital: the emerging venture's most important asset and competitive advantage', *Journal of Business Venturing*, **17**(3), 275–90.

Fedderke, J., R. De Kadt and J. Luiz (1999), 'Economic growth and social capital: a critical reflection', *Theory and Society*, **28**(5), 709–45.

Forbes, D.P. (1999), 'Cognitive approaches to new venture creation', *International Journal of Management Reviews*, **1**(4).

Gartner, W.B. (1985), 'A conceptual-framework for describing the phenomenon of new venture creation', *Academy of Management Review*, **10**(4), 696–706.

Gimeno, J., T.B. Folta, A.C. Cooper and C.Y. Woo (1997), 'Survival of the fittest? Entrepreneurial human capital and the persistence of underperforming firms', *Administrative Science Quarterly*, **42**(4), 750–83.

Granovetter, M.S. (1973), 'The strength of weak ties', *American Journal of Sociology*, **78**(6), 1360–80.

Greve, A. (1995), 'Networks and entrepreneurship: an analysis of social relations, occupational background and use of contacts during the establishment process', *Scandinavian Journal of Management*, **11**(1), 1–24.

Greve, A., M. Benassi and A.D. Sti (2006), 'Exploring the contributions of human and social capital to productivity', paper presented at Sunbelt XXVI conference, Vancouver, BC, 25–30 April, 2006.

Greve, A. and J.W. Salaff (2003), 'Social networks and entrepreneurship', *Entrepreneurship Theory and Practice*, **28**(1), 1–22.

Hansen, E.L. (1995), 'Entrepreneurial networks and new organization growth', *Entrepreneurship Theory and Practice*, **19**(4).

Henley, A. (2007), 'Entrepreneurial aspiration and transition into self-employment: evidence from British longitudinal data', *Entrepreneurship and Regional Development*, **19**(3), 253–80.

Hoang, H. and B. Antoncic (2003), 'Network-based research in entrepreneurship: a critical review', *Journal of Business Venturing*, **18**(2), 165–87.

Koellinger, P., M. Minniti and C. Schade (2007), '"I think I can, I think I can": Overconfidence and entrepreneurial behavior', *Journal of Economic Psychology*, **28**(4), 502–27.

Krueger, N.F., M.D. Reilly and A.L. Carsrud (2000), 'Competing models of entrepreneurial intentions', *Journal of Business Venturing*, **15**(5–6), 411–32.

Lee, C., K. Lee and J.M. Pennings (2001), 'Internal capabilities, external networks, and performance: a study on technology-based ventures', *Strategic Management Journal*, **22**(6–7), 615–40.

Levie, J. and E. Autio (2008), 'A theoretical grounding and test of the GEM model', *Small Business Economics*, **31**(3).

Lin, N. (2001), *Social Capital: A Theory of Social Structure and Action*, New York: Cambridge University Press.

Lin, N. and M. Dumin (1986), 'Access to occupations through social ties', *Social Networks*, **8**(4), 365–85.

Littunen, H. (2000), 'Networks and local environmental characteristics in the survival of new firms', *Small Business Economics*, **15**(1), 59–71.

Murphy, G.B., J.W. Trailer and R.C. Hill (1996), 'Measuring performance in entrepreneurship research', *Journal of Business Research*, **36**(1), 15–23.

Nahapiet, J. and S. Ghoshal (1998), 'Social capital, intellectual capital, and the organizational advantage', *Academy of Management Review*, **23**(2), 242–66.

Neergaard, H. and H. Madsen (2004), 'Knowledge intensive entrepreneurship in a social capital perspective', *Journal of Enterprising Culture*, **12**(2), 105–25.

O'Donnell, A., A. Gilmore, D. Cummins and D. Carson (2001), 'The network construct in entrepreneur research: a review and critique', *Management Decision*, **39**(9), 749–60.

Ostgaard, T.A. and S. Birley (1994), 'Personal networks and firm competitive strategy: a strategic or coincidental match', *Journal of Business Venturing*, **9**(4), 281–305.

Ostgaard, T.A. and S. Birley (1996), 'New venture growth and personal networks', *Journal of Business Research*, **36**(1), 37–50.

Paige, R.C. and M.A. Littrell (2002), 'Craft retailers' criteria for success and associated business strategies', *Journal of Small Business Management*, **40**(4), 314–31.

Podolny, J.M. and J.N. Baron (1997), 'Resources and relationships: social networks and mobility in the workplace', *American Sociological Review*, **62**(5), 673–93.

Reynolds, P.D., N. Bosma, E. Autio, S. Hunt, N. De Bono, I. Servais, P. Lopez-Garcia and N. Chin (2005), 'Global Entrepreneurship Monitor: data collection design and implementation 1998–2003', *Small Business Economics*, **24**(3), 205–31.

Reynolds, P.D. (1997), 'Who starts new firms? Preliminary explorations of firms-in-gestation', *Small Business Economics*, **9**(5), 449–62.
Robinson, K.C. (1999), 'An examination of the influence of industry structure on eight alternative measures of new venture performance for high potential independent new ventures', *Journal of Business Venturing*, **14**(2), 165–87.
Rotefoss, B. and L. Kolvereid (2005), 'Aspiring, nascent and fledgling entrepreneurs: an investigation of the business start-up process', *Entrepreneurship and Regional Development*, **17**(2), 109–27.
Schøtt, T. (2007), *Entrepreneurship in the Regions in Denmark 2006 – studied via Global Entrepreneurship Monitor*, Kolding: University of Southern Denmark.
Schøtt, T. (2009), *Education, Training and Networking for Entrepreneurship in Denmark 2008*, Kolding: University of Southern Denmark.
Watson, J. (2007), 'Modeling the relationship between networking and firm performance', *Journal of Business Venturing*, **22**(6), 852–74.
Westhead, P., M. Wright and D. Ucbasaran (2001), 'The internationalization of new and small firms: a resource-based view', *Journal of Business Venturing*, **16**(4), 333–58.
Witt, P. (2004), 'Entrepreneurs' networks and the success of start-ups', *Entrepreneurship and Regional Development*, **16**(5), 391–412.

7. Structuring the field of social entrepreneurship: a transatlantic comparative approach[1]

Sophie Bacq and Frank Janssen

INTRODUCTION

During recent years, social entrepreneurship has been receiving greater recognition from the public sector, as well as from scholars (Stryjan, 2006; Weerawardena and Sullivan Mort, 2006). Encouraging social initiatives has been on our governments' agenda for a while. European policy makers claim the importance of social enterprises as 'they not only are significant economic actors, but also play a key role in involving citizens more fully in Society and in the creation and reproduction of social capital, by organizing, for example, opportunities for volunteering' (European Commission, 2003). Consequently, several European states have created specific legal forms for this kind of initiatives. On the other hand, famous business schools all around the world have created centres for research and education programmes in social entrepreneurship. So far, academic research in social entrepreneurship 'has largely been focused on defining what it is and what it does, and does not, have in common with commercial entrepreneurship' (Nicholls, 2008: 7).

No doubt that this growing interest toward social entrepreneurship partly results from its innovativeness in treating social problems that are becoming more and more complex (Johnson, 2000; Thompson et al., 2000). Some academic scholars see it as *a way of creating community wealth* (Wallace, 1999) while others consider it as *a means to relieve our modern society from its illnesses* (Thompson et al., 2000), such as unemployment, inequalities in the access to health care and social services (Catford, 1998), squalor, poverty, crime, privation or social exclusion (Blackburn and Ram, 2006). It can also be considered *as a means to subcontract public services* or as *a means to improve these services without increasing the state's intervention* (Cornelius et al., 2007). Moreover, this innovative entrepreneurial practice bears the advantage of blurring traditional boundaries between private and public sectors, giving birth to hybrid enterprises (Johnson, 2000; Wallace, 1999) guided by strategies of double value creation – social and economic (Alter, 2004).

A consensus has thus emerged according to which understanding social entrepreneurship is important (Weerawardena and Sullivan Mort, 2006; Dees, 1998a). However, this concept has long remained poorly defined and its boundaries with other fields of study remained fuzzy (Mair and Martí, 2006). Therefore, this chapter has three objectives. The first objective is to clarify the three main concepts of the field: 'social entrepreneurship' (seen as a process), 'social entrepreneur' (as an individual) and 'social enterprise' (as an organization), since these three notions have been used interchangeably to express the same idea. To that end, we will review the literature from an analytical and critical perspective. The second objective of this chapter is to determine to what extent these concepts differ from traditional or commercial entrepreneurship/entrepreneur/enterprise. If an organization devotes part of its income to a social cause, we cannot necessarily speak of social entrepreneurship. The same holds for all non-profit organizations that adopt managerial practices (Mair and Martí, 2004). Therefore, a person who is in charge of the management of an organization that acts in the social, voluntary or community fields will rather be called 'social enterprise manager' because a social entrepreneur has to meet the entrepreneurial condition (Brouard, 2007). Finally, several approaches of social entrepreneurship seem to emerge. Their differences could be due to their geographical origin. Because Europe and the United States consider the government's role from different perspectives, we assume that both sides of the Atlantic consider the role of social entrepreneurship differently. Consequently, we presuppose that each side focuses on particular elements, such as the individual features or the collective aspects of the initiative. Therefore, the third objective of this chapter is to identify the different schools of thought and practices on both sides of the Atlantic and to determine whether there is a transatlantic divide in the way of approaching social entrepreneurship.

This chapter is organized as follows. The first section presents the practical and academic background of social entrepreneurship as a field of research. In the second section, our method for reviewing the literature is explained. The third section of this chapter presents and discusses the results of our literature review. Finally, the fourth section examines whether there is a transatlantic divide in the way of approaching and defining social entrepreneurship, the social entrepreneur and the social enterprise.

In the next section, we show how social entrepreneurship can learn from the development of entrepreneurship as a legitimate field of research.

1. FROM SOCIAL ENTREPRENEURSHIP AS A PRACTICE TO A LEGITIMATE FIELD OF RESEARCH

Social entrepreneurship practitioners have always existed, everywhere around the world[2] (Roberts and Woods, 2005). Nevertheless, if social entrepreneurship as a practice is far from being new and benefits from a long heritage and a global presence, it has been attracting researchers' attention for a few years only (Dearlove, 2004). Apart from isolated early research on the topic (Waddock and Post, 1991 and Young, 1986, cited in Light, 2005), the term 'social entrepreneurship' emerged, in the academic world, in the late 1990s in the United States (Drayton, 2002; Thompson et al., 2000; Bornstein, 1998; Dees, 1998a; Boschee, 1995) and in the United Kingdom (SSE, 2002; Leadbeater, 1997). In Europe, social enterprises have begun to attract our governments' attention. The concept of 'social enterprise' appeared for the first time in the late 1980s in Italy (Defourny, 2001). Since the mid-1990s, this concept has been more and more widely used in Europe, especially thanks to the works of a European research network, namely EMES.[3]

From an academic point of view, numerous authors agree on the fact that the emerging field of research in social entrepreneurship shows three similarities with the field of entrepreneurship research in its early days. First, social entrepreneurship research is still *phenomenon-driven* (Mair and Martí, 2006). As has been the case for the field of entrepreneurship, social entrepreneurship initiatives have first developed among practioners before attracting researchers' attention. Second, Bruyat and Julien (2001) and Shane and Venkataraman (2000), among others, regretted the *lack of a unifying paradigm* in the field of entrepreneurship. In his seminal article, 'What are we talking about when we talk about entrepreneurship?', Gartner (1988) tackled important questions such as 'has entrepreneurship become a label of convenience with little inherent meaning?' or 'is entrepreneurship just a buzzword, or does it have particular characteristics that can be identified and studied?'. This fuzziness brought up Acs and Audretsch's (2003) question of whether entrepreneurship constitutes a distinctive field of research or a discipline-based research. Filion (1997) moderated this lack of consensus in the field of entrepreneurship regarding the definition of the entrepreneur and the parameters that constitute the paradigm. Indeed, from the reverse point of view, entrepreneurship remains one of the rare topics that attract specialists from a lot of diverse disciplines. Consequently, any researcher is influenced by the premises of their own discipline in considering and defining the entrepreneur. Similarly, one can regret that the absence of a unifying paradigm in the field of social entrepreneurship has led to the proliferation of definitions (Dees, 1998a). 'Is social entrepreneurship a distinctive field of research?', Mair and Martí (2006) ask, or is it based on other disciplines? According to Dees and Battle Anderson (2006), attracting the interest of researchers from other disciplines will be both a source of legitimacy and of new knowledge. Let us stress that interdisciplinarity played a key role in the evolution of entrepreneurship, coming from a marginal field of research to a respected one (Dees and Battle Anderson, 2006). Third, academic research in social entrepreneurship is still at the *infancy stage* (Dees and Battle Anderson, 2006; Dorado, 2006), as the entrepreneurship field was some years ago (Brazael and Herbert, 1999). Entrepreneurship within the field of management sciences had then been characterized as a pre-paradigmatic field (Verstraete and Fayolle, 2004). Social entrepreneurship does not currently bear the explanatory or prescriptive theories that characterize a more mature field of research (Dees and Battle Anderson, 2006).

One can conclude that social entrepreneurship, considered as a sub-theme of entrepreneurship, shows the same weaknesses as the latter at its beginning. That leads us to think that research in the field of social entrepreneurship could replicate the theoretical evolution of its parent-field, entrepreneurship. Therefore, even if the field of entrepreneurship has suffered from the lack of a federating paradigm, research has progressed and, today, some paradigms exist. Entrepreneurship is now recognized as an academic field (Bruyat and Julien, 2001) and has an important scientific community that has produced a significant body of research (Acs and Audretsch, 2003; McGrath, 2003). Indeed, the entrepreneurship field has managed to go beyond the infancy stage to reach the adolescence stage.

However, one could push the argument further and consider entrepreneurship as a sub-field of social entrepreneurship. Verstraete and Fayolle (2004) suggested that four paradigms can be used to delimit the field of entrepreneurship: the paradigm of business opportunity, the paradigm of venture creation, the paradigm of innovation and the paradigm of value creation. If we focus on the last one, it imports to discuss the definition of value. The value created by the entrepreneurial act is more than monetary since almost all ventures create at least some social value. A simple example is that any entrepreneurial process is at the source of job creation even if it is only the entrepreneur's job. Given this definition, entrepreneurship could be considered as being social by essence.

To progress in a new field of research, a clear definition is one of the key issues (Christie and Honig, 2006). As mentioned above, social entrepreneurship, as a very complex idea that carries around a wide range of beliefs and different meanings attached to it, lacks an agreed-upon definition. Therefore, an in-depth analysis of the literature could be useful to identify convergences, as well as divergences, in publications on social entrepreneurship. The next section presents the criteria we used to conduct such a literature review.

2.　LITERATURE REVIEW CRITERIA

Given the various backgrounds and the numerous perspectives used by scholars in their study of social entrepreneurship, literature reviews on the topic have begun to flourish in academic journals and book chapters. For instance, Zahra et al. (2009) recently defined the concept. Acknowledging the complexity induced by the 'breadth of the scholarly communities studying the subject', they listed 20 definitions or descriptions of the phenomenon. Their ambition was not to end up with a statement that encompasses all the dimensions covered in the different approaches but to gather the common points of view. Zahra et al. (2009: 522) therefore suggest that 'social entrepreneurship encompasses the activities and processes undertaken to discover, define, and exploit opportunities in order to enhance social wealth by creating new ventures or managing existing organizations in an innovative manner'.

However, this chapter distinguishes itself from those pieces of work by the two classification criteria we used in order to systematize our literature review on social entrepreneurship. Indeed, following the methodology used by Brush et al. (2008) in their literature review of the outcome variable in entrepreneurship research, we classified research by main themes in the entrepreneurship literature, and looked at the differences in these by geographical origin of the publication. By doing so, we try to deepen the understanding of social entrepreneurship by distinguishing the process of social value creation from the individual or the organization.

First, let us look at the different approaches of social entrepreneurship that have emerged according to their geographical origin. The next section presents them.

2.1　The Geographical Criterion

Attempts to understand social entrepreneurship have been geographically concentrated on both sides of the Atlantic. In Europe the focus of publications has been more on social enterprises and legal forms, whereas American scholars have restricted their study of social entrepreneurship to social entrepreneurs and non-profits' ways of funding. This geographical divide between Europe and the United States can be explained by different Third Sector traditions. Indeed, from a European perspective, the Third

Sector can be viewed as the private, not-for-profit[4] sector and encompasses a large variety of organizations that generally include cooperatives and related enterprises, mutual societies as well as voluntary associations (Defourny and Nyssens, 2008). On the other hand, the American view of the Third Sector is restricted to the associative, non-profit world, that is all organizations that impose a strict prohibition of profit distribution to all persons who own or work in the organization. All profits must be reinvested in the organization's social purpose. Hence, cooperatives, in the heart of the European conception of social entrepreneurship, are excluded from the American perspective, as they do distribute profit – even in a limited way.

More precisely, two independent streams of thought have investigated the nature of social entrepreneurship in the United States, according to Dees and Battle Anderson's (2006) typology. Both schools have emerged in their own particular context and focus on particular aspects of social entrepreneurship.[5] The American Social Innovation School of thought focuses on the establishment of new and better means to tackle social problems or to satisfy social needs. Although many people contributed to the birth of the Social Innovation School, one person and his organization were its driving force: Bill Drayton and Ashoka (Dees and Battle Anderson, 2006). Ashoka was created in 1980 in order to search and bring support to outstanding individuals with ideas for social change. Nevertheless, the term 'social entrepreneur' was not used before the mid-1990s as a substitute for the expressions 'innovator for the public sector' or 'public entrepreneur' which were used before. Since then, many other organizations supporting social entrepreneurs have appeared.[6] These organizations also promote the development of social entrepreneurs' networks and build structures facilitating their access to funds. On the other hand, the American Social Enterprise School of thought focuses on income generation in conducting a social mission. Among the pioneering initiatives of this movement, New Ventures, a consultancy company specialized in the Third Sector, was founded in 1980. The growing interest of non-profit organizations for new financial sources – the traditional ones being grants and subsidies – motivated its creation. Other important initiatives emerged with the aim of professionalizing social enterprises through sharing best practices.

In Europe all approaches gather around the Third Sector and 'social enterprises' even though some national differences remain in terms of field of activities, statutes or modes of governance of social enterprises. Two types of definitions have been established. On the one hand, *conceptual* definitions have been given by international organizations, such as the OECD and the EMES Network, among others. On the other hand, *legal* definitions have been set up by national governments in order to establish clear norms. Conceptual definitions bear the advantage of not being rooted in a specific national legislation and, therefore, are more neutral. Moreover, the EMES Network's broad approach bears the advantage of taking the different European national realities into account. We will use this last perspective in our comparison of the European and American perspectives. From a thematic point of view, three main themes have emerged from the classical literature on entrepreneurship. The next section discusses the criteria relative to the individual, the process and the organization.

2.2 The Thematic Criterion

First, Peredo and McLean (2006) make the hypothesis that defining social entrepreneurship is logically linked to the definition of the entrepreneur in the sense that entrepreneurship is 'what entrepreneurs do when they become entrepreneurs'. Therefore, our first criterion focuses on the individual and consists in identifying similarities and differences among scholars, in the way they weight the importance of the social entrepreneur's role in social entrepreneurship. Following an indicative approach (Casson, 1982), some scholars focused on the motivations of the founder of the social initiative, as well as on his/her particular features. As in the entrepreneurship field of research, these scholars have defined entrepreneurship solely in terms of 'Who the entrepreneur is' (Venkataraman, 1997) whereas, according to Gartner (1988), this question is not necessarily the right one to ask. The question of 'how does the entrepreneur act?' could be a way of differentiating the social entrepreneurial initiatives from other social initiatives (Dees, 1998b).

Second, two dynamic dimensions emerged from the literature on entrepreneurship, related to what Gartner (1988) called the 'process' of entrepreneurship. The first dimension refers to the goal at the basis of the social entrepreneurial creation. Convergences and divergences between the approaches of social entrepreneurship are measured here in terms of intensity of the social mission. The second issue regards the required intensity of the link between the social mission and the productive activities of the entrepreneurial initiative.

Third, following a functional approach (Casson, 1982), some researchers became interested in the organizational aspect of social entrepreneurship. From our literature review, three main dimensions emerged regarding the social enterprise: the centrality of the concept of 'enterprise'; the legal form of the social enterprise; and, linked to this dimension, the limitation or not of profit distribution.

Other dimensions could be found in the literature. By instance, numerous scholars (Gartner, 1985; Miller and Friesen, 1982) found that the environment was an important variable to be taken into account when studying entrepreneurship.

These four dimensions – the individual, the process, the organization and the environment – correspond to Gartner's (1985) framework for studying entrepreneurship.

However, the three variables chosen – the individual, the process and the organization – cover a large part of the issues in social entrepreneurship. The third section of this chapter classifies the American and European scholarship in social entrepreneurship according to these geographical and thematic criteria.

3. ANALYSIS OF THE LITERATURE

For the purpose of our literature review, we have examined the publications of each geographical school regarding the different thematic criteria. As we have seen, some scholars have followed an indicative approach and focused on the motivations of the founder of the social initiative. Let us first examine the importance attached to the personality and role of the social entrepreneur by the different approaches.

3.1   The Individual: The Social Entrepreneur

The social entrepreneur is more or less central to the different schools of thought. The social entrepreneur can be defined as a person whose main objective is not to make profit but to create social value for which he/she will adopt an entrepreneurial behaviour.

The Social Innovation School clearly distinguishes itself from the two others by the importance attached to the individual in its conception of social entrepreneurship. According to this approach, the concept of social entrepreneurship refers to the qualities of innovation (Austin et al., 2006; Mair and Martí, 2004) and creativity of the social entrepreneur in her or his pursuit of opportunities (Weerawardena and Sullivan Mort, 2006; Roberts and Woods, 2005). The main definitions of the social entrepreneur according to this school of thought are compiled in Appendix B. There seems to be an agreement among the Social Innovation School's scholars on several features of the social entrepreneur.[7] According to this school, social entrepreneurs:

- Adopt a *visionary* and *innovative* approach (Roberts and Woods, 2005; Skoll, cited in Dearlove, 2004; Sullivan Mort et al., 2003; De

Leeuw, 1999; Catford, 1998; Dees, 1998a; Drayton in Bornstein, 1998; Schuyler, 1998; Schwab Foundation, 1998). According to the Schumpeterian narrative of entrepreneurship, social entrepreneurs are essentially 'social innovators' (Nicholls and Cho, 2008).

- Are characterized by a *strong ethical fibre* (Catford, 1998; Drayton in Bornstein, 1998).
- Show a particular ability to detect *opportunities* (Sullivan Mort et al., 2003; Thompson et al., 2000; Catford, 1998; Dees, 1998a).
- Play a key role as 'Society's *change agents*' (Chell, 2007; Sharir and Lerner, 2006; Skoll in Dearlove, 2004; Thompson et al., 2000; Dees, 1998a; Schuyler, 1998). The Schumpeterian definition of the entrepreneur definitely is at the basis of this school's conception since social entrepreneurs can be considered as individuals who reform or revolutionize traditional production schemes of social value creation in moving resources towards places which offer superior return for society (Dees and Battle Anderson, 2006).
- Without being limited by *resources* currently at hand; otherwise, they gather them and use these to 'make a difference' (Peredo and McLean, 2006; Sharir and Lerner, 2006; Thompson et al., 2000; Dees, 1998a; Schuyler, 1998).

To sum up, according to this view, the social entrepreneur is a visionary individual who is able to identify and exploit opportunities; to leverage the resources necessary to the achievement of his/her social mission and to find innovative solutions to social problems of his/her community that are not adequately met by the local system.

However, the centrality of the individual figure in the Social Innovation School does not mean that other approaches of social entrepreneurship do not pay any attention at all to the social entrepreneur although for the Social Enterprise School and the EMES Network, social entrepreneurship is a more collective action. For the former, the initiative must come from a non-profit organization or from the state. Here, the social entrepreneur plays a secondary role as the one who organizes and manages social-purpose activities. Nicholls (2008: preface, p. xiii) very recently wrote that the focus on 'hero entrepreneurs' is 'effectively the tip of a socially entrepreneurial iceberg [. . .] most social entrepreneurship is in reality the product of groups, networks, and formal and informal organizations'.

The EMES approach does not exclude the possibility for some leader or charismatic entrepreneur to play a key role in the enterprise, but generally these persons are supported by a group whose members are responsible for the public benefit mission of the social enterprise (Defourny and Nyssens, 2006). But in the European perspective in general, social entrepreneurship is more a collective action, 'where the social entrepreneur is embedded in a network of support/advice that helps this new way of entrepreneurship succeed' (Hulgard and Spear, 2006: 88–9). Spear (2006) argues that individualistic entrepreneurship in worker cooperatives is rather the exception than the rule. For the EMES Network, the social enterprise is an initiative that comes from a group of citizens – what Hulgard (2008) calls the 'active citizenship' – self-help dynamics, public–associative partnerships, and so on (Defourny, 2004). Moreover, research about community entrepreneurship (Johannisson and Nilsson, 1989; Stöhr, 1990) attests to the collective aspect usually ascribed to entrepreneurship in Europe.

Being of first or second importance depending on the school of thought, the social entrepreneur seems to bear several features. Nevertheless, one could ask whether these features are specific to social entrepreneurs. What defines an element is a set of peculiar characteristics that enable it to be distinguished from other elements, be they commercial entrepreneurship or other non-entrepreneurial social activities. Therefore, a comparative approach is essential in the process of defining a field and its core concepts.

Despite all these attempts to define social entrepreneurs, it seems that they share many characteristics with 'commercial' entrepreneurs: they have the same focus on vision and opportunity and the same ability to convince and empower others to help them turn their ideas into reality (Catford, 1998). We agree with Dees (1998a) according to whom social entrepreneurs would be a 'sub-species' of the entrepreneurs' family. However, although there is a lot of overlap between social entrepreneurs and their commercial counterparts – particularly leadership, vision, drive and opportunism – the main difference is that 'social entrepreneurs usually have a vision of something that they would like to solve in the *social sector* or a *socio-moral motivation* in their entrepreneurial focus and ambition' (Nicholls, 2008: 20). On the other hand, business entrepreneurs look at a problem from a purely economic point of view (Dearlove, 2004) whereas social entrepreneurs' acts will always be linked to an objective of social value creation (Sharir and Lerner, 2006; Sullivan Mort et al., 2003; Dees, 1998a; Schwab Foundation, 1998). It is possible to compare the two types of entrepreneurs according to several variables. Thalhuber (1998) suggests using four criteria to distinguish between social and commercial entrepreneurs. The former draw their strengths from collective wisdom and experience rather than from personal competences and knowledge; they focus on long-term capacity rather than short-term financial gains; their ideas are limited by their mission; they see profit as a means in people's service that has to be reinvested in future profit rather than an end to be distributed to shareholders. Finally, Brouard (2006) adds that social entrepreneurs risk the organization's assets rather than personal and investors' funds, and see their freedom limited by donors rather than employers.

As in the entrepreneurship field of research, some scholars tried to define social entrepreneurship without referring to the person but to the process. The next section investigates the process of social entrepreneurship.

3.2   The Process: Social Entrepreneurship

First, the mission is at the heart of the venture creation process. Be it expressed in terms of 'social change' (Mair and Martí, 2004), 'social transformation' (Roberts and Woods, 2005), 'social value creation' (Austin et al., 2006; Weerawardena and Sullivan Mort, 2006) or 'social impact', the social mission is a central element for each of the perspectives. Appendix C presents numerous definitions of social entrepreneurship we can find in the American literature. Indeed, the European literature has focused more on the organizational aspect of social entrepreneurship than on the process.

For Dees (1998a), social entrepreneurship combines the passion of a *social mission* with an image of *business-like discipline*. Some authors add the characteristic of *sustainability* to the social initiative (Weerawardena and Sullivan Mort, 2006; Mair and Martí, 2004). For the Social Innovation School, social value creation and sustainable social improvements prevail on profit and wealth generation. For the Social Enterprise School also, the pursuit of social goals must be the first objective of social entrepreneurship – along with the pursuit of profit motives. The social nature of the initiative is guaranteed by the fact that, according to this approach, it is necessarily structured as a non-profit organization. Hence, any profit is allocated to the fulfilment of a social mission. Here, the social mission embraces all the social activities which non-profits can be involved in. Europeans rather stress the fact that social entrepreneurship most often takes place within the Third Sector (Defourny and Nyssens, 2008). According to the EMES Network, social entrepreneurship initiatives must have an explicit objective of service to community that embraces social and environmental questions. In the European legislations in general, social enterprises must be driven by their social goals. Despite some differences, the three schools of thought clearly agree on the fact that the social mission is at the heart of social entrepreneurship.

Second, some researchers investigated whether there has to be an intense link between the social mission and the productive activities. Two approaches require a direct link between the means and the end: the Social Innovation School and the EMES Network. According to the latter, 'the nature of the economic activity must be linked to the social mission' (Defourny and Nyssens, 2006: 12). In Europe in general, the productive activity must usually be related to the mission. In contrast, the Social Enterprise School, as well as the British tradition, do not require the link between the organization's social end and its activities to be direct. For the partisans of this school of thought, social entrepreneurship consists in the implementation, by non-profit organizations, of commercial dynamics developed in order to finance their social activities. According to Nicholls (2008: 11), 'social entrepreneurs subsidize their social activities either through exploiting profitable opportunities in the core activities of their not-for-profit venture or via for-profit subsidiary ventures and cross-sector partnerships with commercial corporations'. In other words, according to this approach, profit-generating activities must not necessarily be linked with the social mission of the non-profit organization. For the two other schools, a link between the activity and the mission is a central differentiating element.

Finally, what makes social entrepreneurship different from its commercial form? Whereas some researchers (Mair and Martí, 2004; Dees, 1998a) rather looked at the common points, others compared social entrepreneurship and commercial entrepreneurship. Some of them (Roberts and Woods, 2005; Marc, 1988) stressed its innovating side in terms of collection, use and combination of resources in building, evaluating and pursuing opportunities in a perspective of social transformation. For Austin et al. (2006), the distinction between social and commercial entrepreneurship should not be dichotomous but rather continuous. Therefore, they proposed a systematic approach to compare social and commercial entrepreneurship, based on four differentiating variables: market failure, mission, resource mobilization and performance measurement. Their proposition was four-fold. First, 'market failure will create differing entrepreneurial opportunities for social and commercial entrepreneurship' (Austin et al., 2006: 3). Second, the mission will be a fundamental criterion to distinguish between social and commercial entrepreneurship. Third, there will be prevailing differences between both approaches in the way human and financial resources are mobilized and managed. Fourth, measuring social performance will be a fundamental differentiator since it will make accountability and relations with stakeholders more complex. Brouard (2006) based his comparison on the social and commercial roles of the entrepreneurial initiatives. For him, the commercial role is represented by two dimensions, namely the presence of commercial exchanges and the repartition of commercial profit. He believes that social entrepreneurship must pay exclusive, or at least majority, attention to the social role, commercial role being accessory. Moreover, he suggests that there can be commercial exchanges but that the entirety or the majority of the commercial profit has to be reinvested in the social mission rather than distributed to shareholders. The main difference between social entrepreneurship and corporate social responsibility lies in the fact that the latter does not give primacy to the social role although it is aware of it. Let us stress that the importance of this difference may vary between the different approaches, as we will see in the next section devoted to the social venture.

3.3   The Organization: The Social Enterprise

American and European conceptions of the social enterprise are slightly different. Appendix D presents the main definitions of the social enterprise from the different geographical perspectives. The different schools mainly differ in the way they approach the enterprise concept, the organizational form and profit distribution.

We define this concept of 'enterprise' as an activity marked by an economic risk. In Europe, researchers of the EMES Network elaborated a common definition of the social enterprise in order to analyse the various national realities. Their definition is based on two series of indicators. On the one hand, four criteria reflect the economic and entrepreneurial dimensions of the social initiatives considered: (1) a continuous activity of goods and/or services production and sale; (2) a high degree of autonomy; (3) a significant level of economic risk;[8] and (4) a minimum amount of paid work. On the other hand, five indicators encapsulate the social dimensions of the initiatives: (1) an explicit aim to benefit the community; (2) an initiative launched by a group of citizens; (3) a decisional power not based on capital ownership; (4) a participatory nature including all the activity's stakeholders; and (5) limited profit distribution. This definition is not normative but rather an ideal-type.

In the United States, the social enterprise remains a broad and often quite vague concept referring primarily to market-oriented economic activities serving a social goal (Defourny and Nyssens, 2006). The Social Enterprise School also considers the 'enterprise' as central. This approach focuses on the double (sometimes triple) bottom line of social entrepreneurship organizations. Social entrepreneurs are those who balance between moral imperatives and the profit motives (Boschee, 1995) or articulate a compelling social impact theory with a plausible business model and commercial objectives. This approach defines social enterprises as being non-profit organizations that set up profit-generating activities in order to survive financially and become more independent of donations and subsidies they receive. The two main elements that characterize a social enterprise for the partisans of the Social Enterprise School are the fact that it combines a social objective – creating social value – with an entrepreneurial strategy – applying business expertise and market-based skills to non-profit organizations. This school of thought aims at the sustainability of social enterprises and promotes complete self-sufficiency of non-profits, which can be reached only through income generation and not through dependency on public and private sectors (Boschee and McClurg, 2003). Indeed, according to Boschee (2001), the 'ideal' way to tackle a social need is to answer it autonomously without being accountable to stakeholders. In contrast to the European perspective,[9] the Social Enterprise School only stresses the risks associated with market income.

Finally, as mentioned above, the American Social Innovation School focuses on the social entrepreneur and his/her qualities, rather than on the organization and its specificities. According to this approach, the social enterprise is an activity set up by a social entrepreneur and there is no mention of any criterion of economic risk.

Therefore, we conclude that the concept of 'enterprise' is central for the EMES network as well as for the Social Enterprise School.

Another important issue that arose from our literature review is the question of the legal organizational form of the social enterprise. Does the social mission of the social enterprise imply that it cannot exist under any other legal organizational form than the non-profit form?

According to the Social Innovation School, the social enterprise can adopt either a non-profit or a for-profit organizational form. For Austin et al. (2006), as well as Mair and Martí (2004), social enterprises should not be limited to any specific legal form. According to these authors, the choice should rather be dictated by the nature of the social needs addressed and the amount of resources needed. To Mair and Martí (2004), the important element is the entrepreneurial spirit that gives the initiatives their social entrepreneurial nature. This perspective has resulted in the emergence of various hybrid organizational forms: independent, they can generate profit, employ people and hire volunteers, as well as adopt innovative strategies in their pursuit of social change. The advantages of these hybrid organizations include, among others, a higher market response rate, higher efficiency and innovation rates, as well as a larger capacity to mobilize resources (Dees and Battle Anderson, 2006; Haugh, 2005).

On the other hand, for the Social Enterprise School, at least at its beginning, social enterprises had to be non-profits that used an earned income strategy in order to generate revenue in support of their charitable mission. Earned income can be defined as 'income derived from selling products or services' (Battle Anderson and Dees, 2008: 145) to contrast with the idea of philanthropic donations or government subsidies. However, since the mid-1990s the Social Enterprise School has considered a social enterprise as any business that trades for a social purpose (Austin et al., 2006).

Finally, in some European countries, a specific legal form has been created in order to encourage and support social enterprises. The Italian case has demonstrated how the state may encourage social enterprises' growth thanks to the introduction of specific laws (Borzaga and Santuari, 2001). Indeed, by legally recognizing the 'social cooperatives' in 1991, Italy saw their number increase significantly. Following the Italian example, other European countries have introduced new legal forms that reflect the entrepreneurial approach adopted by an increasing number of non-profits. In 1995, Belgium introduced the status of 'social purpose company'. In Portugal (1997), we talk of 'social solidarity cooperatives', in France (2002) of 'cooperative societies of collective interest' and in Finland (2003) of 'work insertion social enterprises' (Defourny and Nyssens, 2006). More than ten years after the impulse given by Italy to social enterprises, the British Blair government defined the 'Community Interest Company' as an independent organization having social and economic objectives, which aims at playing a social role as much as reaching financial durability through business (DTI, 2001). This new legal form represents a hybrid organizational type, part not-for-profit, part equity offering limited company. Despite all these newly created legal forms, most social enterprises across Europe still adopt legal forms that have existed for a long time, namely associations or cooperatives – or traditional business forms (Defourny and Nyssens, 2008).

Directly linked to the legal form, profit distribution is also an important issue for social enterprises.

The Social Innovation School does not impose any constraint regarding profit distribution. According to this movement, if the social entrepreneur's activity generates benefits, these will preferably be reinvested in the social object, but this is not a strict obligation. Only the final increase of the social added value is important.

In contrast, the American Social Enterprise School forbids any profit distribution as, according to the definition of non-profit organizations, social enterprises cannot distribute profit to their directors or members. Profit was therefore entirely dedicated to the social objective. In its later version, the Social Enterprise School considers social enterprises as any business, which, consequently, authorizes some profit distribution to owners or workers. Alter (2004), in her 'Hybrid Spectrum Model', presented the different options of social strategies for hybrid organizations, characterized by the fact that they generate social as much as economic value. These strategies depend on three criteria: the enterprise's objective, the scope of its responsibility towards shareholders and the ends to which profit is dedicated. Between these two extremes (non-profits and traditional for-profits), Alter (2004) distinguished four types of hybrid organizations. On the one hand, *social enterprises* and *non-profits having income generating activities*[10] try to have a social impact on society. On the other hand, *socially responsible organizations'* and *practising social responsibility organizations'* primary objective is the search for profit. Therefore, in this model, social enterprises are characterized by a social mission, a high responsibility towards stakeholders and the reinvestment or their income in social programmes or operational costs, in contrast with profit distribution to shareholders, totally prohibited by this school.

Finally, the European approach advocates a limit to profit distribution. According to the EMES Network, the social enterprise, in its choice of the way it will distribute benefits, must avoid a behaviour that would lead to profit maximization. Hence, the social enterprise can distribute profit, but in a limited manner.

The next section concludes whether, according to our analysis of the literature, there is a transatlantic divide in the way of approaching social entrepreneurship.

CONCLUSION: A TRANSATLANTIC DIVIDE OR A MORE COMPLEX PICTURE?

Social entrepreneurship can be seen as a source of solutions to certain illnesses of our modern societies. The utility of social enterprises as an instrument for governments has been recognized, for example, in the UK where a lending agency for social enterprises has been set up. Be they as a way to subcontract public services or as a means to improve these services without increasing the state's domain (Cornelius et al., 2007), social entrepreneurship initiatives are growing in number and importance. Unfortunately, from an academic point of view, research in the field of social entrepreneurship has long remained descriptive and, sometimes, partisan.

From our in-depth literature review on social entrepreneurship, we have identified three main schools of thought. Two schools studying the phenomenon of social entrepreneurship from different perspectives have emerged in the United States. The Social Innovation School stresses the importance of the social entrepreneur as an individual and focuses on his/her features. The Social Enterprise School claims that this kind of organization will survive by conducting profit-generating activities in order to finance social value creation. The European tradition approaches social entrepreneurship by creating specific legal forms for social enterprises. On the other hand, three major themes have also emerged from the classical literature in entrepreneurship: the individual, the process and the organization. The review of the definitions of the main concepts of the field enabled us to identify six criteria that we used in order to analyse common points and differences between the different approaches: the entrepreneur; the intensity of the social mission; the intensity of the link between the organization's activities and its first goal; the importance of the enterprise as an organizational structure; its legal form; and the limitation of profit distribution. Crossing the three schools of social entrepreneurship with the six above-mentioned criteria, we obtain a 6 × 3 matrix. Table 7.1 summarizes the results of our literature review in terms of the position of each school of thought of social entrepreneurship regarding each thematic criterion.

To sum up, we observed that the *figure of the entrepreneur* is central only to the Social Innovation School of thought that highlights individual profiles, whereas, in Europe, the focus is rather on collective modes of organization and less on individuals. The social *mission* is clearly acknowledged as the primary objective of social entrepreneurship, even if it has been expressed in different ways by all the three approaches. Although the Social Innovation School and the EMES Network require a direct *link between the enterprise's social mission and its productive activities*, the Social Enterprise School advocates that the link between social mission and income-generating activities can be more or less strong. The flag of 'social enterprise' is probably the most controversial (Defourny and Nyssens, 2008). Indeed, the *social enterprise* is a key element in the European tradition as well as for the Social Enterprise School according to which social enterprises are self-financed undertakings with a social aim. The latter considers non-profit social enterprises whereas the European tradition imposes some constraints regarding the *legal form*. Therefore, linked to the legal framework, *profit distribution* is almost totally prohibited by the Social Enterprise School and partially limited in the EMES approach in order to protect the primacy of the social mission. The Social Innovation School does not impose any constraint: the choice regarding the legal form and profit distribution should rather be dictated by the nature of the social needs addressed and the amount of resources needed.

Before starting this work, one could have thought that there would have been a clear-cut transatlantic divide in the way of approaching and defining social entrepreneurship. This assumption could be based on the way Europe and the United States consider the government's role and, consequently, social entrepreneurship's role. Indeed, if the American and European literatures agree on the fact that the first goal of social entrepreneurship must be the creation of social value, one can clearly distinguish them on basis of the central role played by public policies in Europe compared to the government-detached American approach. However, there is no such divide. Even within the United States, there are different

Entrepreneurship research in Europe

Table 7.1   Classification of geographical schools of thought of social entrepreneurship by thematic criteria

Themes		Criteria	AMERICAN TRADITION		EUROPEAN TRADITION
			The Social Innovation School	The Social Enterprise School	The EMES Network
INDIVIDUAL	1.	The entre-preneur	Central figure	Secondary importance	Collective dynamics: initiative launched by a group of citizens
PROCESS	2.	The mission	The innovation process is primarily oriented to a soci(et)al change	These organizations allocate market resources to the fulfilment of a social mission	Explicit aim to benefit the community
	3.	Link social mission-productive activities	Direct: innovative strategies to tackle social needs are implemented through the provision of goods and services	No constraint: the trading activity is simply considered as a source of income, so SE can develop business activities unrelated to the social mission to provide financial resources	Direct: the productive activity is related to the social mission of the SE
ORGANIZATION	4.	The enterprise	Secondary importance: activity set up by a social entrepreneur	Central: stress on the risks associated with market income	Central: significant level of economic risk
	5.	The legal form	No clear constraint: the choice regarding the legal form should be	1st Early version: focus on non-profits 2nd Later version: stress on any	Some constraints: new legal forms and specific frameworks have been created to

Table 7.1   (continued)

Themes	Criteria	AMERICAN TRADITION		EUROPEAN TRADITION
		The Social Innovation School	The Social Enterprise School	The EMES Network
		dictated by the nature of the social needs addressed and the amount of resources needed	business that trades for a social purpose: for-profit company, public authority, . . .	encourage and support social enterprises + in some cases, use of traditional business legal forms
	6. Profit distribution	No constraint	1st Early version: non-distribution constraint 2nd Later version: limited	Limited

Source: Partially adapted from Degroote (2008).

conceptions. These conceptions are based on strong social convictions and have resulted in various definitions, making it harder to circumvent the concept of social entrepreneurship clearly.

In terms of directions for future research in the field of social entrepreneurship, this implies that social entrepreneurial ventures as a research object are not different on both sides of the Atlantic and that the field of social entrepreneurship can be seen as a global one. However, we have also observed differences within the United States, which could mean that, as long as definitions are not completely reconciled, researchers should clearly announce the perspective from which they study the phenomenon.

This work was a first attempt to advance the structuration of this new broad field of research. It has also raised future research avenues. In our comparative analysis with the United States, we have considered the European publications as approaching the phenomenon with one voice. However, several perspectives actually coexist in Europe. Evidence lies in the fact that Northern and Southern Europe have shown different approaches to entrepreneurship in general. Therefore, a geographical analysis of the different approaches of social entrepreneurship in Europe would be of prime interest. The various geographical European situations could result in different clusters corresponding to national, transnational or regional areas. Finally, tensions between the social mission and market requirements have been recognized by numerous authors as the central definitional element of social entrepreneurship. However, little research has been conducted so far on the way this can be managed. Therefore, the role of management practices in solving these tensions should be examined more deeply.

NOTES

1. Some parts of this chapter constitute an early version of a manuscript that has been accepted for publication in *Entrepreneurship and Regional Development*, special issue on Community-based, Social & Societal Entrepreneurship.
2. Florence Nightingale, a British pioneer, fought to improve the hospital conditions during the Crimean War in the nineteenth century, making the mortality rate drop from 40 per cent to 2 per cent. Roshaneh Zafar, founder of the Kashf Foundation, has fought for the economic condition of women in Pakistan by opening thousands of micro-credit institutions (Dearlove, 2004). Fundación Social in Colombia was established in 1911 with the aim of generating and devoting revenues to the creation of social value (Fowler, 2000).
3. In 1996, university research centres and researchers from the fifteen member states of the European Union set up a scientific network whose name, 'EMES', refers to the title of its first research programme on the 'Emergence of social enterprises in Europe'.
4. A 'not-for-profit' means any venture whose very first aim is a social purpose rather than profit making. Hence, a not-for-profit can be profitable and distribute profit in a limited way in agreement with its social mission, in contrast with purely 'non-profit' enterprises.
5. The reader will find a classification of the main authors of each of these two approaches in Appendix A.
6. Among the most important ones, let us cite Echoing Green (1987), The Schwab Foundation for Social Entrepreneurs (1998), The Skoll Foundation (1999) and The Manhattan Institute's Social Entrepreneurship Initiative (2001).
7. The words in boldface in Appendix B represent these features.
8. According to EMES, social enterprises must bear a significant level of economic risk, which means that 'the financial viability of the social enterprise depends on the efforts of its members to secure adequate resources to support the enterprise's social mission' and that 'these resources can have a hybrid character and come from trading activities, from public subsidies and from voluntary resources obtained thanks to the mobilization of social capital' (Defourny and Nyssens, 2008, 2006).
9. With the exception of the United Kingdom where, according to the CIC legislation, it is commonly admitted that 50 per cent of the total income of a social enterprise must be market-based.
10. This kind of hybrid organization is very close to Fowler's (2000) idea of 'complementary social entrepreneurship'.

REFERENCES

Acs, Z.J. and D.B. Audretsch (2003), 'Introduction to the Handbook of Entrepreneurship Research', in Z.J. Acs and D.B. Audretsch (eds), *Handbook of Entre-*

preneurship Research: An Interdisciplinary Survey and Introduction, Dordrecht: Kluwer Academic Publishers, pp. 3–20.

Acs, Z.J. and K. Kallas (2007), 'State of literature on small to medium-size enterprises and entrepreneurship in low-income communities', Discussion Paper on Entrepreneurship, growth and public policy no. 0307, Jena, Germany: Group Entrepreneurship, Growth and Public Policy.

Alter, K. (ed.) (2004), *Social Enterprise Typology*, Virtue Ventures LLC.

Alvord, S.H., L.D. Brown and C.W. Letts (2004), 'Social entrepreneurship and social transformation: an exploratory study', *Journal of Applied Behavioral Science*, **40**(3), 260–82.

Austin, J., H. Stevenson and J. Wei-Skillern (2006), 'Social and commercial entrepreneurship: same, different, or both?', *Entrepreneurship Theory and Practice*, **31**(1), 1–22.

Battle Anderson, B. and G. Dees (2008), 'Rhetoric, reality, and research: building a solid foundation for the practice of social entrepreneurship', in A. Nicholls (ed.), *Social Entrepreneurship: New Models of Sustainable Social Change*, Oxford: Oxford University Press, pp. 144–80.

Blackburn, R. and M. Ram (2006), 'Fix or fixation? The contributions and limitations of entrepreneurship and small firms to combating social exclusion', *Entrepreneurship and Regional Development*, **18**(1), 73–89.

Bornstein, D. (1998), 'Changing the world on a shoestring', *The Atlantic Monthly*, **281**(1), 34–9.

Borzaga, C. and A. Santuari (2001), 'Italy: from traditional co-operatives to innovative social enterprises', in C. Borzaga and J. Defourny (eds), *The Emergence of Social Enterprise*, London: Routledge, pp. 166–81.

Boschee, J. (1995), 'Social entrepreneurship: some nonprofits are not only thinking about the unthinkable, they're doing it – running a profit', *Across the Board, The Conference Board Magazine*, **32**(3), 20–25.

Boschee, J. (2001), 'Eight basic principles for nonprofit entrepreneurs', *Nonprofit World*, **19**(4), 15–18.

Boschee, J. and J. McClurg (2003), 'Toward a better understanding of social entrepreneurship: some important directions', working paper, available at http://www.se-alliance.org/better_understanding.pdf.

Brazael, D.V. and T. Herbert (1999), 'The genesis of entrepreneurship', *Entrepreneurship Theory and Practice*, **23**(3), 29–45.

Brock, D.D. (ed.) (2006) *Social Entrepreneurship Teaching Resources Handbook*, Kentucky: Entrepreneurship for the Public Good, Berea College.

Brouard, F. (2006), 'L'entrepreneuriat social, mieux connaître le concept', paper presented at the Annual Conference of the Canadian Council for Small Business and Entrepreneurship, Trois-Rivières.

Brouard, F. (2007), 'Réflexions sur l'Entrepreneuriat Social', paper presented at the Administrative Sciences Association of Canada, Ottawa.

Brush, C.G., T.S. Manolova and L.F. Edelman (2008), 'Separated by a common language? Entrepreneurship research across the Atlantic', *Entrepreneurship Theory and Practice*, **32**(2), 249–66.

Bruyat, C. and P.-A. Julien (2001), 'Defining the field of research in entrepreneurship', *Journal of Business Venturing*, **16**(2), 165–80.

Casson, M. (ed.) (1982), *The Entrepreneur – An Economic Theory*, Oxford: Martin Robertson.

Catford, J. (1998), 'Social entrepreneurs are vital for health promotion – but they need supportive environments too', *Health Promotion International*, **13**(2), 95–7.

Chell, E. (2007), 'Social enterprise and entrepreneurship, towards a convergent theory of the entrepreneurial process', *International Small Business Journal*, **25**(1), 5–26.

Christie, M.J. and B. Honig (2006), 'Social entrepreneurship: new research findings', *Journal of World Business*, **41**(1), 1–5.

Cooney, K. (2006), 'The institutional and technical structuring of nonprofit ventures: case study of a US hybrid organization caught between two fields', *Voluntas*, **17**(2), 143–61.

Cornelius, N., M. Todres, S. Janjuha-Jivraj, A. Woods and J. Wallace (2007), 'Corporate social responsibility and the social enterprise', *Journal of Business Ethics*, **76**(1), 117–35.

Dart, R. (2004), 'The legitimacy of social enterprise', *Nonprofit Management and Leadership*, **14**(4), 411–24.

Dearlove, D. (2004), 'Interview: Jeff Skoll', *Business Strategy Review*, **15**(2), 51–3.

Dees, G. (1998a), 'The meaning of "Social Entrepreneurship"', *Kauffman Foundation*, pp. 1–5.

Dees, G. (1998b), 'Enterprising nonprofits', *Harvard Business Review*, **76**(1), 54–6.

Dees, G. and B. Battle Anderson (2006), 'Framing a theory of social entrepreneurship: building on two schools of practice and thought', *ARNOVA Occasional Paper Series – Research on Social Entrepreneurship: Understanding and Contributing to an Emerging Field*, **1**(3), 39–66.

Defourny, J. (2001), 'From Third Sector to social enterprise', in C. Borzaga and J. Defourny (eds), *The Emergence of Social Enterprise*, London/NY: Routledge, pp. 1–28.

Defourny, J. (2004), 'L'émergence du concept d'entreprise sociale', *Reflets et Perspectives de la Vie Économique*, **43**(3), 9–23.

Defourny, J. and M. Nyssens (2006), 'Defining social enterprise', in M. Nyssens (ed.), *Social Enterprises, At the Crossroads of Market, Public Policies and Civil Society*, London: Routledge, pp. 3–26.

Defourny, J. and M. Nyssens (2008), 'Conceptions of social enterprise in Europe and the United States: convergences and divergences', paper presented at the EMES International Summer School, Corte, 3–7 July.

Degroote, N. (2008), 'L'enterprise sociale aux Etats-Unis et en Europe: analyse comparative de cinq approches', Master's Thesis, Thesis director: J. Defourney.

De Leeuw, E. (1999), 'Healthy cities: urban social entrepreneurship for health', *Health Promotion International*, **14**(3), 261–9.

Dorado, S. (2006), 'Social entrepreneurial ventures: different values so different process of creation, no?', *Journal of Developmental Entrepreneurship*, **11**(4), 319–43.

Drayton, W. (2002), 'The citizen sector: becoming as entrepreneurial and competitive as business', *California Management Review*, **44**(3), 120–32.

Drucker, P. (1985), *Innovation and Entrepreneurship*, New York: Harper and Row.

DTI (2001), 'Researching social enterprise', Final Report to the Small Business Service, available at http://www.dti.gsi.gov.uk/.

Emerson, Jed and Fay Twersky (1996), *New Social Entrepreneurs: The Success, Challenge and Lessons of Non-profit Enterprise Creation*, San Francisco: Roberts Foundation, Homeless Economic Development Fund.

European Commission (2003), *The Social Situation in the European Union*, Brussels: Commission of the European Union.

Filion, L.J. (1997), 'Le champ de l'entrepreneuriat: historique, evolution, tendances', *Revue International P.M.E.*, **10**(2), 129–72.

Fowler, A. (2000), 'NGDOs as a moment in history: beyond aid to social entrepreneurship or civic innovation?', *Third World Quarterly*, **21**(4), 637–54.

Gartner, W.B. (1985), 'A conceptual framework for describing the phenomenon of new venture creation', *Academy of Management Review*, **10**(4), 696–706.

Gartner, W.B. (1988), '"Who is an entrepreneur?" is the wrong question', *American Journal of Small Business*, **12**(4), 11–32.

Guclu, A., G. Dees and B. Battle Anderson (2002), 'The process of social entrepreneurship: creating opportunities worthy of serious pursuit', working paper, Center for the Advancement of Social Entrepreneurship (CASE).

Haugh, H. (2005), 'A research agenda for social entrepreneurship', *Social Enterprise Journal*, **1**(1), 1–12.

Haugh, H. and P. Tracey (2004), 'The role of social enterprise in regional development', paper presented to the Social Enterprise and Regional Development Conference, Cambridge-MIT Institute, University of Cambridge.

Hulgard, L. (2008), 'Discourses of social entrepreneurship in USA and Europe – variations of the same theme?', paper presented at the EMES International Summer School, Corte, 3–7 July.

Hulgard, L. and R. Spear (2006), 'Social entrepreneurship and the mobilization of social capital in European social enterprises', in M. Nyssens (ed.), *Social Enterprises: At the Crossroads of Market, Public Policies and Civil Society*, London/NY: Routledge, pp. 85–108.

Johannisson, B. and A. Nilsson (1989), 'Community entrepreneurship – networking for regional development', *Entrepreneurship and Regional Development*, **1**(1), 1–19.

Johnson, S. (2000), 'Literature review on social entrepreneurship', working paper, Canadian Centre for Social Entrepreneurship (CCSE): pp. 1–16, available at http://www.ccsecanada.org/.

Kerlin, J.A. (2006), 'Social enterprise in the United States and Europe: understanding and learning from the differences', *Voluntas*, **17**(3), 246.

Kramer, M. (2005), 'Measuring innovation: evaluation in the field of social entrepreneurship', Skoll Foundation, Boston: Foundation Strategy Group.

Leadbeater, C. (ed.) (1997), *The Rise of the Social Entrepreneur*, London: Demos.

Light, P. (2005), 'Searching for social entrepreneurs: who they might be, where they might be found, what they do', paper presented at the Association for Research on Nonprofit and Voluntary Associations annual conference, 17–18 November.

Mair, J. and I. Martí (2004), 'Social entrepreneurship: what are we talking about? A framework for future research', working paper, IESE Business School, University of Navarra, pp. 1–14.

Mair, J. and I. Martí (2006), 'Social entrepreneurship research: a source of explanation, prediction and delight', *Journal of World Business*, **41**(1), 36–44.

Mair, J. and E. Noboa (2006), 'Social entrepreneurship: how intentions to create a social venture are formed', in J. Mair, J.A. Robinson and K. Hockerts (eds), *Social Entrepreneurship*, Basingstoke, UK and New York: Palgrave Macmillan, pp. 121–35.

Marc, F. (1988), 'Nouvel entrepreneuriat et mission sociale de l'entreprise', paper presented at the International Conference, Montpellier.

McGrath, R.G. (2003), 'Connecting the study of entrepreneurship and theories of capitalist progress: an epilogue', in Z.J. Acs and D.B. Audretsch (eds), *Handbook of Entrepreneurship Research*, Boston/Dordrecht/London: Kluwer Academic Publishers, pp. 515–31.

Miller, D. and P.H. Friesen (1982), 'Innovation in conservative entrepreneurial firms: two models of strategic momentum', *Strategic Management Journal*, **3**, 1–25.

Nicholls, A. (ed.) (2008), '*Social Entrepreneurship: New Models of Sustainable Social Change*, Oxford: Oxford University Press (paperback edition).

Nicholls, A. and A.H. Cho (2008), 'Social entrepreneurship: the structuration of a field', in A. Nicholls (ed.), *Social Entrepreneurship: New Models of Sustainable Social Change*, Oxford: Oxford University Press (paperback edition), pp. 99–118.

Peredo, A.M. and M. McLean (2006), 'Social entrepreneurship: a critical review of the concept', *Journal of World Business*, **41**(1), 56–65.

Roberts, D. and C. Woods (2005), 'Changing the world on a shoestring: the concept of social entrepreneurship', *University of Auckland Business Review*, Autumn, pp. 45–51.

Robinson, J. (2006), 'Navigating social and institutional barriers to markets: how social entrepreneurs identify and evaluate opportunities', in J. Mair, J. Robinson and K. Hockerts (eds), *Social Entrepreneurship*, Basingstoke, UK and New York: Palgrave Macmillan, pp. 95–120.

School for Social Entrepreneurs (SSE) (2002), available at http://www.sse.org.uk/.

Schuyler, G. (1998), 'Social entrepreneurship: profit as means, not an end', *Kauffman Center for Entrepreneurial Leadership Clearinghouse on Entrepreneurship Education Digest*, **98**(7), 1–3.

Schwab Foundation (1998), available at http://www.schwabfound.org/.

Shane, S. and S. Venkataraman (2000), 'The promise of entrepreneurship as a field of research', *Academy of Management Review*, **25**(1), 217–26.

Sharir, M. and M. Lerner (2006), 'Gauging the success of social ventures initiated by individual social entrepreneurs', *Journal of World Business*, **41**(1), 6–20.

Smallbone, D., M. Evans, I. Ekanem and S. Butters (2001), 'Researching social enterprise', Centre for Enterprise and Economic Development Research, Middlesex University.

Spear, R. (2006), 'Social entrepreneurship: a different model?', *International Journal of Social Economics*, **33**(5/6), 399–410.

Stöhr, W.B. (ed.) (1990), *Global Challenge and Local Response: Initiatives for Economy Regeneration in Contemporary Europe*, London/NY: The United Nations University – Mansell.

Stryjan, Y. (2006), 'The practice of social entrepreneurship: notes toward a resource-perspective', in C. Steyaert and D. Hjorth (eds), *Entrepreneurship as Social Change: A Third Movements in Entrepreneurship Book*, Cheltenham, UK and Northampton, MA, USA: Edward Elgar, pp. 35–55.

Sullivan Mort, G., J. Weerawardena and K. Carnegie (2003), 'Social entrepreneurship: towards conceptualization', *International Journal of Nonprofit and Voluntary Sector Marketing*, **8**(1), 76–88.

Thalhuber, J. (1998), 'The definition of social entrepreneur', National Centre for Social Entrepreneurs, pp. 1–3.

Thompson, J.L. (2002), 'The world of the social entrepreneur', *International Journal of Public Sector Management*, **15**(4/5), 412–31.

Thompson, J.L. and B. Doherty (2006), 'The diverse world of social enterprise: a collection of social enterprise stories', *International Journal of Social Economics*, **33**(5/6), 361–75.

Thompson, J.L., G. Alvy and A. Lees (2000), 'Social entrepreneurship: a new look at the people and the potential', *Management Decision*, **38**(5), 328–38.

Tracey, P. and N. Phillips (2007), 'The distinctive challenge of educating social entrepreneurs: a postscript and rejoinder to the special issue on entrepreneurship education', *Academy of Management Learning and Education*, **6**(2), 264–71.

Venkataraman, S. (1997), 'The distinctive domain of entrepreneurship research', in J. Katz (ed.), *Advances in Entrepreneurship, Firm Emergence and Growth* 3, Greenwich, CT: JAI Press, pp. 119–38.

Verstraete, T. and A. Fayolle (2004), 'Quatre paradigmes pour cerner le domaine de recherche en entrepreneuriat', paper presented at the 7th Congrès International Francophone en Entrepreneuriat et PME, Montpellier, 27–29 October.

Wallace, S.L. (1999), 'Social entrepreneurship: the role of social purpose enterprises in facilitating community economic development', *Journal of Developmental Entrepreneurship*, **4**(2), 153–74.

Weerawardena, J. and G. Sullivan Mort (2006), 'Investigating social entrepreneurship: a multidimensional model', *Journal of World Business*, **41**(1), 21–35.

Young, D.R. (2001), 'Organizational identity in non-profit organizations: strategic and structural implications', *Nonprofit Management & Leadership*, **12**(2), 139–57.

Zahra, S.A., E. Gedajlovic, D.O. Neubam and J.M. Shulman (2009), 'A typology of social entrepreneurs: motives, search processes and ethical challenges', *Journal of Business Venturing*, **24**(5), 519–32.

APPENDICES

Appendix A: Which Author belongs to which School?

In the United States, two independent streams of practice can explain the interest for social entrepreneurship. These two streams resulted in two schools of thought that investigated the nature of social entrepreneurship: the Social Innovation School of thought, on the one hand, and the Social Enterprise School of thought, on the other hand (Dees and Battle Anderson, 2006). Table 7A.1 presents a classification of the main authors of each of these two approaches.

Table 7A.1   Classification of the main authors in the American streams of social entrepreneurship

Social Innovation School	Social Enterprise School
Alvord et al. (2004)	Alter (2004)
Austin et al. (2006)	Boschee (1995)
Bornstein (1998–2004)	Boschee and McClurg (2003)
Catford (1998)	Emerson and Twersky (1996)
Chell (2007)	Guclu et al. (2002)
De Leeuw (1999)	Haugh and Tracey (2004)
Dees (1998)	Stryjan (2006)
Drayton (2002)	Tracey and Philips (2007)
Drucker (1985)	
Kerlin (2006)	
Kramer (2005)	
Leadbeater (1997)	
Mair and Martí (2004; 2006)	
Mair and Noboa (2006)	
Peredo and McLean (2006)	
Roberts and Woods (2005)	
Robinson (2006)	
Schuyler (1998)	
Schwab (1998)	
Sharir and Lerner (2006)	
Skoll in Dearlove (2004)	
Smallbone et al. (2001)	
Sullivan Mort et al. (2003)	
Thompson et al. (2000)	
Weerawardena and Sullivan Mort (2006)	
Young (2001)	

Appendix B: The Individual: Definitions of the Social Entrepreneur

Table 7A.2   Definitions of the 'social entrepreneur' according to the two American schools of thought

Social Innovation School	Social Enterprise School
Social entrepreneurs combine street activism with professional skills, **visionary insights** with pragmatism, and **ethical fibre** with tactical trust. They see **opportunities** where others only see empty buildings, unemployable people and unvalued resources. (Catford, 1998: 96)	**Non-profit executives** who pay increased attention to market forces without losing sight of their underlying mission, to somehow **balance moral imperatives and the profit motives** – and that balancing act is the heart and soul of the movement. (Boschee, 1995: 1)
Social entrepreneurs play the role of **change agents in the social sector**, by: adopting a **mission** to create and sustain **social value** (not just private value); recognizing and relentlessly pursuing new **opportunities** to serve that mission; engaging in a process of continuous **innovation**, adaptation, and learning; acting boldly without being limited by **resources** currently at hand; and exhibiting heightened accountability to the constituencies served and for the outcomes created. (Dees, 1998a: 3–4)	Social entrepreneurs must be able to **articulate** a compelling **social impact theory** and a plausible **business model**. (Guclu et al., 2002, in Acs and Kallas, 2007: 30)
Ashoka's social entrepreneur is a **path breaker** with a powerful new idea, who combines **visionary** and real-world problem-solving creativity, who has a strong **ethical fiber**, and who is 'totally possessed' by his or her vision of change. (Drayton, in Bornstein, 1998: 37)	Individuals who **combine social and commercial objectives** by developing economically **sustainable solutions** to social problems. It requires social entrepreneurs to identify and exploit **market opportunities** in order to develop products and services that achieve **social ends**, or to **generate surpluses** that can be reinvested in a social project. (Tracey and Phillips, 2007: 264)
Individuals who have a **vision** for social change and who have the financial **resources** to support their ideas. . .[who] exhibit all the **skills of successful business people** as well as **a powerful desire for social change**. (Schuyler, 1998: 1)	

Table 7A.2   (continued)

Social Innovation School	Social Enterprise School
Someone who: identifies and applies practical solutions to social problems. . .; **innovates** by finding a new product, service or approach. . ., focuses. . . on **social value creation**. . .; resists being trapped by the constraints of ideology and discipline; has a **vision**, but also a well-thought out roadmap as to how to attain the goal. (Schwab Foundation, 1998)	
Rare individuals with the ability to analyze, to **envision**, to communicate, to empathize, to enthuse, to advocate, to mediate, to enable and to empower a wide range of disparate individuals and organizations. (De Leeuw, 1999: 261)	
People who realize where there is an **opportunity** to satisfy some unmet need that the state welfare system will not or cannot meet, and who gather together the necessary **resources** (generally people, often volunteers, money and premises) and use these to 'make a difference'. (Thompson et al., 2000: 328)	
Social entrepreneurs are first driven by the **social mission** of creating better social value than their competitors which results in them exhibiting **entrepreneurially virtuous behaviour**. Secondly, they exhibit a **balanced judgment**, a coherent unity of purpose and action in the face of complexity. Thirdly, social entrepreneurs explore and recognize **opportunities** to create better social value for their clients. Finally, social entrepreneurs display **innovativeness, proactiveness** and **risk-taking propensity** in their key decision making. (Sullivan Mort et al., 2003: 82)	

Table 7A.2 (continued)

Social Innovation School	Social Enterprise School
At the Skoll Foundation we call social entrepreneurs **'society's change agents'**: the pioneers of innovation for the social sector. Social entrepreneurs usually have a **vision** of something that they would like to solve in the social sector. (Skoll, in Dearlove, 2004: 52)	
Visionary, passionately **dedicated** individuals. (Roberts and Woods, 2005: 49)	
Social entrepreneurship is exercised where **some person or group** aims either exclusively or in some prominent way to **create social value** of some kind, and pursue that goal through some combination of (1) recognizing and exploiting **opportunities** to create this value, (2) employing **innovation**,(3) tolerating **risk**, and (4) declining to accept limitations in available **resources**. (Peredo and McLean, 2006: 64)	
The social entrepreneur is acting as a **change agent** to create and sustain **social value** without being limited to **resources** currently at hand. (Sharir and Lerner, 2006: 7)	

Note: The chronological order has been chosen in order to shed light on the evolution of the concept across time. This note is valuable for Table 7A.3 (the concept of 'social entrepreneurship') and Table 7A.4 (the concept of 'social enterprise'). The European perspective is not tackled in Appendices B and C as it mainly focuses on the organizational aspect of the phenomenon of social entrepreneurship.

Appendix C: The Process: Definitions of Social Entrepreneurship

Table 7A.3   Definitions of 'social entrepreneurship' according to the two American schools of thought

Social Innovation School	Social Enterprise School
A vast array of economic, educational, research, welfare, social and spiritual **activities** engaged in by various organizations. (Leadbeater, 1997)	Social entrepreneurship is viewed as a category of entrepreneurship that primarily (a) is engaged in by **collective actors**, and (b) involves, in a central role in the undertaking's resource mix, socially embedded resources [. . .] and their conversion into (market-) convertible resources, and vice-versa. (Stryjan, 2006: 35)
It combines the passion of a **social mission** with an image of **business-like discipline**, innovation and determination. (Dees, 1998a: 1)	
A process consisting in the **innovative** use and combination of resources to explore and exploit **opportunities**, that aims at catalyzing **social change** by catering to basic **human needs** in a **sustainable manner**. (Mair and Martí, 2004: 3)	
Social entrepreneurship encompasses the notions of 'construction, evaluation and pursuit of **opportunities**' as means for a '**social transformation**' carried out by visionary, passionately dedicated individuals. (Roberts and Woods, 2005: 49)	
Innovative, social value creating activity that can occur *within or across the nonprofit, business, and/or public/ government sectors*. (Austin et al., 2006: 1)	
The **innovative** use of resource combinations to pursue **opportunities** aiming at the creation of organizations and/or practices that **yield and sustain social benefits**. (Mair and Noboa, 2006)	

Table 7A.3   (continued)

Social Innovation School	Social Enterprise School
• A behavioural phenomenon expressed in a **NFP organization** context aimed at **delivering social value** through the exploitation of perceived **opportunities**. • Social entrepreneurship is a **bounded multidimensional construct** that is deeply rooted in an organization's **social mission**, its drive for **sustainability** and highly influenced and shaped by the **environmental dynamics**. Opportunity recognition is embedded in these three dimensions. • Social entrepreneurship strives to achieve **social value creation** and this requires the display of **innovativeness, proactiveness** and **risk management** behaviour. • Social entrepreneurs' behaviour in regard to **risk** is highly constrained by their primary objective of **building a sustainable organization** and hence does not support Dees' view that social entrepreneurs do not allow the lack of initial resources to limit their options. Finally, social entrepreneurs can indeed remain **competitive whilst fulfilling their social mission**. (Weerawardena and Sullivan Mort, 2006: 22, 32)	

Appendix D: The Organization: Definitions of the Social Enterprise

Table 7A.4 Definitions of the 'social enterprise' according to the different schools of thought

Social Innovation School	Social Enterprise School	European Conceptual Approaches
Enterprises set up for a **social purpose** but **operating as businesses** and in the voluntary or nonprofit sector. However, according to him, the **main world** of the social entrepreneur is the **voluntary (NFP) sector**. (Thompson, 2002)	Organizations positioned in **two different organizational fields** – each necessitating different internal organizational technologies – to elucidate the structural tensions that can emerge inside these new **hybrid models**. (Cooney, 2006: 143)	Organizations with an explicit aim to **benefit the community, initiated by a group of citizens** and in which the **material interest** of capital investors is **subject to limits**. (Defourney and Nyssens, 2006)
Social enterprises enact **hybrid non-profit and for-profit activities**. (Dart, 2004: 415)		An independent organization that has **social and economic objectives** which aims to fill a **social role** as well as reach **financial durability** through commerce. (DTI, 2001)
[. . .] a range of organizations that trade for a **social purpose**. They adopt one of a **variety of different legal formats** but have in common the principles of pursuing **business-led solutions to achieve social aims**, and the reinvestment of surplus for community benefit. Their objectives focus on socially desired, **non financial goals** and their outcomes are the **non financial measures** of the implied demand for and supply of services. (Haugh, 2005: 3)		

Table 7A.4 (continued)

Social Innovation School	Social Enterprise School	European Conceptual Approaches
Non-profit, for-profit or cross-sector Social Entrepreneurial Ventures are social because they aim to address **a problem the private sector has not adequately addressed**; they are entrepreneurial because their **founders have qualities identified with entrepreneurs**. (Dorado, 2006: 327)		
Social enterprises have a **social purpose**; assets and wealth are used to create **community benefit**; they pursue this with **trade in a market place**; **profits and surpluses** are **not distributed** to shareholders; 'members' or employees have some **role in decision making and/or governance**; the enterprise is seen as **accountable to both its members and a wider community**; there is a **double- or triple-bottom-line** paradigm: the most effective social enterprises demonstrate healthy financial and social returns. (Thompson and Doherty, 2006: 362)		
Social entrepreneurial organizations must clearly address **value positioning strategies**, and take a **proactive posture** as well as providing superior service maximizing **social value creation**. (Weerawardena and Sullivan Mort, 2006: 21)		

PART III

The Process of Creating and Developing
Entrepreneurial Organizations

8. Mapping internationalization paths of technology-based SMEs: cases of Estonian ICT and biotechnology companies*

Kalev Kaarna and Tõnis Mets[1]

INTRODUCTION

Building descriptive models of internationalization, which incorporate the accelerated internationalization of technology-based companies, has led to the convergence of different research streams. Criticism of over 30-year-old or older stage models of incremental internationalization, such as the U-model (Johanson and Vahlne, 1977) and I-model (Bilkey and Tesar, 1977), has led to the introduction of a new research field known as 'International Entrepreneurship' (IE) (McDougall and Oviatt, 2000). McDougall and Oviatt (2000) see convergence between International Business (IB) research and entrepreneurship research. The first stream of research has widened their area of interest from multinational corporations to SMEs. Entrepreneurship researchers, on the other hand, have started to study the cross-border activities of entrepreneurs in addition to developments in their home country.

Despite the common interests, the two fields have not merged successfully and IE still lacks not only a common theoretical basis but also a common, widely accepted definition, which would broaden the scholarly field beyond start-ups and SMEs (Keupp and Gassmann 2009; Aspelund et al., 2007). In this chapter IE is defined as a dynamic process of recognizing and exploiting entrepreneurial opportunities across national borders. For semantic reasons we use a term 'entrepreneurial internationalization' for labelling companies that follow this process.

Keupp and Gassmann (2009) concluded in their literature analysis of 179 articles, selected from 7627, that International Entrepreneurship has '(a) conflicting viewpoints about the entrepreneurial component of internationalization, (b) conflicting explanations of why early and rapid internationalization is possible, (c) knowledge gaps resulting from the unilateral empirical focus on small firms, and (d) knowledge gaps from the imbalance of IB and entrepreneurship theory in IE.'

Regarding causality, most research has been focused on the causal links between antecedents (such as managers' socio-cognitive properties and cultural distance) and outcomes (such as patterns of internationalization and performance) of internationalization. Other links and influences have received little attention (Keupp and Gassmann, 2009).

Due to the phenomenological nature and initial definition of the field by McDougall in 1994 (McDougall et al., 1994), the majority of research has been focused on SMEs, which are new, small, young and can venture abroad right from their inception (Keupp and Gassmann, 2009). These companies are labelled in many categories. Most common are Born Globals (BG) and International New Ventures (INV). For semantic reasons the BG label is preferred in the current chapter.

Despite the significant number of articles about the BG phenomenon, little has been done regarding categorizing or differentiating BG companies inside the category, even though the companies are found to be heterogeneous and there are more differentiating factors than universal characteristics of the companies and their internationalization paths (Aspelund et al., 2007). The main paths of internationalization recognized are still international market-entry-timing-related: gradual, BG, and Born-again Global (BAG).

The gradual path is the slow path from home country to closely related countries to global markets and is described by U-model and I-model (see next section of the chapter). BG companies internationalize rapidly and often have little or no presence in the home market. One of the reasons is that knowledge- and technology-intensive companies target market niches of a size viable for earning profits solely on a global scale. Such rapid internationalization is especially important for technology-based companies from very small countries, where the market is too small to feed R&D (push factor), while the demand of large global markets works as a real pull-factor (Luostarinen and Gabrielsson, 2004). BAG companies internationalize rapidly later, after building up domestic support (Bell et al., 2001). These companies are considered responsive as the second attempt is initiated by an external event such as a change of owners or managers (Bell et al., 2003). But in essence there is no other major difference between BG and BAG than the date of initiating a rapid internationalization strategy.

Some other labels for companies not fitting under a BG or gradual path are also used, but these have not gained wider notice or usage. One of such labels is 'inward internationalizers', who import components from global sources and internationalizing rather rapidly (Gabrielsson et al., 2008).

Due to the gaps and problems in the body of knowledge of IE listed above, there is a definite need for new approaches, which would help to merge the gradual internationalization view of international business theory and chaotic view of the entrepreneurship research field. Also, approaches allowing differentiating internationalization paths of BG companies would help to enlarge the scope of IE beyond companies selected based on size (SMEs) and market entry timing (instant internationals). Internationalization models with such features would help the advance towards building common theoretical bases for IE and would have significant descriptive power for all types of IE paths.

The purpose of the current chapter is to propose and test a model for mapping the internationalization paths of companies according to two dimensions: market extent and complexity of knowledge. The qualitative mapping model allows the division of the internationalization path into phases (gradual approach of IB), but also allows the mapping of chaotic path changes (entrepreneurial approach). The model also allows the differentiation of internationalization paths of companies in more ways than just gradual, BG or BAG. A longitudinal case study approach is used to evaluate the model for mapping internationalization paths over 15–18 years. Such a longitudinal approach is not common in the IE field and is suggested to gain better insight into the processes (Keupp and Gassmann, 2009).

DEFINING THE EVOLVING CONCEPT OF INTERNATIONAL ENTREPRENEURSHIP

The IE research field dates its beginnings back to 1994, when Oviatt and Mcdougall defined International New Ventures as 'a business organization that, from inception, seeks to derive significant competitive advantage from the use of resources and the sale of outputs in multiple countries'. IE as a research field was labelled first by McDougall and Oviatt in 2000.

The field is phenomenological in nature as it started from the observations that significant numbers of SMEs do not follow the incremental paths of internationalization proposed by gradual models (Oviatt and McDougall, 1994). Such gradual models are the Uppsala model (U-model) (Johanson and Vahlne, 1977, 1990) and the Innovation related model (I-model) (Andersen, 1993; Cavusgil, 1980). The gradual models are stage models, where companies internationalize and overcome obstacles step-by-step. The main knowledge and learning-related issue in stage models is learning about the markets. The home market is considered a test bed for the development of the product/service, which then is replicated in the international market (Cavusgil, 1980; Johanson and Vahlne, 1990).

The criticism of gradual models started in the 1980s, but intensified in the 1990s. It was found that the majority of companies tend not to follow the U-model stages in their internationalization process (Turnbull, 1987) and all general stages are not necessary for all companies (Reid, 1983). Researchers have tried to overcome the gap in theory through introducing new concepts, which would better describe the rapid internationalization paths of companies (see Table 8.1). As seen from Table 8.1 and stated in literature reviews (Aspelund et al., 2007; Keupp and Gassmann, 2009), the majority of the concepts and hence research in the field of IE are based on the 1994 definition of the International New Venture. The field of study is equated with 'the study of new small and young firms that venture abroad' (Keupp and Gassmann, 2009).

The first attempt to redefine the field of IE was made in 2000 when McDougall and Oviatt formulated IE as 'a combination of innovative, proactive and risk-seeking behaviour that crosses national borders and is intended to create value in organizations. The study of IE includes research on such behaviour and research comparing domestic entrepreneurial behaviour in multiple countries' (McDougall and Oviatt, 2000). Since 2003 the same authors started using another definition 'IE is the discovery, enactment, evaluation, and exploitation of opportunities – across national borders – to create future goods and services. It follows, therefore, that the scholarly field of international entrepreneurship examines and compares – across national borders – how, by whom, and with what effects those opportunities are acted upon' (Oviatt and McDougall, 2005).

Researchers like Shane and Venkataraman (2000), and Coviello (2006) and Mathews and Zander (2007) have tried to add the dynamic process component to the definition of IE. Yet these attempts have been unnoticed by most empirical studies, which continue to use the definition of INV from 1994 (Keupp and Gassmann, 2009).

We agree with the approach of broadening the definition and emphasizing the dynamic nature of the process. In this chapter we will define IE as a dynamic process of recognizing and exploiting entrepreneurial opportunities across national borders. The scholarly field of IE examines and compares, how, by whom, and with what effects these cross-border entrepreneurial opportunities are acted upon. Instant internationalization is one research area of the field.

Table 8.1   Concepts for describing internationalization paths

Year	New concept/term
1975	Firm first develops in the domestic market and internationalization is the consequence of a **series of incremental decisions**. Stage model based on **four stages** (Johanson and Wiedersheim-Paul, 1975).
1977	• Stage model based on **experiential knowledge** about markets and increasing foreign market commitments (key factor: psychic distance) (later labelled Uppsala-Model) (Johanson and Vahlne, 1977). • Stage model based on **management intention** and psychic distance of markets (later labelled Innovation-related Model) (Bilkey and Tesar, 1977).
1985	**'Short route' strategy** (later termed 'leapfrogging') means that companies tend to shorten the time between different stages in the hypothesized establishment chain (agent, sales subsidiary, manufacturing subsidiary) and skip some stages altogether (Hedlund and Kverneland, 1985).
1989	**Innate exporters** are corporations established expressly from their inception to serve foreign markets (Ganitsky, 1989).
1993	**Born-Globals** (BGs) are companies which started exporting, on average, only two years after their foundation, compete successfully against larger companies globally, and gain most of their revenues from international markets (Rennie, 1993).
1994	**International New Ventures** (INVs) are business organizations that, from inception, seek to derive significant competitive advantage from the use of resources and the sale of outputs in multiple countries (Oviatt and McDougall, 1994).
1995	**Global Start-ups are** 'a type of international new venture that coordinates many organizational activities across many countries' and are international at inception. A Global Start-up can also be termed *innate exporter, born international, infant international*, and *international new venture* (Oviatt and McDougall, 1995).
1999	• **Instant Exporters or Instant Internationals** are SMEs which rapidly become involved in international markets through having international activities within the first year of being in business (McAuley, 1999). • **International Entrepreneurs** label is based on the concept of INV and groups of young firms tending to experience the first cross-border links or contacts with or soon after the foundation date of the firm (Jones, 1999).
2000	• **Accelerated internationalization** refers to the phenomenon of firms engaging in international business activities earlier in their organizational life cycles than they have done historically (Shrader et al., 2000).

Table 8.1 (continued)

Year	New concept/term
	• **International Entrepreneurship** (IE) is 'a combination of innovative, proactive and risk-seeking behaviour that crosses national borders and is intended to create value in organizations. The study of IE includes research on such behaviour and research comparing domestic entrepreneurial behaviour in multiple countries' (McDougall and Oviatt, 2000)
2001	• **Instant Internationals** are entrepreneurially-inclined start-up companies able to pursue global strategies (Fillis, 2001).
	• **Born-again Global (BAG)** companies internationalize rapidly later on, after building up domestic support (Bell et al., 2001).
2003	• **Born-Internationals** are based on the INV definition and refer to new SMEs, which plan from inception to export goods or services as an integral part of their strategy (Kundu and Katz, 2003).
	• **Micromultinationals** (mMNE) are SMEs that control and manage value-added activities through constellation and investment modes in more than one country. The mMNE does not have to necessarily *own* its value-added activities abroad, but can control and manage them (Dimitratos et al., 2003).
2005	**Early Internationalizing Firms** is a term used to refer to companies deemed as INVs, global start-ups or BG firms, which are, by definition, international at inception (Rialp et al., 2005).

IDENTIFYING THE DETERMINANTS AND THE PATH OF INTERNATIONALIZING

The summary of key determinants covered in the literature and main paths of internationalization are presented in Figure 8.1. The axes represent the two main characteristics of entrepreneurial internationalization emphasized in IE literature since the 1990s: entry time to international market related to the establishing date of the company, and the market extent of the company on the scale from local to global.

Figure 8.1 also represents the main groups of determinants influencing the internationalization path of technology-based SMEs: product, operation, market, entrepreneur and the team, and environment. Different authors have listed different independent variables and there are several approaches for categorizing the variables (Aspelund et al., 2007; Keupp and Gassmann, 2009). In the current chapter we have based the categorization of variables on the POM-strategy model.

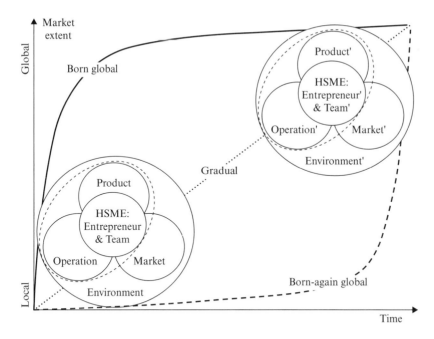

Source: Mets (2009).

Figure 8.1   Main paths and determinants of the internationalization of high-technology SMEs internationalization

The globalization strategy comprises three sub-strategies or fields: the product (P), the operation mode (O) and the market (M). The POM-strategy itself engenders a global marketing strategy, which consists of pricing, distribution and customer strategy (Luostarinen and Gabrielsson, 2004). Based on research on the IE field, we have identified two categories in the POM-strategy: entrepreneurs and environment.

The socio-cognitive properties of entrepreneurs are considered to be crucial determinants of internationalization (Christensen, 2003; Keupp and Gassmann, 2009). The environment category incorporates both general trends and changes in market opportunities, legislation, communication and transportation (Madsen and Servais, 1997), but also the availability of financing, which is considered a crucial issue for technology-based SMEs (Moen et al., 2008).

Although Figure 8.1 summarizes the existing view on IE, it does not explicitly incorporate learning processes, opportunity recognition and exploitation. These phenomena are interrelated, as one of the most important outcomes of entrepreneurial learning is effective recognition of opportunities (Politis, 2005; Corbett, 2005; Hitt et al., 2001; Shane and Venkataraman, 2000). In addition to opportunity recognition, learning new capabilities helps firms to compete effectively, survive and grow (Autio et al., 2000). Gradual models of internationalization have emphasized learning about external factors such as market characteristics, regulations and so on. Entrepreneurial theory and growth theories of firms place an equal importance on internal learning. A company has to learn about alternative uses of its own internal resources as this would open up opportunities and be an incentive for expansion (Foss, 1999; Penrose, 1959). Technology-based companies are found to create value largely based on their internal capabilities, and technology capabilities are one of the key determinants of a company's growth (Lee et al., 2001).

In cases of technology-based SMEs, scarcity of resources raises the issue of leverage. SMEs can't afford to learn about all possible opportunities and all possible independent technologies. Integrating new knowledge domains with existing knowledge allows SMEs to leverage their scarce resources and gain an advantage over global competitors. Such knowledge leverage is especially important in cases when company managers see and want to realize opportunities even if the necessary resources are currently not available.

In cases of BG the research of IE has focused on studying the market leverage: an advantage is gained from offering products and services over a wider number of markets. The aspect of leveraging internal knowledge should also be taken into account. In the next section we offer an approach to map these leverage effects and internationalization paths of companies.

MODEL FOR MAPPING INTERNATIONALIZATION PATHS OF TECHNOLOGY COMPANIES

In general, leverage is defined as the exploitation of organizational financial and non-financial resources and capacity to their full extent in order to increase profits (Crainer, 1999; Thompson, 2001; Hamel and Prahalad, 1993). In order to stretch resources to their optimal limits, higher skills and performance need to be created, developed and spread over the whole organization.

Market leverage is based on the assumption that technology companies' products and services have often zero (in the case of information goods) or very low marginal costs after the development or production of initial units. As for technology-based companies, the market in each geographical region might be small, in which case they have to operate in several

		low	medium	high
Market extent	high	Market diversification of single domain high-tech	Market diversification of multi-domain high-tech	Market diversification of integrated systems
	medium	Market duplication of single domain high-tech	Market duplication of multi-domain high-tech	Market duplication of integrated systems
	low	Single domain high-tech on home market	Multi-domain high-tech on home market	Integrated systems on home market

low   medium   high
Complexity of knowledge

Source: Authors.

Figure 8.2   Model for mapping entrepreneurial internationalization

markets in order to earn profits. Due to low marginal costs, every new market will significantly leverage (the impact increases with each added market) the profit margins of the company. Although the market leverage holds true only under certain conditions, it indicates that a similar leverage effect could be expected for the knowledge domains.

Knowledge leverage is achieved through integrating multiple domains of knowledge in order to be able to offer customers services or products at a significantly higher level. The higher level of service/production cannot be achieved through using only a single domain of knowledge. Integration of different domains of knowledge results is new knowledge, which is valued significantly more highly than the sum of integrated domains. Such 'lever-aged knowledge' can be duplicated or multiplied to different markets.

The matrix in Figure 8.2 describes the strategic options of entrepre-neurial internationalization in terms of knowledge and market leverage.

Labelling quadrants by two axes (Complexity of knowledge, Market extent) in a three-scale measure (L-low; M-medium; H-high) we can describe different ways to leverage knowledge according to the interna-tionalization paths described in IE. The BG company is ready to move

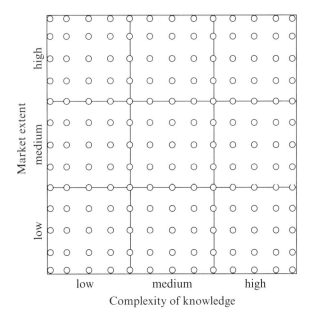

Figure 8.3   Possible positions of change in internationalization and knowledge

into the quadrant HH or even to start from there, leveraging its business model at the inception. BAG company can follow a more fluctuating trajectory, for example: LL-LM-LL-ML-HL-HM-HH.

In order to make qualitative mapping more comparable, 5 × 5 positions were determined for each matrix cell (see Figure 8.3). The rules used for mapping were as follows:

1.   start from the middle position of a cell;
2.   movement is relative to the previous position;
3.   during the mapping of the next movement, if possible, all already mapped positions are taken into account (in addition to previous position).

CASE STUDIES OF THREE ESTONIAN TECHNOLOGY-BASED COMPANIES

The companies in focus were chosen due to their relative success in internationalization and different internationalization paths.

Regio AS has four fields of activity: mapping, geospatial data, geographical information systems (GIS) and mobile positioning. The company is situated in the south-Estonian city of Tartu, which has about 100 000 inhabitants.

MicroLink is an IT company, which became the biggest IT firm in the Baltic States. Its services ranged from selling PCs to ISP and system development services, and e-business. MicroLink was founded in the Estonian capital, Tallinn, which currently has about 400 000 inhabitants.

Asper Biotech is a leading Estonian biotechnology company. Asper's business model is conducting research projects for the world's science, research and development organizations. The main offerings include custom genotyping services, genotyping software, genotyping hardware, and genotyping consumables. The company is situated in Tartu.

Data Collection Methods and Analysis

A substantial volume of publicly available information from newspapers, the companies' homepages (http://www.regio.ee/, http://www.microlink. ee, http://www.asperbio.com), and the commercial register, including the company's annual reports, were gathered and analysed. As Regio's international activities are carried out under the trademark 'Reach-U', the web page http://www.reach-u.com/ was also studied. Public information, including interviews with CEOs available in the Estonian newspapers and journals, were also used.

The generally accessible public information permitted mapping of the main material facts of the companies' history, and a study of the balance sheets and management reports to the business register, the main decisions taken and the resulting developments. It was also possible to derive from the public data the major milestones, strategy, organization structure, technology, skills and knowledge in every period. The main task of the interviews was to ascertain the historical facts and the roles of the key figures.

The final text was completed after a critical comparison and analysis of different sources: annual reports, interviews, newspapers, web pages and students' graduate theses. In the following section we describe the cases of Regio, MicroLink and Asper. The facts taken from the companies' homepages and annual reports (1999–2006) are usually not specially referenced, but where necessary, the specific facts have been referenced.

Regio

Regio's internationalization can be divided into six periods. The internationalization path of Regio is presented in Figure 8.4. The changes in revenue, export and profits are presented in Figure 8.5.

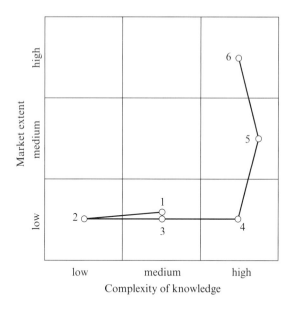

Figure 8.4   Internationalization path of Regio

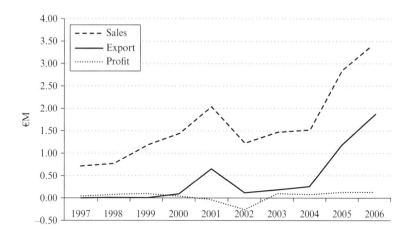

Figure 8.5   Performance indicators of Regio (million euros)

1.   R&D and postcards, 1988–89

The company was started as a small state-owned enterprise in the late 1980s. The first CEO, Rivo Noorkõiv, was appointed by the government. In 1989 Regio was transformed into a private joint stock company.

Regio was established as an R&D company carrying out regional studies, publishing them, and producing postcards (Noorkõiv, 2006).

2. Starting cartography, 1989–91

Regio launched their Estonian maps production. The first Estonian road map during the 50 years of the Soviet regime was produced in 1989 (Püttsepp, 1997). This led to the postcard production unit employees deciding to leave and set up their own business in 1990, as they did not want to subsidize all the R&D activities.

3. Building up geo-information systems, 1992–94

By 1994 Regio had moved completely to digital mapping, and began using satellite-based global positioning systems (GPS). Teet Jagomägi was appointed the CEO of the company after returning to Estonia from studying 3D software programming in the USA (Jagomägi, 2005). All the developments were financed through mortgages on personal homes of the management team.

The first export deals were made to produce travel guides to Germany (Noorkõiv, 2006). These were one-off deals and had no significant impact on the company's total sales.

4. Rapid sales growth, partnership building and taking in risk capital, 1995–99

Regio became a software and ICT company and invested in Differential GPS (DGPS) technology. In 1998 Regio was the biggest GIS software supplier in Estonia, and in the Estonian IT sector it had the second-highest growth rate in profit. Continuing an annual sales growth of over 50 per cent required breaking into international markets. An investment deal was made with the American risk capital fund Baltics Small Equity Fund (BSEF). Regio's managers were hoping to use risk capitalist networks for rapid internationalizing. The risk capitalists required the use of consultants and forced Regio's managers to be active, start internal reporting and seminars, learn new skills, and redefine the meaning of cartography (Noorkõiv, 2006).

In 1999 Regio won the tender from Ericsson AB to develop mobile positioning software (MPS) for the Estonian Rescue Centre. Regio's E-112 emergency GSM application became the first mobile positioning system implementation in the world, making it possible to locate mobile phone users (Kodres, 2006).

Despite BSEF investment, Regio needed an additional 450000 euros to launch their positioning system as a product in the international market. In 2000 Regio merged with the Finnish corporation Digital

Open Network Environment OY (DONE) quoted on the Helsinki Stock Exchange, to provide financing and internationalization solutions. BSEF exited the project by exchanging their Regio shares for cash (Noorkõiv, 2006). Regio's ambition to gain a market opening through risk capitalist networks had not been realized.

5.   Becoming a member of a listed company, DONE corporation, 2000–02
Regio developed the first MPS. The PinPoint software improved positioning accuracy by up to two to eight times. In 2000 Regio began to resell IKONOS satellite photos and to offer the hosting service of the mapserver (ASP). The brand Reach-U was established for international marketing. In 2001 Regio was integrated into the sales network of Ericsson AB. The MPS product portfolio was sold to DNA, a telecoms operator in Finland (Rozental, 2002a).

6.   Becoming independent again and growing global, since 2002
In February 2002 Regio's mother company went bankrupt. Regio managers repurchased the company and bought licences for some technologies developed by Reach-U, which were necessary for Regio to continue the contract with Ericsson AB. As Regio did not take over all the personnel, competences and projects from the mother company, there was a slight decrease in knowledge to which Regio had access (see Figure 8.4). The trademarks of Reach-U and Mgine Technologies were also purchased (Rozental 2002b).

In June 2002 Ericsson agreed to offer Reach-U middleware and mobile applications via its global network. In 2003 the first big contract was signed with Orange Slovakia to deliver the Reach-U location-based services (LBS) package for providing services to 2.7 million subscribers. In 2004 Ericsson agreed to open its sales channel for Reach-U LBS applications. (Walmsley, 2004). In 2005 Regio delivered mobile positioning to Saudi Arabia, and LBS solutions for Orange Romania's more than six million subscribers. In January 2006 Reach-U signed a deal with one of the leading operators in North Africa.

Since the sixth period Regio's product portfolio, consisting of LBS middleware and more than 10 LBS applications, has been used around the world by such mobile operators as: Etisalat (United Arab Emirates), Mobily (Saudi Arabia), Dishnet (India), Orange (Slovakia / Romania), EMT (Estonia), Elisa (Finland) and Elisa Vodafone (Estonia).

At first glance Regio might look like a BAG company: they first attempted exporting in the early 1990s, but they made their first significant sales in international markets only in 2002 and became truly global in 2005. Yet Regio does not fit the definition of a BAG as the company

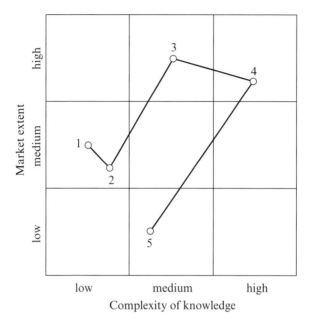

Figure 8.6   Internationalization path of MicroLink

had the intention of becoming international from early on, working for several years on developing competences and products to break into the international market. Only through combining the different knowledge domains of cartography, map design, GPS and LBS was Regio able to develop systems that had a global appeal. It is a case of active opportunity recognition and exploitation, not the reactive behaviour of BAG companies. Therefore we would label the internationalization trajectory of Regio as 'Learn Global' – a company reaching out to international markets rapidly after several years of intentional learning and combining different knowledge domains.

MicroLink

MicroLink's internationalization can be divided into five periods. The internationalization path of MicroLink is presented in Figure 8.6. The changes in revenue, export and profits are presented in Figure 8.7.

1.   PC assembling, retail and wholesale, 1991–95
The company was founded in August 1991 with the vision of becoming a Pan-Baltic computer assembly company. Up to 1995, MicroLink's

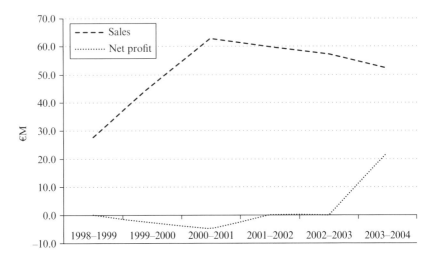

Figure 8.7 Performance indicators of MicroLink (million euros)

activities were concentrated on PC assembly, and wholesale and retail distribution of computer equipment in the Baltic. The company built an extensive resellers' and maintenance network across the Baltic countries, pioneering the concept of using authorized dealers in PC sales in Estonia as early as 1992.

2. System integration and Internet businesses, 1995–98
In 1995 activities were expanded into system integration and Internet businesses, which soon became the core activities of the company. In 1996 MicroLink sold its computer wholesale operations to the global distribution firm CHS Electronics.

3. Capitalization, mergers and growing global, 1998–99
A new management team led by Allan Martinson was appointed in the first half of 1998. It was the start of a Mergers and Acquisitons (M&A) strategy. In the course of 19 months, MicroLink merged with or acquired 19 companies, among them some of the region's largest, and exceeded the limits of SME definition. In 1998, it merged with Astrodata, Estonia's second largest IT company. This led to the revision of MicroLink's operations and structure, in order to consolidate the business and to be more flexible.

MicroLink identified a need to capitalize the company in order to be best positioned in the expected consolidation of the Baltic IT sector. In February 1999, MicroLink raised €3 million by the private placement of the company's shares. The investor was the Baltic Investment Fund, for whom new shares were issued to the value of €2.3 million.

In 1999 it bought Fortech and Var (Latvia's two largest IT companies), acquired five ISP providers in Estonia, Latvia and Lithuania, and merged them into one Internet holding company, Delfi (Reid, 2000). Through obtaining Fortech, MicroLink became shareholder of SAF Tehnika, which was an active player in the global microwave communication technology market (TBT, 2007). Yet MicroLink considered SAF as a financial investment and had no ambitions to stay in the global company for long. (Kokk, 2001).

After this M&A MicroLink officially declared IT services and Internet activities as its core businesses, and PC and cable assembly to be secondary businesses. The company then aimed at achieving a leading position in the Baltic IT services and Internet market through aggressive M&A activities. For this, MicroLink went through a second round of equity financing raised through the private placement of €3.8 million in October 1999. The investor was the Baltic Republics Fund, which obtained equal portions of old and new shares.

4. Focus on core business, 2000–03

In order to focus on its businesses MicroLink sold a 16 per cent stake in a financial accounting software provider, AS Columbus IT Partner Eesti, and 66.7 per cent interest in the cable assembly division MicroLink Electronics in 2000.

In August 2000 the company issued 60 233 new shares, most of which went to the company's employees who used their option scheme. Also in August MicroLink's shareholders completed a €3.3 million private placement of shares with the Baltic Post Privatisation Fund, BBL Finland and other financial investors.

Enforced by significant losses, MicroLink continued restructuring and in the financial year 2001/2002 divided its activities into five business areas, namely Systems division, Computers & Services division, Data division, New Media and Wireless Broadband Equipment divisions. Together these business units covered most of the needs of Top-1000 companies and public sector institutions in all Baltic countries, where the company was also a clear market leader. MicroLink Computers continued to be the leading PC manufacturer, and Delfi the leading portal. SAF Tehnika had successfully established its position as an important player in the world microwave communication market.

In June 2001, MicroLink made its third largest share issue, bringing the company proceeds to €3.1 million. All main shareholders of the company subscribed for the shares.

5. Exit of investors, 2004–05
In 2004 Delfi portals were sold to the Findexa group from Norway, and SAF Tehnika was listed on the Riga Stock Exchange with MicroLink exiting.

In June 2004 MicroLink announced a record unaudited net profit of €22.4 million for the financial year 2003/2004 due to the sale of Delfi portals and the exit from SAF Tehnika. In June Janis Bergs was appointed new MicroLink CEO.

In August 2004 MicroLink sold its share of Doclogiksas to Alna and continued as a partner reselling and implementing the software.

In October 2005 the Baltic telecoms company, Elion, Lattelekom and Lietuvos Telekomas, acquired the MicroLink group. The sale was conditional on regulatory competition board approvals in all three countries. Today, the Estonian branch of MicroLink is fully owned by Elion, a member of the Eesti Telekom Group.

In general the MicroLink case matches the definition of a BG, as entrepreneurs had the intention to become international from the very start and the company did actually become global to an extent. Yet at the same time MicroLink does not fit the BG label as it did not want to become truly global, and wanted to stay Pan-Baltic. Also, due to the IT bubble, it was able to acquire significant amounts of financial resources and grow rapidly beyond the scale of an SME through aggressive M&A. because of this, MicroLink does not even fit under the definition of MicroMultinational.

Asper Biotech

Asper's internationalization can be divided into four periods. The internationalization path of Asper is presented in Figure 8.8. The changes in revenue, export and profits are presented in Figure 8.9.

1. Product platform development, 1999–2000
The company was founded in 1999 by two scientists, who believed that the genotyping services market would soon move into a rapid growth phase. During its first years the company developed its Arrayed Primer Extension method based on genotyping technology. The first stage of technological development was finalized in 1999 and the first genotyping contracts were signed with Estonian and French clients. Clients were found through the scientists' personal networks.

Two risk capital funds invested in Asper: BSEF in 2000, and SEAF Central and Eastern European Growth Fund in 2001. Asper also obtained a low interest loan from a public body.

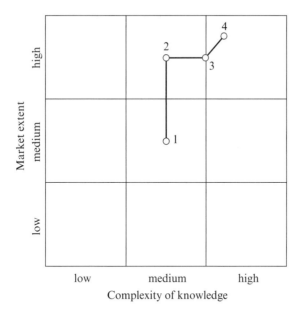

Figure 8.8   Internationalization path of Asper

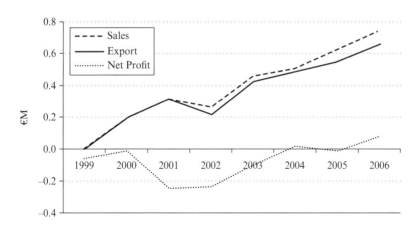

Figure 8.9   Performance indicators of Asper (million euros)

2.   Start of systematic sales network development, 2001–02

In 2001 Asper was selling to the USA, eight European and two Asian countries. The €30 000 project of high-density genotyping was finished. In 2001 the genotyping tests and technology were branded Genorama. A dedicated marketing team was created and the building of global sales representatives network was started. Some of the pressure for these changes came from investors.

In 2001 Deloitte & Touche recognized Asper as one of the fastest-developing technology companies in Central Europe. Asper received a Genomics Award for its Genorama QuattroImager genotyping system.

3. Starting usage of public funds for R&D, 2003–04

In 2003 Asper participated as a partner in several European Union 6th Framework Programme (FP) project proposals. Two of the projects were launched in 2004. Asper recognized FP as a 'market' and continued to participate in different projects as a service provider. By 2006 Asper was a partner in nine different FP6 R&D projects.

Asper optimized its organization structure and processes, and reduced the number of employees from 30 to 25. Asper also upgraded to ISO 9001:2000. The development of genotyping technology for research diagnostics (including diagnosing eye diseases) was started.

4. Focus and start of niche market strategy, 2003–06

Management reevaluated and decreased the value of investments by 30 per cent on their balance sheet. Instead of participating in FP6 projects as a service provider, Asper focuses on providing marketing services based on Asper's library of DNA tests (Kask, 2007). In 2005 Asper launched their patented trademark Asper Ophthalmics (AO) for marketing DNA tests for diagnosing eye diseases that do not yet have a cure, a niche that is unattractive to big biotechnology companies.

The launch of AO has been encouraging and has led Asper to start developing its competence in the field of DNA-based diagnostics. Also pharmacogenetics is seen as a lucrative area for developing competence for personnel (Kask, 2007).

The Asper case fits the BG definition most closely. Financially (see Figure 8.9) the current strategy choices have not yet paid off. It is still unclear how well Asper can leverage their existing knowledge of genotyping, eye disease diagnostics and marketing in order to earn significant ROI.

Comparison of Cases

None of the three companies followed their original intentions for very long. Regio switched from producing postcards and maps to GPS and LBS positioning solutions, MicroLink from PC assembly to M&A strategy in ICT systems and the services sector, whilst Asper switched from

APEX technology platform to DNA-based diagnostics. In financial terms Regio and MicroLink have been successful in the realization of their goals. In 2006 Asper was in the process of building a DNA-diagnostics service business model.

According to the POM strategy model all companies changed their products and as a result of this they also changed their operations. In all cases risk capitalists forced entrepreneurs and managers to make changes in management and/or organization structures.

Market access was realized differently: Regio's marketing is based on Ericsson's sales network, MicroLink used M&A, and Asper is building its own distributors' network.

The environment had a significant impact on access to finance and starting position. The height of the dot.com bubble in 1999 was probably a major reason why Regio and MicroLink found investment.

Post-Soviet Estonia as an environment also influenced the starting position of the entrepreneurs: neither Regio's nor Microlink's entrepreneurs had any business experience. Asper's scientists had international networking experience, but no business experience. The second round of managers at Regio, MicroLink and Asper had personal experience in international networking. MicroLink's new CEO, Allan Martinson, also had business experience in building up the Baltic News Service and attracting investment to the company from Dow Jones and the Swedish Bonnier media group in 1994.

The internationalization paths of all three companies differed, and only Asper's path matched the definition of Born Global. MicroLink and Regio had some characteristics of BG and BAG accordingly, but did not completely fit under these profiles.

CONCLUSIONS AND DISCUSSIONS

The three cases analysed support the suggestion that the IE field of research should move beyond instant internationals and SMEs (Keupp and Gassmann, 2009), and start differentiating between companies currently deemed to be BG companies. Regio had a vision and intention to become global, but it took several years to leverage different knowledge domains, build globally competitive products, and launch them rapidly on to the global market. MicroLink grew rapidly into a large company, but still continued the entrepreneurial behaviour of seeking and realizing new opportunities. Although Asper and MicroLink could both be labelled BG companies, their internationalization paths were very different.

The proposed model for mapping internationalization paths according to market extent and knowledge complexity allows the differentiation of internationalization paths, and there is potential to group BG companies according to their path shapes into more homogeneous groups. Regio's path could be labelled 'Learn Global': seeing the opportunity but lacking the means to realize it, forcing the company into intentional and focused learning for several years to develop globally appealing products and only then internationalize rapidly.

The model also allows the division of the internationalization path into periods (gradual approach) and at the same time mapping all the turns and changes in the internationalization trajectory (chaotic entrepreneurial approach). This suggests a potential for better integrating international business and entrepreneurship theories in the framework of IE.

Further research is required in order to test the model on a large number of companies and also non-technology-based companies. In the case of the latter, the complexity of knowledge should be redefined to match the non-technical background of companies. Also, in future analyses the enhanced POM-strategy model should be better integrated with the internationalization path model in order to gain deeper insight into the interrelatedness between determinants of changes in the internationalization paths.

Understanding how leverage effects can shape the internationalization paths allows companies and policy makers to choose better strategies and develop support measures for preferred internationalization paths.

NOTES

*   This research has been partially financed by the EU's Sixth Framework Programme project 'Knowledge and Competitiveness in the Enlarged EU', the Estonian Ministry of Education projects SF 0180037s08 and T0107, and the Estonian Science Foundation grant projects 5840, 6853 and 8546.
1.   Both authors contributed equally to the writing of this chapter and are cited as being mutually agreed.

BIBLIOGRAPHY

Andersen, O. (1993), 'On the internationalization process of firms: a critical analysis', *Journal of International Business Studies*, **24**(2), 209–31.
Aspelund, A., T.K. Madsem and Ø. Moen (2007), 'A review of the foundation, international marketing strategies, and performance of international new ventures', *European Journal of Marketing*, **41**(11/12), 1423–48.
Autio, E., H.J. Sapienza and J.G. Almeida (2000), 'Effects of age at entry,

knowledge intensity, and imitability on international growth', *The Academy of Management Journal* **43**(5), 909–24.

Bell, J., R. McNaughton and S. Young (2001), '"Born-again Global" firms. An extension to the "Born Global" phenomenon', *Journal of International Management*, **7**, 173–89.

Bell, J., R. McNaughton, S. Young and D. Crick (2003), 'Towards an integrative model of small firm internationalization', *Journal of International Entrepreneurship*, **1**, 339–62.

Bilkey,W.J. and G. Tesar (1977), 'The export behaviour of smaller-sized Wisconsin manufacturing firms', *Journal of International Business Studies*, **8**(1), 93–8.

Cavusgil, S.T. (1980), 'On the internationalization process of firms', *European Research*, **8** November, 272–81.

Chesbrough, H. and R.S. Rosenbloom (2002), 'The role of the business model in capturing value from innovation: evidence from Xerox Corporation's technology spin-off companies', *Industrial and Corporate Change*, **11**(3), 529–55.

Christensen, P.R. (2003), 'International entrepreneurship: a new concept and its research agenda', in E.G.i Garrigosa (ed.), *Creacion de Empresas: Homenaje al Profesor José Maria Veciana Vergas*, Barcelona: Universitat Autónoma de Barcelona, Servei de Publicacions, pp. 649–68.

Corbett, A.C. (2005), 'Experiential learning within the process of opportunity identification and exploitation', *Entrepreneurship Theory and Practice*, July, 473–91.

Coviello, N.E. (2006), 'The network dynamics of international new ventures', *Journal of International Business Studies*, **37**, 713–31.

Crainer, S. (1999), *Handbook of Management*, London: Financial Times.

Dimitratos, P., J. Johnson, J. Slow and S. Young (2003), 'Micromultinationals: new types of firms for the global competitive landscape', *European Management Journal*, **21**(2), 164–74.

Fillis, I. (2001), 'Small firm internationalization: an investigative survey and future research directions', *Management Decision*, **39**(9), 767–83.

Forsgren, M. (2002), 'The concept of learning in the Uppsala internationalization process model: a critical review', *International Business Review*, **11**(3), 257–77.

Foss, N.J. (1999), 'Edith Penrose, economics and strategic management', *Contributions to Political Economy*, **18**(1), 87–104.

Gabrielsson, M., V. Kirpalani, P. Dimitratos, C. Solberg and A. Zucchella (2008), 'Born globals: propositions to help advance the theory', *International Business Review*, **17**(4), 385–401.

Ganitsky, J. (1989), 'Strategies for innate and adoptive exporters: lessons from Israel's case', *International Marketing Review*, **6**(5), 50–65.

Hamel, G. and C.K. Prahalad (1993), 'Strategy as stretch and leverage', *Harvard Business Review*, March–April, 75–84.

Hedlund, G. and A. Kverneland (1985), 'Are strategies for foreign markets changing? The case of Swedish investment in Japan', *International Studies of Management & Organization*, **15**(2), 41–59.

Hitt, M.A., R.D. Ireland, S.M. Camp and D.L. Sexton (2001), 'Strategic entrepreneurship: entrepreneurial strategies for wealth creation', *Strategic Management Journal*, **22**, 479–91.

Jagomägi, T. (2005), *Teet Jagomägi*, Curriculum Vitae for the Seminar for 'Äripäev', 24 March.

Johanson, J. and J.-E. Vahlne (1977), 'The internationalization process of the firm:

a model of knowledge development and increasing foreign market commitments', *Journal of International Business Studies*, **8**(1), 23–32.

Johanson, J. and J.-E. Vahlne (1990), 'The mechanism of internationalization', *International Marketing Review*, **7**(4), 23–32.

Johanson, J. and F. Wiedersheim-Paul (1975), 'The internationalization of the firm: four Swedish cases', *Journal of Management Studies*, **12**, 305–22.

Jones, M.V. (1999), 'The internationalization of small high-technology firms', *Journal of International Marketing*, **7**(4), 15–41.

Kask, I. (2007), *Interview*, 20 July, by Kalev Kaarna.

Keupp, M.M. and O. Gassmann (2009), 'The past and the future of international entrepreneurship: a review and suggestions for developing the field', *Journal of Management*, **35**(3), 600–633.

Kodres, G. (2006), 'Internationalization of Estonian technology-intensive sector: the case of three companies', Master's thesis in Entrepreneurship and Technology Management, Tartu: University of Tartu.

Kokk, A. (2001), 'MicroLinki suur dilemma', *Director*, 7, pp. 8–14.

Kundu, Sumit K. and J.A. Katz (2003), 'Born-Internationals SMEs: BI-level impacts of resources and intentions', *Small Business Economics*, **20**, 25–47.

Lee, C., K. Lee and J.M. Pennings (2001), 'Internal capabilities, external networks, and performance: a study of technology-based ventures', *Strategic Management Journal*, **22**(6/7), 615–40.

Luostarinen, R. and M. Gabrielsson (2004), 'Finnish perspectives of international entrepreneurship', in L.-P. Dana (ed.), *Handbook of Research on International Entrepreneurship*, Cheltenham, UK and Northampton, MA, USA: Edward Elgar, pp. 383–403.

Madsen, T.K. and P. Servais (1997), 'The internationalization of Born Globals: an evolutionary process?', *International Business Review*, **6**(6), 561–83.

Mathews, J.A. and I. Zander (2007), 'The international entrepreneurial dynamics of accelerated internationalization', *Journal of International Business Studies*, **38**, 1–17.

McAuley, A. (1999), 'Entrepreneurial instant exporters in the Scottish arts and crafts sector', *Journal of International Marketing*, **7**(4), 67–82.

McDougall, P.P., S. Shane and B.P. Oviatt (1994), 'Explaining the formation of international new ventures: the limits of theories from international business research', *Journal of Business Venturing*, **9**(6), 469–87.

McDougall, P.P. and B.M. Oviatt (2000), 'International entrepreneurship: the intersection of two research paths', *Academy of Management Journal*, **43**, 902–908.

Mets, T. (2008), 'Regio – a learned global knowledge company: case from Estonia', in R. Aidis and F. Welter (eds), *The Cutting Edge: Innovation and Entrepreneurship in New Europe*, Cheltenham, UK and Northampton, MA, USA: Edward Elgar, pp. 54–73.

Mets, T. (2009), 'Creating a global business model for knowledge-intensive SMEs: the small transition country cases', *Economics & Management*, **14**, 466–75.

MicroLink, (2005). 'Closing of purchase of IT-provider *MicroLink*', press release 30 November, available at: http://www.telekom.ee/index.php?lk=1004&uudis=209 (accessed 30 December 2009).

Moen, Ø., R. Sørheim and T. Erikson (2008), 'Born Global firms and informal investors: examining investor characteristics', *Journal of Small Business Management*, **46**(4), 536–49.

Noorkõiv, R. (2006), *Interview*, 8 December, by T. Mets.
Oviatt, B.M. and P.P. McDougall (1994), 'Toward a theory of international new ventures', *Journal of International Business Studies*, **25**(1), 45–64.
Oviatt, B.M. and P.P. McDougall (1995), 'Global start-ups: entrepreneurs on a worldwide stage', *Academy of Management Executive*, **9**(2), 30–43.
Oviatt, B.M. and P.P. McDougall (2005), 'The internationalization of entrepreneurship', *Journal of International Business Studies*, **36**, 2–8.
Penrose, E.T. (1959), *The Theory of the Growth of the Firm*, Oxford: Basil Blackwell.
Politis, D. (2005), 'The process of entrepreneurial learning: a conceptual framework', *Entrepreneurship Theory and Practice*, July, 399–424.
Püttsepp, J. (1997), 'Teet Jagomägi: Olen Kasvanud Kaartide Sees', *Postimees*, 17 September.
Reid, D. (2000), 'Money is no issue', *Central European*, **10**(2), March, 15.
Reid, S. (1983), 'Managerial and firm influence of export behaviour', *Journal of the Academy of Marketing Science*, **11**(3), 323–32.
Rennie, M.W. (1993), 'Global competitiveness: Born Global', *McKinsey Quarterly*, **4**, 45–52.
Rialp, A., J. Rialp and G.A. Knight (2005), 'The phenomenon of early internationalizing firms: what do we know after a decade (1993–2003) of scientific inquiry?', *International Business Review*, **14**(2), 147–66.
Rozental, V. (2002a), 'Teet Jagomägi: Regio tagasi ostmine oli hea tehing', *Äripäev online*, 18 March 2002, available at: http://www.ap3.ee/Print.aspx?PublicationId=0f3f62f5-3bc4-4301-8c82-3c8718e41881 (accessed 30 December 2009).
Rozental, V. (2002b), 'Jagomägi ostis Regio pankrotipesast välja', *Äripäev Online*, 19 March 2002, available at: http://www.ap3.ee/?PublicationId=31503ED6-39D4-4163-9D98-74AA1E3959CE&code=2121/uud_uudidx_212104 (accessed 30 December 2009).
Senge, P. (1990), *The Fifth Discipline: The Art and Practice of the Learning Organization*, Sydney: Random House.
Shane, S. and S. Venkataraman (2000), 'The promise of entrepreneurship as a field of research', *Academy of Management Review*, **25**, 217–26.
Shrader, R.C., B.M. Oviatt and P.P. McDougall (2000), 'How new ventures exploit trade-offs among international risk factors: lessons for the accelerated internationalization of the 21st century', *Academy of Management Journal*, **43**(6), 1227–47.
TBT (2007), 'Latvian firms after world market share', TBT 28 May 2007, available at: www.baltictimes.com/news/articles/17612/ (accessed 30 December 2009).
Thompson, J.L. (2001), *Strategic Management*, 4th edn, London: Thomson Learning.
Turnbull, P. (1987), 'A challenge to the stages theory of the internationalization process', in P.J. Rosson and S.D. Reid (eds), *Managing Export Entry and Expansion*, New York: Praeger, pp. 21–40.
Walmsley, K. (2004), 'Partner profile: Reach-U connects with success', 2 December 2004, available at: http://www.ericsson.com/mobilityworld/sub/articles/case_studies/04dec01 (accessed 30 December 2009).

9. Exploring firm growth as a process of creation

Tuija Mainela, Vesa Puhakka and Sakari Sipola*

INTRODUCTION

Firm growth is regarded as one of the key issues in economic development of nations, and growth is at the top of the target list in many companies (Haour, 2005). In practice, some firms manage to achieve temporary spurts of growth but are not able to keep up a sustained, profitable growth process (Christensen and Raynor, 2003). This is especially true in high-technology industries where technological change is considered to be one of the main drivers of growth (Schumpeter, 1934; Solow, 1956; Romer, 1986). During the turn of the millennium great expectations were placed on the growth potential of new technology firms (See Hoch et al., 1999; Messerschmitt and Szyperski, 2003). However, technological uncertainty and other industry characteristics caused many of them to fail and expectations were proven too optimistic.

On these grounds it is not surprising that firm growth has attracted a lot of interest among researchers (see Davidsson and Wiklund, 1999; Delmar et al., 2003). Many theories about the growth of the firm have been proposed since Penrose (1959) depicted hers, but none of them has been widely approved by the academic society (Barringer et al., 2005; Davidsson et al., 2006). On the basis of prior research we know about quite a variety of different factors and mechanisms that have influence on firm growth but as a whole our knowledge is limited and fragmented (Delmar, 1997).

To advance our understanding of firm growth more attention should be paid to the consideration of the nature of growth as a phenomenon and research object. Researchers tend to approach growth as a linear phenomenon that can be described through natural law like causal relationships and measured through numeric values that grow in value over time. Consequently, we are able to measure growth but cannot explain why, where and how firms grow (Davidsson et al., 2006). However, growth could also be seen as a multilayered change process where growth is created by entities acting in events, which create even the phenomenon itself along time (Van de Ven and Poole, 2005). Research based on process epistemology searches for necessary causality, generalization based on versatility and flexibility of explanations, temporal order and discontinuations of explanations and layers of causalities (Langley, 1999; Van de Ven and Poole, 2002, 2005). Therefore, studying growth is not only a methodological issue (see Davidsson et al., 2006) but an ontological and epistemological issue concerning how to approach the organizing behaviour of human beings (Van de Ven and Poole, 1995, 2005).

In the present study, we contribute to research on firm growth in three particular ways. First, we demonstrate that firm growth is inherently about change and thus should be approached using processual methods. Secondly, we suggest that firm growth consists of interlaced behaviours to act on or enact an opportunity that form the generative mechanisms driving the creation of growth. Thirdly, we argue that growth is a process embedded in a particular context. This way we bring new knowledge on how firm growth can be conceptualized and approached. We propose that new understanding on firm growth could be achieved through examining processually over time the different kinds of opportunity-driven behaviours of the firm in relation to its environment. Our modelling of firm growth emphasizes type of opportunity, entrepreneurial behaviours for its realization and contextual determinants, dynamism and episodic nature of firm development. In the end, our conceptualization offers insight into how firms learn and develop capabilities for creating and sustaining competitiveness in rapidly changing and uncertain modern business environments.

The chapter is structured as follows: in the second section we analyse prior research on firm growth and elaborate on firm growth as a process of creation. In the third section we build a conceptual model and develop propositions of firm growth. We conclude with discussion on the applicability of the model in future research on firm growth.

REVISITING GROWTH RESEARCH

Growth of entrepreneurial firms has been under the spotlight in a number of studies (see reviews in Delmar, 1997; Davidsson and Wiklund, 1999). The discussion as a whole can be described as a complex one starting from the point that growth as a multifaceted phenomenon (Delmar et al., 2003) has made researchers constantly make new definitions for growth. Different definitions, in turn, have created a great diversity of studied variables. In the end, there is considerable lack of reliability and comparability of the results and fragmentation of previous research. Zahra et al. (2006) conclude that as a whole 'the previous research has not provided a compelling explanation for the ability of some new and established companies to continuously create, define, discover and exploit entrepreneurial opportunities'.

Recent entrepreneurship research can actually be seen to lead us to approach firm growth as a process of entrepreneurial opportunity discovery and enactment (Eckhardt and Shane, 2003; Sarasvathy, 2001; Shane and Venkataraman, 2000). As seen in the review by Barringer et al. (2005) this viewpoint is rare in research on firm growth. Instead, elements like founder characteristics, firm attributes, business practices and human resource management practices have been connected to firm growth. For example, entrepreneurial orientation is a firm attribute that has been linked with founders' motivation to grow their businesses and then the likelihood of growth to be realized (Wiklund, 1998; Wiklund and Shepherd, 2005). Firm growth is typically defined as growth in some quantities that describe the firm (Penrose, 1959), such as growth of sales (for example Autio et al., 2000; Barringer et al., 2005) or growth of personnel (for example Greiner, 1972). Connected to these measures, prior studies on firm growth have mostly applied the positivistic, variance-based methods. This kind of research aims at explaining and predicting what happens in a social reality by searching natural law like regularities and causality within research phenomenon (see Burrell and Morgan, 1979).

On the other hand, it has been emphasized that most phenomena in the social world take place in spatiotemporal open systems in which events do not follow a determined and recurrent pattern (Tsoukas, 1989). This makes it difficult to find general causalities and patterns of growth that would be applicable on the firm level. To overcome this problem, some research has applied a process approach on growth studying different overlapping episodes that are not tied to certain sequence of execution or time in a firm's life-cycle (for example Tsoukas and Chia, 2002; Barringer et al., 2005). This moves the focus from static description of growth towards analyses of growth as a spatiotemporal process including different behavioural processes. We apply the latter definition of growth stressing the behaviours of the involved individuals and the emergent nature of growth. This way of seeing growth offers a basis for a real-time study of how and why firms grow (Davidsson and Wiklund, 1999).

In addition to emphasizing the processual approach to growth, we stress global industries and international markets as the most typical context for growth of high-tech firms. High-tech business is one of the major drivers of innovation and economic growth. By definition the high-tech firms produce products and services with leading-edge technologies (see for example Bell, 1995). This typically means that the firms are highly specialized, high quality producers with products having short life cycles and specialized niche markets spread thinly across the world (Bell, 1995; Crick and Jones, 1998; Madsen and Servais, 1997). High-tech business, however, is not only about commercialization of new technologies, but more broadly about the interplay between new technologies and the business context in which business processes and ways of organizing new ventures are constantly redefined (Carayannis et al., 2006). High-tech business is, therefore, malleable and there is no single route to growth, but the actions of the involved actors co-produce the outcome (Liao et al., 2005).

In sum, we propose that growth research should examine how growth comes into existence through entrepreneurial behaviours in a dynamic business environment in an attempt to combine technological innovations with new venture creation to add new economic value. To create further understanding of the emergence of high-tech firm growth we focus, in the following, on the types of business opportunities (for example Sarasvathy et al., 2002), the types of entrepreneurial behaviours (for example Liao et al., 2005) and certain contextual issues (for example Zahra, 2007) as the determinants of high-tech firm growth.

MODEL DEVELOPMENT

In this part of the chapter we present the theoretical elements that constitute the basis for the conceptual model of firm growth as an emergent process of creation. The elements are based on prior research on entrepreneurship, organizational change and firm growth. There are not many studies which aim to build a comprehensive view on firm growth. We depict firm growth as a process of creation instead of focusing on the relationships between single variables in measurable growth. Recently, Davidsson (2003) has provided a similar kind of holistic view to entrepreneurship literature and Barringer et al. (2005) on growth studies. Our framework consists of (1) types of opportunities; (2) types of growth behaviours; (3) contextual issues of resources, strategizing practices and environment; and (4) the outcome of the process. The presented conceptualization of firm growth emphasizes the multidimensionality, emergent nature and context-dependence of firm growth.

There are some basic assumptions that must be stated before explaining the framework in detail. First of all, we see entrepreneurial process as an integrated aspect of the growth process. Entrepreneurship can be understood as new venture creation both in an existing firm and in a new firm

(Amit et al., 1993). In both cases it is a question of by whom, how and with what consequences opportunities to bring into existence future goods and services are discovered and exploited (Shane and Venkataraman, 2000; Venkataraman, 1997). This is directly connected to the importance of examining the opportunity-driven behaviours of involved actors in the creation of growth. Furthermore, the firm behaviour is strongly related to its business environment and therefore it is necessary to study the emergence of growth in a certain context. All the decisions are made in relation to the business environment based on the available information at that moment.

Type of business opportunity is directly interlinked with the method of opportunity exploitation and related growth behaviours of the firm (Sarasvathy et al., 2002; Saemundsson and Dahlstrand, 2005). First, if the initial situation (for example technology) and the goal (for example target market) are both known, the opportunity needs to be recognized. The process of recognizing the opportunity is rational, based on decision-making in a given problem-solving space, and typically there is a question of refining existing solutions. The role of the entrepreneur is to behave as an improver of the existing situation. The outcome, when recognized and realized, is clear and visible and in some sense past-oriented. Second, when either initial situation (technology) or the goal (market) is unknown, the opportunity is more open and needs to be discovered. The process of discovering an opportunity is about solution-making, discovering the most suitable option and decision-making in a semi-complicated situation. The task is to discover logic between the existing, but scattered, pieces of information and the role of an entrepreneur is to be a developer of a workable solution. The outcome of opportunity discovery is present-oriented and can be seen as a new solution to an existing situation. The third type of opportunity involves an unknown starting point as well as an unknown end-result and the opportunity needs to be created through inventions. These kinds of business opportunities are, thus, not yet open because some of the elements are not yet possible or compatible with other elements. The process of creating an opportunity is about creating new realities along the way and about sense-making and social construction of the situation. The creation of growth through opportunity-driven behaviours in relation to different types of opportunities is summarized in Table 9.1.

In the classification of the business opportunities there is primarily the question of the novelty of the business opportunity. Novelty, in turn, is evaluated in relation to the business environment. Sarasvathy et al. (2002) emphasize the uncertainty of the business environment as the main feature influencing the entrepreneur's behaviour (see also Vesalainen and Pihkala, 1996). In opportunity recognition uncertainty is rather low and the future can be forecast up to a certain point. What the organization

Table 9.1   Process of growth creation in relation to type of opportunity

	Opportunity recognition	Opportunity discovery	Opportunity creation
Opportunity	Business opportunities, which exist and are open for exploitation or have to be refined	Business opportunities, which are open but some of the elements wait to be discovered	Business opportunities, which are not yet open because some of the elements are not yet possible or compatible with existing elements
Behaviours	Refining existing Rational analysis Decision-making in a given problem-solving space Searching inefficiencies from the existing businesses and trying to operate more efficiently than others	Solution-making Need-finding Discovering the most suitable option Decision-making	Creating new realities Creating along the way Learning by doing Sense-making
Outcome	Past-oriented Clear and visible solutions 'This is what customers need and how more value can be created to them'	Present-oriented New solutions to existing problems New applications for existing solutions Existing realities are often difficult to perceive 'What this is all about?'	Future-oriented New realities No best or most suitable solution No predetermined form of value creation 'What is going to be real in 10 years or so?'

needs to do is a roadmap that minimizes future risks and guarantees the planned business actions. In opportunity discovery, uncertainty of the environment is moderate and there is a chance to invent an opportunity through strategic thinking and maybe trial and error to find new ways of working. In opportunity creation, both supply and demand sides of the opportunity are unknown. Uncertainty of the environment is high and the role of the entrepreneur is to behave as a challenger and a web-weaver of various interests. The outcomes are future-oriented new realities of which it is impossible to say if they are the best or the most suitable solutions. As the opportunity is only to emerge, its outcome is also to be seen over time. The prediction of the future and setting of goals are secondary activities. Instead opportunities consist primarily of ideas, beliefs and needs that evolve along the journey towards an emerging goal. We propose the following relationships to drive the creation of growth:

P1:   Firm growth is a process of creation, in which the type of the opportunity is intertwined with the behaviours for its realization.

P2:   The more novel the business opportunity as interpreted in relation to the business environment, the more the creation of growth is a process of sense-making and creation of influence without knowledge of future.

On the basis of the opportunity type, entrepreneurs and their businesses become related to specific other actors in the business environment and as well develop the opportunity as a response to actions of others in the environment (Davidsson, 2003). Capability to create unique customer value is often emphasized in growth of high-tech firms especially (Hoch et al., 1999; Kim and Mauborgne, 1997), but as important can be the social and professional relationships of the entrepreneur that provide information, support and a basis for learning (Johannisson, 1990). Entrepreneurs gather information about development of the business environment on a broad and narrow scale by investigating products and services on the markets, their distribution channels, competitors and upcoming trends (Cadotte and Woodruff, 1994). Entrepreneurs try to find gaps and niches that are not crowded by competitors but still big enough business-wise (De Koning and Muzyka, 1996). They search information through behaviours, such as environmental scanning (for example Aguilar, 1967; Miller, 1983; De Koning and Muzyka, 1996), proactive searching (for example Cooper, 1981; Christensen et al., 1994; Hills, 1995) and innovative behaviour (for example Gilad, 1984; Peterson, 1985). Information through this kind of activities is needed to be able to react to or predict environmental changes (McKee et al., 1989).

P3:   The creation of growth is a process of acting in response to changes in environment as well as to create change in the environment.

The identification and effectuation of new opportunities is crucial for continued growth (Penrose, 1959; Sarasvathy, 2001). In relation to these

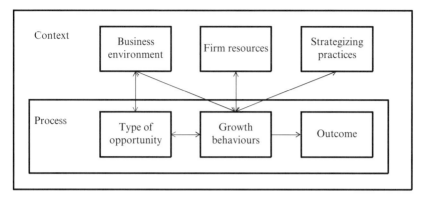

Figure 9.1   Proposed model of firm growth as a process of creation

behaviours entrepreneurs network to access various resources (Garnsey, 1998) as well as coordinating the resources to create multiple innovations (Brown and Eisenhardt, 1997) and establish the core competences of the firm (Hamel and Prahalad, 1990). Especially important resources that form the basis for growth behaviours have been seen in the characteristics of individuals, such as prior industry experience in the same industry as the current business (MacMillan and Day, 1987; Siegel et al., 1993), technical and market knowledge (Autio and Lumme, 1998), educational background (Cooper and Gimeno-Gascon, 1992), broadness of social network (Shaw and Conway, 2000) and attitude towards change (Tsoukas and Chia, 2002). In the end all the involved individuals form a collection of resources for the creation of growth (Penrose, 1959). The resources also develop and take shape during the activities. A firm typically aligns its usage of resources in the strategy (Grant, 1991), which reflects the level of entrepreneurial orientation in the firm (Wiklund and Shepherd, 2005), the importance of seeking growth (Kim and Mauborgne, 1997) as well as the future vision (Brown and Eisenhardt, 1997). It also matters whether the firm thinks mainly through causation or effectuation processes (Sarasvathy, 2001). The related strategizing practices influence time and effort used to search for opportunities to grow.

P4:   Resources as a basis for growth are a flexible collection of internal and external, individual and firm-level assets to be used in need.

P5:   Strategizing practices of a firm are related to the extent of growth-orientated behaviours of a firm.

Above we have described and proposed certain features for firm growth as a process of creation. We summarize the model in Figure 9.1.

Finally, we need to discuss the outcome of the proposed context-embedded behavioural process. We see organizations as human, social processes that inherently involve change, develop over time and create timeless internal identities (Van de Ven and Poole, 2005; Rehn et al., 2007). Further, we lean on Sarasvathy's (2001) notion that organizations are merely means-driven rather than goal-driven and therefore it is the meaning-building rather than goal achievement that we should understand also in relation to growth. Therefore, the outcome that is of interest in this kind of growth research is the continuous renewal and change through which the organization can be seen to create and re-create itself over time (Tsoukas and Chia, 2002). Then firm growth is a social construction of emergence and re-emergence of an organization with different features that are connected to economic value creation as narrated by the involved individuals (Van de Ven and Poole, 2005).

P6:   Outcome of the process of growth is a changing manifestation of a firm's ability to create and re-create economic value in a dynamic business context.

Our conceptualization of firm growth builds primarily on the interlaced behaviours to act on or enact an opportunity. These opportunity-driven behaviours form the generative mechanisms driving the creation of growth. They are the microprocesses that create change in the organization (Tsoukas and Chia, 2002). It is important to see the elements and propositions as dynamic in nature. The context in which the creation of economic value happens is changing, and thus growth is the embodiment of the resource configurations that are also likely to change. Growth as an outcome is therefore a result of the growth creation process as manifested in the behaviours and value propositions of that moment.

DISCUSSION

In the present chapter we have attempted to model firm growth as a process of creation. We conceptualized growth as an opportunity-driven behavioural process that is embedded in a particular, dynamic context. Our modelling of firm growth calls for research designs that allow for processual examination of growth at the level of behaviours by individuals. For future research we suggested four primary theoretical elements and their interaction to create the growth-creating process. The contents of these elements are unique in every firm because there are different kinds of resources, information, skills and ways of behaving involved (cf. Hayek, 1945). In the end, every firm has its own way of creating growth and that is what should be of interest to us. There is not one model which could describe growth in such a way that it would be right for every company (cf. Davidsson, 2003).

Our modelling of firm growth enables examination of growth as an integral part of entrepreneurship and takes place as a result of entrepreneurial behaviour. It builds on the behaviours to search for, discover, effectuate and enact business opportunities, which has been seen as the core of entrepreneurship (Shane and Venkataraman, 2000).

The model is applicable in research that approaches growth as an emergent process of creation over time instead of seeing growth as a measurable feature of an organization. Our capability to measure growth as the number of personnel or amount of sales should be supported by understanding of the underlying mechanisms that produce the growth creation process of the moment. The search for the generative mechanisms driving the growth creation is the core of our modelling and the suggested processual research approach on firm growth. It is connected to a view that past growth does not predict future growth; growth is not a general law-like phenomenon. It is also because the dynamism of present-day business environments requires constant renewal from the firms, and the competitive advantages are only temporal. Therefore, it is important to try to dig deeper into what kinds of mechanisms are actually beneath growth creation. In our view firm growth is more about reciprocal relationships and interplay between certain elements than it is about causal relationships between certain variables.

The importance of context implies that at one point in time the capabilities and factors behind competitiveness that created growth are an embodiment of that spatiotemporal situation between firms, markets and growth behaviours. This situation is always dynamic and after a period of time, the outcome, measurable growth, is related to different, re-defined or renewed, configurations of capabilities, resources and practices in relation to opportunities that are evaluated and enacted in a social dialogue.

Growth behaviour of a firm can be expressed in many ways because it depends on firm-specific content of theoretical elements in the framework. The essential thing for a firm is to recognize different mechanisms such as organizational learning and different information-gathering behaviours, and to build an environment with these mechanisms. This builds the standing point and environment in which the growth behaviour can take place. The behaviour occurs relative to the firm's physical and immaterial resources, which offer many possibilities but at the same time set up constraints to their execution. In this case, the growth behaviour can consist of removing those constraints or trying to find new opportunities. This highlights the firm's ability to create and exploit opportunities, which can be thought to be at the core of growth creation. It can be proposed that the theoretical framework illustrates the symbiosis between the behaviour and resources. The former creates and exploits opportunities and the latter makes them possible to execute.

The study will have implications for both scholars and practitioners. Scholars can develop the presented theoretical elements further and conduct empirical research with the help of the propositions on the nature of the growth-creation process. This would build the idea of opportunity-driven growth-generating behaviours. Practitioners can consider their behaviours and processes in relation to the conceptual framework and maybe start to question and further develop their current practices. The conceptual model is not strongly industry-specific although high-tech industries have been emphasized. Therefore, we could suggest the model to allow for examination of many kinds of growth creation processes in any business context characterized by dynamism.

NOTE

*   The authors have contributed equally to the chapter. The financial support of the Foundation for Economic Education is gratefully acknowledged.

REFERENCES

Aguilar, F.J. (1967), *Scanning the Business Environment*, New York: Macmillan Co.
Amit, R., L. Glosten and E. Muller (1993), 'Challenges to theory development in entrepreneurship research', *Journal of Management Studies*, **30**(5), 815–34.
Autio, E. and A. Lumme (1998), 'Does the innovator role affect the perceived potential for growth? Analysis of four types of new, technology-based firms', *Technology Analysis & Strategic Management*, **10**(1), 41–54.
Autio, E., H. Sapienza and J. Almeida (2000), 'Effects of age at entry, knowledge intensity, and imitability on international growth', *Academy of Management of Journal*, **43**, 909–24.
Barringer, B., F. Jones and D. Neubaum (2005), 'A quantitative content analysis of the characteristics of rapid-growth firms and their founders', *Journal of Business Venturing*, **20**(5), 663–87.
Bell, J. (1995), 'The internationalization of small computer software firms. A further challenge to "stage" theories', *European Journal of Marketing*, **29**(8), 60–75.

Brown, S. and K. Eisenhardt (1997), 'The art of continuous change: linking complexity theory and time-paced evolution in rentlessly shifting organisations', *Administrative Science Quarterly*, **42**(1), 1–34.

Burrell, G. and G. Morgan (1979), *Sociological Paradigms and Organizational Analysis*, London: Heinemann.

Cadotte, E. and R. Woodruff (1994), 'Analysing market opportunities for new ventures', in G. Hills (ed.), *Marketing and Entrepreneurship: Research Ideas and Opportunities*, Westport, CT: Greenwood Press.

Carayannis, E., D. Popescu, C. Sipp and M. Stewart (2006), 'Technological learning for entrepreneurial development (TL4ED) in the knowledge economy (KE): case studies and lessons learned', *Technovation*, **26**(4), 419–43.

Christensen, C. and M. Raynor (2003), *Innovator's Solution*, Cambridge, MA: Harvard University Press.

Christensen, P.S., O.O. Madsen and R. Peterson (1994), 'Conceptualizing entrepreneurial opportunity identification', in G. Hills (ed.), *Marketing and Entrepreneurship: Research Ideas and Opportunities*, Westport, CT: Greenwood Press.

Cooper, A.C. (1981), 'Strategic management: new ventures and small business', *Long Range Planning*, **14**(5), 39–45.

Cooper, A.C. and F.J. Gimeno-Gascon (1992), 'Entrepreneurs, processes of founding and new firm performance', in D. Sexton and J. Kasarda (eds), *The State of the Art in Entrepreneurship*, Boston, MA: PWS Publishing.

Crick, D. and M. Jones (1998), 'Design and innovation strategies within "successful" high tech firms', *Marketing Intelligence & Planning*, **17**(3), 161–8.

Davidsson, P. (2003), 'The domain of entrepreneurship research: some suggestions', in J. Katz and D. Shepherd (eds), *Advances in Entrepreneurship, Firm Emergence and Growth (Volume 6): Cognitive Approaches to Entrepreneurship Research*, New York: Elsevier.

Davidsson, P., F. Delmar and J. Wiklund (2006), *Entrepreneurship and the Growth of Firms*, Cheltenham, UK and Northampton, MA, USA: Edward Elgar.

Davidsson, P. and J. Wiklund (1999), 'Theoretical and methodological issues in the study of firm growth', Jönköping International Business School, *Working Paper Series, 1999-6*.

De Koning, A. and D. Muzyka (1996), 'The convergence of good ideas: when and how do entrepreneurial managers recognize innovative business ideas?', in N. Churchill, W. Bygrave, J. Butler, S. Birley, P. Davidsson, W. Gartner and P. McDougall (eds), *Frontiers of Entrepreneurship Research*, Wellesley, MA: Babson College.

Delmar, F. (1997), 'Measuring growth: methodological considerations and empirical results', in R. Donckels and A. Miettinen (eds), *Entrepreneurship and SME Research: On Its Way to the Next Millennium*, Brookfield, VA: Aldershot.

Delmar F., P. Davidsson and W.B. Gartner (2003), 'Arriving at the high-growth firm', *Journal of Business Venturing*, **18**(2), 189–216.

Eckhardt, J.T. and S. Shane (2003), 'Opportunities and entrepreneurship', *Journal of Management*, **29**(3), 333–49.

Garnsey, E. (1998), 'A theory of the early growth of the firm', *Industrial and Corporate Change*, **13**(3), 523–56.

Gilad, B. (1984), 'Entrepreneurship: the issue of creativity in the market place', *Journal of Creative Behavior*, **18**(3), 151–61.

Grant, R.M. (1991), 'The resource-based theory of competitive advantage: implications for strategy formulation', *California Management Review*, **33**(2), 114–35.

Greiner, L.E. (1972), 'Evolution and revolution as organizations grow', *Harvard Business Review*, **50**(4), 37–45.

Hamel, G. and C.K. Prahalad (1990), 'The core competence of the corporation', *Harvard Business Review*, **68**(3), 79–91.

Haour, G. (2005), 'Israel, a powerhouse for networked entrepreneurship', *International Journal of Entrepreneurship and Innovation Management*, **5**(1/2), 39–48.

Hayek, F.A. (1945), 'The use of knowledge in society', *American Economic Review*, **35**(4), 519–30.

Hills, G. (1995), 'Opportunity recognition by successful entrepreneurs: a pilot study', in M. Hay, W. Bygrave, S. Birley, N. Churchill, R. Keeley, B. and W. Wetzel, Jr. (eds), *Frontiers of Entrepreneurship Research*, Wellesley, MA: Babson College.

Hoch, D.J, C.R. Roeding, G. Purkert, S.K. Lindner and R. Mueller (1999), *Secrets of Software Success: Management Insights from 100 Software Firms around the World*, Boston: Harvard Business School Press.

Johannisson, B. (1990), 'Economies of overview-guiding the external growth of small firms', *International Small Business Journal*, **9**(1), 32–44.

Kim, W.C. and R. Mauborgne (1997), 'Value innovation: the strategic logic of high growth', *Harvard Business Review*, **75**(1), 102–12.

Langley, A. (1999), 'Strategies for theorizing from process data', *Academy of Management Review*, **24**(4), 691–710.

Liao, J., H. Welsch and W.-L. Tan (2005), 'Venture gestation paths of nascent entrepreneurs: exploring the temporal patterns', *Journal of High Technology Management Research*, **16**, 1–22.

MacMillan, I.C. and D.L. Day (1987), 'Corporate ventures into industrial markets: dynamics of aggressive entry', *Journal of Business Venturing*, **2**(1), 29–39.

Madsen, T. and P. Servais (1997), 'The internationalization of born globals: an evolutionary process?', *International Business Review*, **6**(6), 561–83.

McKee, D.O., P.R. Varadarajan and W.M. Pride (1989), 'Strategic adaptability and firm performance: a market-contingent perspective', *Journal of Marketing*, **53**(3), 21–35.

Messerschmitt, D.G. and C. Szyperski (2003), *Software Ecosystem: Understanding an Indispensable Technology and Industry*, Cambridge, MA: MIT Press.

Miller, D. (1983), 'The correlates of entrepreneurship in three types of firms', *Management Science*, **29**, 770–91.

Penrose, E.T. (1959), *The Theory of the Growth of the Firm*, Oxford: Oxford University Press.

Peterson, R. (1985), 'Creating contexts for new ventures in stagnating environments', in J. Hordanay, E. Shils, J. Timmons and K. Vesper (eds), *Frontiers of Entrepreneurship Research*, Wellesley, MA: Babson College.

Rehn, A., L. Strannegård and K. Tryggestad (2007), 'Putting process through its paces', *Scandinavian Journal of Management*, **23**(3), 229–32.

Romer, P.M. (1986), 'Increasing returns and long-run growth', *Journal of Political Economy*, **94**(5), 1002–37.

Saemundsson, R. and Å. Dahlstrand (2005), 'How business opportunities constrain young technology-based firms from growing into medium-sized firms', *Small Business Economics*, **24**, 113–29.

Sarasvathy, S. (2001), 'Causation and effectuation: toward a theoretical shift from economic inevitability to entrepreneurial contingency', *Academy of Management Review*, **26**(2), 243–88.

Sarasvathy, S, N. Dew R. Velamuri and S. Venkataraman (2002), 'Three views of entrepreneurial opportunity', in Z.J. Acs and D.B. Audretsch (eds), *Entrepreneurship Handbook*, Boston/Dordrect: Kluwer Academic Publishers.

Schumpeter, J.A. (1934), *The Theory of Economic Development*, Cambridge, MA: Harvard University Press.

Shane, S. and S. Venkataraman (2000), 'The promise of entrepreneurship as a field of research', *Academy of Management Review*, **25**(1), 217–26.

Shaw, E. and S. Conway (2000), 'Networking and the small firm', in S. Carter and D. Jones-Evans (eds), *Enterprise and Small Business*, Harlow: Prentice Hall.

Siegel, R., E. Siegel and I.C. MacMillan (1993), 'Characteristics distinguishing high-growth ventures', *Journal of Business Venturing*, **8**(2), 169–80.

Solow, R.M. (1956), 'A contribution to the theory of economic growth', *Quarterly Journal of Economics*, **70**, 65–94.

Tsoukas, H. (1989), 'The validity of idiographic research explanations', *Academy of Management Review*, **14**(4), 551–61.

Tsoukas, H. and R. Chia (2002), 'On organisational becoming: rethinking organisational change', *Organisation Science*, **13**(5), 567–82.

Van de Ven, A. and M.S. Poole (1995), 'Explaining development and change in organisations', *Academy of Management Review*, **20**, 510–40.

Van de Ven, A. and M.S. Poole (2002), 'Field research methods', in J. Baum (ed), *Companion to Organizations*, Oxford: Blackwell Publishers.

Van de Ven, A. and M.S. Poole (2005), 'Alternative approaches for studying organisational change', *Organisation Studies*, **27**(11), 1617–38.

Venkataraman, S. (1997), 'The distinctive domain of entrepreneurship research: an editor's perspective', in J. Katz and R. Brockhaus (eds), *Advances in Entrepreneurship, Firm Emergence and Growth*. Greenwich, CT: JAI Press.

Vesalainen, J. and T. Pihkala (1996), 'Perceived barriers to innovation in Finland', paper presented at the 26th European Small Business Seminar, Vaasa, Finland.

Wiklund, J. (1998), 'Entrepreneurial orientation as predictor of entrepreneurial behaviour and performance in small firms: longitudinal evidence', in P.D. Reynolds, W.B. Bygrave, N.M. Carter, S. Manigart, C.M. Mason, G.D. Meyer and K.G. Shaver (eds), *Frontiers of Entrepreneurship Research*, Wellesley, MA: Babson College.

Wiklund, J. and D. Shepherd (2005), 'Entrepreneurial orientation and small business performance: a configurational approach', *Journal of Business Venturing*, **20**, 71–91.

Zahra, S.A. (2007), 'Contextualizing theory building in entrepreneurship research', *Journal of Business Venturing*, **22**, 443–52.

Zahra, S.A., H. Sapienza and P. Davidsson (2006), 'Entrepreneurship and dynamic capabilities: a review, model and research agenda', *Journal of Management Studies*, **43**(4), 917–55.

10. The influence of organizational characteristics on intentions of employees towards corporate entrepreneurship

Olga Belousova*

INTRODUCTION

Corporate entrepreneurship (CE) is often recognized as beneficial for organizations. In a race for newness and diversity, modern companies employ an entrepreneurial approach to their strategies (Kuratko et al., 2005). Indeed, being innovative, risk-taking and ready to pioneer has proved to contribute well to the financial performance and strategic value of big corporations as well as small and medium enterprises (Covin and Slevin, 1989; Dess et al., 1997; Lumpkin and Dess, 2001; Wiklund and Shepherd, 2005).

Therefore, we are interested in learning more about the way organizations become more innovative and entrepreneurial. More specifically, we are eager to understand how organizations stimulate such behaviours among their employees. Indeed, individual innovation behaviour is recognized as crucial in fostering continued entrepreneurship (Aldrich, 1999).

In this chapter we focus on factors *within* the organization that influence employees' decisions to engage in entrepreneurial behaviours. One way to approach this issue is to look at intentions of employees to engage in specific behaviours. Intentions are known to be formed by three types of beliefs: behavioural, normative and control. Further we look at organizational factors that influence these beliefs. We map the existing research on factors stimulating entrepreneurship and formulate several hypotheses. Our main hypothesis is that the entrepreneurial orientation of the business (reflecting the way the entrepreneurial strategy is exercised within the business) should directly and positively influence employees' intentions towards entrepreneurial behaviours. To our knowledge, this link has not yet been extensively discussed in the literature on corporate entrepreneurship.

The chapter is organized as follows. The first section provides an in-depth literature review on the subject. The second section proposes a conceptual model and offers hypotheses for further investigation. The chapter ends with a short discussion.

1. REVIEW OF THE LITERATURE

This section proceeds in three parts: a discussion on the nature of corporate entrepreneurial activity, and two subsequent discussions on individual intentions to engage in CE and the organizational context that is supposed to influence these intentions. The clarification of the nature of corporate entrepreneurship is necessary, because often it is recognized as entrepreneurship within organizations, although this approach may lead to some important features implied by the context being overlooked.

As presented in the introduction, we focus on the interaction between organization and an individual employee in the context of stimulating corporate entrepreneurial behaviour. Figure 10.1 presents this idea.

1.1 CE: A Mix between Organizational and Entrepreneurial Behaviours

Although the concept of corporate entrepreneurship seems to be self-evident, different definitions are used to deal with this concept and findings are borrowed from different contexts.

One of the views on corporate entrepreneurship considers it to be essentially an entrepreneurial activity which takes place in the context of an organization (Sharma and Chrisman, 1999).

Entrepreneurship (individual, or independent, as we refer to it in this chapter) is about 'carrying out new combinations by introducing new

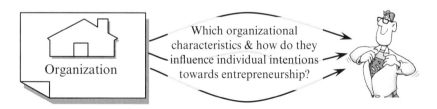

Figure 10.1   Scope of the chapter

products or processes, identifying new markets or sources of supply, or creating new types of organizations' (Schumpeter, 1939). One of the modern definitions focuses on the ability of entrepreneurs to overcome obstacles on the way to the realization of their ideas: 'A process by which individuals [. . .] pursue opportunities without regard to the resources they currently control' (Stevenson and Jarillo, 1990).

Stevenson and Gumpert (1985) outlined six conceptual dimensions which gave greater understanding of the nature of entrepreneurship. To do this they contrasted the entrepreneurial process with administration. The scope of these dimensions was further elaborated by subsequent authors. Table 10.1 summarizes the evidence from the literature (the first six dimensions listed in the table were proposed by Stevenson and Gumpert, 1985). In contrast to administrative activity, entrepreneurial activity is seen to be more dynamic and growth-oriented, driven primarily by opportunity perception and aimed at new value creation, whereas administrative activity is perceived to be more stabilizing and control-oriented. The question is, therefore, whether all these dimensions would hold for corporate entrepreneurship.

Although corporate entrepreneurship incorporates most of the above-mentioned characteristics of independent entrepreneurship, it takes place in a different context: a context of an organization.

The organizational context is said to influence the way motives, time orientation and desire for status and autonomy are formulated by individual corporate entrepreneurs as opposed to the independent entrepreneurs (Antoncic and Hisrich, 2003; Hisrich, 1990; Jennings et al., 1994; Morris et al., 1994).

Looking from the process perspective, corporate entrepreneurs need to deal with existing routines and policies and to 'sell' the innovation within the firm. Therefore, several further dimensions serve to individualize the process of corporate entrepreneurship and distinguish it from individual entrepreneurship (see Table 10.2). Although it is not stated explicitly, the organizational context might also influence other elements of entrepreneurial activity such as opportunity perception, commitment and control of resources.

At the organizational level several further features have been studied as being specific to corporate entrepreneurship. Vesper (1984) draws our attention to the role of *employee's initiative* from below in the organization to undertake something new (Sharma and Chrisman, 1999). Hornsby et al. (2002) write about the ability of a firm to acquire *innovative skills and capabilities*. Zahra (1991) sees the entrepreneurial activity as a combination of formal and *informal activities* aimed at creating new business within established firms through product and process innovations as well as through

Table 10.1   Administration vs entrepreneurship

Administrative	Conceptual dimension	Entrepreneurial
Driven by controlled resources	Strategic orientation	Driven by perception of opportunity
Evolutionary with long duration	Commitment to opportunity	Revolutionary with short duration
A single stage with complete commitment to decision	Commitment of resources	Many stages with minimal exposure at each stage
Ownership or employment of required resources	Control of resources	Episodic use or rent of required resources
Hierarchy	Management structure	Flat, with multiple informal networks
Based on responsibility and seniority	Reward philosophy	Based on value creation
Safe, slow, steady	Growth orientation	Rapid growth is top priority; risk accepted to achieve growth
Opportunity search restricted by resources controlled; failure punished	Entrepreneurial culture	Promoting broad search for opportunities
Slow, according to existing procedures and policies	Action mode	Fast, proactive, persistent
Coordinating	Primary skill	Organizing (creating the processes for a new organization)

Sources: Brown et al. (2001); Morris et al. (1994); Stevenson and Gumpert (1985).

market development. Here the focus is therefore on the informal nature of CE, and on the importance of going beyond the assigned function, showing initiative and learning.

The variety of features highlighted in this section contributes to the understanding that corporate entrepreneurship is a complex phenomenon and a specific field of research. Therefore, in this chapter we try to follow the argument of Zahra (2007), that the research on different kinds of entrepreneurship should be contextualized, and borrowed methods should be relevant and adjusted to the field.

In the next section we review the approaches to the study of the

Table 10.2   Independent entrepreneurship vs corporate entrepreneurship

Independent entrepreneurship	Conceptual dimension	Corporate entrepreneurship
Stand-alone	Occurrence	Within an existing firm
On creating an organization *ex nihilo*	Focus	On developing innovation within a company
Investor's risk (money) High personal risk (money, time)	Risk-taking	Company risk (resources) Medium/low personal risk (career, reputation)
Organizing (creating the processes/teams for a new organization)	Primary skill	'Pushing' (activity is restricted to existing team members, and by routines and procedures in organization)

Sources: Morris et al. (1994, 2000); Stevenson and Jarillo (1990).

individual's intentions towards entrepreneurship and discuss how they could be applied to the domain of corporate entrepreneurial behaviours of employees.

1.2   Individual Level: Intentional Models

It is commonly accepted in the entrepreneurial literature that engagement in entrepreneurial behaviour can be analysed through the lens of intentions: new ventures do not arise from the air; they are the product of individuals' consequent actions. Studying intentions allows a researcher to understand the process of taking a decision to become an entrepreneur as well as to analyse the underlying beliefs of an individual who has to take this decision.

Among the models of intentions, two mainstreams can be outlined: the first aims to adapt a more general model from psychology to the field of entrepreneurship (Ajzen and Fishbein, 1980; Bird, 1988; Boyd and Vozikis, 1994); the second evolved within the entrepreneurship domain (Shapero and Sokol, 1982; Krueger et al., 2000).

Within the first stream, there are two major theories: the theory of planned behaviour and the model of Bird. Here we review the theory of planned behaviour (TPB).

1.2.1 Theory of planned behaviour

According to the *theory of planned behaviour*, human action is guided by three kinds of beliefs: behavioural beliefs, normative beliefs and control beliefs.

Behavioural beliefs are beliefs about the future outcomes of the behaviour. They produce a favourable or unfavourable attitude towards the behaviour.

Normative beliefs are beliefs about the normative expectations of others as well as motivation to comply with these expectations. They result in a perceived social pressure or a subjective norm.

Control beliefs are beliefs about the presence of factors that may facilitate or impede performance of the behaviour and the perceived power of these factors. The picture drawn by these beliefs gives rise to *perceived* control over one's own behaviour.

The interplay between these three beliefs forms intent towards a certain behaviour. Given a sufficient degree of *actual* control over the behaviour, people are expected to carry out their intentions when the opportunity arises. As a general rule, the stronger the intention to engage in a behaviour, the more likely its performance should be. Intention is thus assumed to be the immediate antecedent of behaviour.

Historically, the theory of planned behaviour evolved as an extension of the theory of *reasoned action* (Ajzen and Fishbein, 1980). The original model suggested that a person's behavioural intention depended on his/her attitude about the behaviour as well as subjective norms, but dealt only with those behaviours that were under a person's volitional control. Therefore, actions that were at least in part determined by factors beyond individuals' voluntary control fell outside the boundary conditions established for the model. Thus, the introduced control aspect bears the burden of all the interactions between a person and the environment.

The theory of planned behaviour has proven its applicability in such domains as eating habits, engaging in physical activities, safety behaviours as well as entrepreneurship (Ajzen, 2001; Fayolle et al., 2006; Krueger and Carsrud, 1993).

1.2.2 Shapero's entrepreneurial event model

The second stream has evolved on the side of entrepreneurship. One such model is Shapero's model of the 'Entrepreneurial Event' (EE) (Krueger et al., 2000). This model is 'implicitly an intention model, specific to the domain of entrepreneurship' (ibid.).

According to the EE model, people judge the activity in terms of *desirability* of the outcomes and *feasibility* of the process. Perceived desirability is the personal attractiveness, whereas perceived feasibility is the degree to which one feels personally capable of performing this behaviour. Although desirability and feasibility are necessary, they are not sufficient. The model also includes 'propensity to act', that is one's willingness to retain control over one's life ('I will do it if I want to'). If the person is not ready to act to implement their own decisions and achieve their own goals, they will not engage in entrepreneurial activity, even if it is perceived as desirable and feasible.

Shapero also makes an important remark about the possible influence of some precipitating event – trigger – that changes the perception of the situation by the individual and provides the impetus to behave entrepreneurially when other conditions are conductive to such behaviour (Hornsby et al., 1993). The precipitating event was formally introduced as a part of the model slightly later, in the work of Krueger and Carsrud (1993). The authors mention as well that the influence of exogenous factors remains a critical and as yet insufficiency explored factor.

1.2.3   Resolving the issue of applicability: role identity approach

Although the approaches are constantly elaborated and adjusted to different fields, it is still questionable as to whether they can be applied to the field of *corporate* entrepreneurship.

Ajzen asserts that the behaviour, to which the model is applied, should be defined in terms of its *target, action, context* and *time* elements. Talking about corporate entrepreneurship we confront the following issues:

- *Target and Action*: according to Sharma and Chrisman (1999), based on the outcome and the process one can distinguish between three types of corporate entrepreneurship (process and product innovation, new venture creation, or strategic renewal). Which of them do we usually mean, when we say 'corporate entrepreneurship'? Which of them do the employees mean? Which of them is desirable for the company?
- *Context*: Although it is commonly accepted that entrepreneurship and corporate entrepreneurship possess the same spirit of entrepreneuring, there are still some differences implied by the context of a firm. Furthermore, the context is individual for each company and thus the notion of an 'entrepreneurial role' takes on a special, very subjective meaning.
- *Timing*: Timing of a corporate entrepreneurial project depends highly on the situation within the company, decisions of management and even the workload of the entrepreneur for his/her main (formal) job. Charng et al. (1988) argued that in order to predict

consistent and repetitive behaviours as well as behaviour that may not necessarily occur soon, the theory of Fishbein and Ajzen should be augmented with *identity theory* elements.

Therefore, a clear specification of the purpose of corporate entre-preneuring, the context where it occurs and timing of this activity are necessary for the theory of planned behaviour to be applied to studying corporate entrepreneurial intentions.

Following Charng et al. (1988) we discuss the potential input that iden-tity theory could bring to the research in the field.

The initial concept of identity arose in the domain of sociology in the second half of the twentieth century and was developed by such authors as Stryker (1968), McCall and Simmons (1978) and Turner (1978).

The identity theory, similar to the intentions approach, also views behaviour as a result of a decision process. By clearly defining and con-fronting values, qualities and functions of a corporate entrepreneur alongside those that are associated with other organizational behaviours, a potential corporate entrepreneur is expected to achieve a better under-standing of the purpose and methods of the activity, stick to this image (role) and persist with this image in face of situational challenges. As in theatre, a role can be understood through a set of prescribed activities, reactions and general rules. Nowadays there is a certain stream of research dedicated to the application of role identity to entrepreneurship aiming to investigate formation of role perceptions in entrepreneurs; models of role perceptions; and genesis of entrepreneurial role perceptions.[1]

An important aspect here is the availability of the role model that serves a prototype or an example for the potential corporate entrepre-neur, allowing him or her to develop their understanding of an activity. Scholars constantly focus on the importance of role models (Davidsson, 1995; Murnieks and Mosakowski, 2007), but the empirical evidence sug-gests that the sole presence of role models does not lead to the formation of intentions. At the same time, Krueger (2007) claimed that the entre-preneurial role identity belief is one of the most important beliefs in the structure of entrepreneurial intentions. Therefore the focus of the analysis moves from the *presence* to the *acceptance* or *rejection* of the entrepre-neurial role.

Thus, through clarification of functions and behaviours associated with corporate entrepreneurship in a given company this approach allows us to define the corporate entrepreneurial behaviour in terms of target, activity, context and timing, thus providing us with a tool for examining corporate entrepreneurial intentions of employees within organizations.

1.2.4   Discussion

While research on the intentional models has worked out different views on the core variables, the models have similar basics: they entail an attitudinal component and an element of control. Krueger et al. (2000) tested the models of Ajzen and Shapero against each other and found support for both of them.

Further, the model of Ajzen and Fishbein (TPB) has received wider attention in the entrepreneurial literature. Therefore, when talking about intentions further in this chapter, we assume the framework provided by TPB.

Regarding the issue of applicability of intentional models to the field of corporate entrepreneurship, we argue, the framework should be adjusted according to the dimensions of target, activities, context and timing. As discussed in the previous section, one way to do that could be study closely the role (as a set of behaviours and functions) of a corporate entrepreneur and to seek evidence that an employee accepts this role and is going to perfom it in face of situational challenges.

Several potential approaches to this are possible. A classic approach consists in building a semantic differential: role A vs role B (in our case it could be a comparison of entrepreneur vs administrative employee) (Burke and Tully, 1977). This procedure requires the researcher to name all the characteristics of the entrepreneur role which distinguish it from the administrative role. A similar exercise is presented in Table 10.1, where we compare both archetypes.

Another approach consists in 'gathering' an image of a corporate entrepreneur based on specific individual behaviours associated with corporate entrepreneuring. For example: innovator (Welbourne et al., 1998), creative worker (Farmer et al., 2003), or an innovation champion (Markham, 1998). This type of analysis can be based on the more elaborated procedure of Callero (1992). It requires, though, a list of actions describing the desired behaviour and a Likert-type scale with 'true/not true' statements.

So far, we suggest that using a model based on the principles that have proven their applicability within the domain of entrepreneurship and adjusting it through an in-depth study of the behaviours of corporate entrepreneurs could be a viable research option for corporate entrepreneurship.

Next we review the literature on organizational context, seeking to answer the question regarding which factors could influence employees and stimulate them to engage in corporate entrepreneurship.

1.3   Organizational Context

Organizational context is defined as the set of administrative and social mechanisms that shape behaviours of actors in the organization, over which the top management have some control (Birkinshaw, 1999). The following sections present two different approaches to describing the organizational context for entrepreneurship: the first outlines specific areas (such as reward system or management support) and discusses them independently; the other approaches the way entrepreneurial strategy is realized in the organization along several dimensions (such as risk taking or innovativeness).

1.3.1   Individual organizational factors
The question regarding which factors influence innovative behaviour of employees has been the subject of considerable research, study and analysis. As listed in Kuratko et al. (1990), among particular factors which are associated with *success* in corporate entrepreneurial ventures, there are issues such as financial factors, incentive and control systems, market and entry approaches, and market-driven vs technology-driven demand. Souder (1981) found that the presence of six specific management practices was associated with the positive outcomes in 100 new ventures in 17 organizations. These factors were early identification of intrapreneurs, formal licence (or authority to proceed), sponsorship, appropriate location, discretionary powers, and informal influence. Among *obstacles* to corporate entrepreneuring MacMillan et al. (1986) cited operational difficulties, inadequate planning, unrealistic corporate expectations, inadequate corporate support, and misreading the market.

Kuratko et al. (1990) outlined a set of factors that were consistent throughout the writings in this field (Hornsby et al., 1993) and could be used effectively by researchers as well as by practitioners. The factors were: rewards (goals, feedback, emphasis on individual responsibility and results); management support (willingness of managers to facilitate entrepreneurial projects); resources (including time) and their availability; organizational structure (such as arrangement of workflow, communication, and authority relationships (Covin and Slevin, 1991)); finally, risk taking and tolerance for failure should it occur. In their study Kuratko et al. (1990) found that the outlined factors could be downscaled to three upper-level factors: management support for intrapreneurship (including risk taking), organizational structure, and rewards and research availability (including resources and time).

Three years later Hornsby et al. (1993) expanded on this classification by adding parameters such as organizational boundaries[2] and work discretion.[3] The time availability then became an independent factor.

In order to understand whether the research during the last 15 years in the field has found some other categories of internal determinants of corporate entrepreneurship, we made a new literature review on the topic. We found that managers can influence entrepreneurial behaviour of employees through:[4]

- *Management support:* The willingness of senior management to facilitate and promote entrepreneurial activity in the organization, including championing innovative ideas as well as providing necessary resources, expertise or protection. Also includes risk-acceptance and encouragement.
  Successful practices include: supporting creativity, initiative and innovation; encouraging; being an example; protecting – from bureaucracy or distractions; sponsoring and displaying readiness to find resources if needed; as well as being reasonable while dealing with entrepreneurial mistakes.
- *Organizational structure:* An arrangement of workflow, communication, and authority relationships. The structure must foster the administrative mechanisms by which ideas are evaluated, chosen and implemented.
  Successful practices include: locating the project appropriately within company (embedding or loosening from formal structure); establishing communications within and outside the company; arranging the workflow within the project.
- *Resources:* Availability of financial, time and information resources for innovative activities – those are the resources needed for any project.
  Successful practices include: establishing financial support (grants, loosely committed resources, protection); creating informational infrastructure and checking availability of the necessary information (previous projects experience, contact data, reliable experts etc.); providing adequate time resources to think and create.
- *Rewards:* Goals, feedback, emphasis on individual responsibility as well as rewards based on results. Includes monetary and non-monetary gains from engaging in corporate entrepreneurial activity.
- *Networking and people:* Social networks allowing acquisition of required information, knowledge and skills, access to resources; also includes the 'quality' of people involved.
  Successful practices include: making sure entrepreneurial teams have broad networks with weak ties for finding necessary expertise or resources; developing deep, strong ties for long-term relationships and complex knowledge transfer; recruiting people with entrepreneurial DNA; watching team completeness and dynamics.

● *Work design:* Includes the content of work itself and the discretion of the potential corporate entrepreneurs to make decisions about performing their own work in the way that they believe is most effective.

Our analysis has allowed us to refresh the set of factors that are recommended as important success determinants of new entrepreneurial projects within the company, to understand the mechanisms of their influence and to enhance the theoretical schemes with practical experiences and examples.

The review of theoretical contributions and case studies provided some evidence that the factors affect the organization in a snowball manner. As such, mistakes in placing the project within the organization can lead to communication and subordination problems. Later on this can result in fundraising problems, for example: which department should give money for the equipment, how much time does it take to acquire the needed resources, is the project staffed properly (Bresman, 2001). And this is not only related to the depth of a company's pocket (Abetti, 2000). Miller and Friesen (1982) and Ancona et al. (2002) argue that only a combination of factors can be seen as supportive for successful new initiatives.

Further, Kuratko et al. (1993) assert: 'in establishing the drive to innovate inside today's corporations, one approach is to concentrate on developing a climate conducive to corporate entrepreneurs'. As cited in Anderson and West (1998), Reichers and Schneider (1990) define organizational climate as 'the shared perception of the way things are done around here. More precisely, climate is shared perceptions of organizational policies, practices, and procedures'. Furthermore, Anderson and West (1998), making reference to the accumulated scholarly work, argue in favour of research into facet-specific climates (climate for change, climate for quality, climate for innovation, and so on).

In the corporate entrepreneurship literature such a construct is known as entrepreneurial orientation (Lumpkin and Dess, 1996): it represents key entrepreneurial processes that answer the question of how new ventures are undertaken (Lee and Peterson, 2000). We discuss this in more detail below.

1.3.2 Entrepreneurial orientation

Talking about the organization and its influence on corporate entrepreneurship, Miller first suggested that an entrepreneurial firm is one that 'engages in product market *innovation*, undertakes somewhat risky ventures, and is first to come up with *proactive* innovations, *beating* competitors to the punch' (Miller, 1983, quoting Lumpkin and Dess, 1996).

Since that time, numerous researchers have based their studies of entrepreneurship at the organizational level on Miller's (1983) conceptualization, referring to it as entrepreneurial strategic orientation (Wiklund and Shepherd, 2005), entrepreneurial or strategic posture (Covin and Slevin, 1989).

The initial works in entrepreneurial orientation (EO) considered the concept in the terms of a new entry: 'An EO refers to the processes, practices, and decision-making activities that lead to new entry' (Lumpkin and Dess, 1996). Later researchers shifted to a more general definition of the concept, referring to it as the methods, practices and decision-making styles used to act entrepreneurially (Lee and Peterson, 2000):

- Lumpkin and Dess (2001) open their article by naming entrepreneurial orientation 'strategy making processes and styles of firms that engage in entrepreneurial activities';
- Covin et al. (2006) define entrepreneurial orientation as a 'strategic construct whose conceptual domain includes certain firm-level outcomes and management-related preferences, beliefs, and behaviors as expressed among a firm's top-level managers';
- Lee and Peterson (2000) argue 'this approach stresses the entrepreneurial process and the role of top management philosophies regarding entrepreneurship'.

Entrepreneurial orientation, thus, represents key entrepreneurial processes that answer the question of *how* new ventures are undertaken, whereas the term 'entrepreneurship' refers to the content of entrepreneurial decisions by addressing *what* is undertaken. It involves a willingness to innovate to rejuvenate market offerings, to take risks to try out new and uncertain products, services and markets, and to be more proactive than competitors toward new marketplace opportunities (Wiklund and Shepherd, 2005).

The underlying dimensions can be described as follows (Lumpkin and Dess, 2001):

- *Autonomy* can be defined as independent action by an individual or a team aimed at bringing forth a business concept or vision and carrying it through to completion.
- *Innovativeness* refers to a willingness to support creativity and experimentation in introducing new products/services, and novelty, technological leadership and R&D in developing new processes.
- *Risk taking* means a tendency to take bold actions such as venturing into unknown new markets, committing a large portion of resources to ventures with uncertain outcomes, and/or borrowing heavily.
- *Pro-activeness* is an opportunity-seeking, forward-looking perspective involving introducing new products or services ahead of the

Table 10.3   Operationalizations of the EO construct

	Miller and Friesen (1982)	Miller (1983)	Miller and Friesen (1983)	Covin and Slevin, (1988, 1989, 1991)	Miles and Arnold (1991)	Zahra and Covin (1995)	Lumpkin and Dess (1996, 2001)	Wiklund and Shepherd (2003)	Keh et al. (2007)	Kollmann et al. (2007)	Hughes and Morgan (2007)	Madsen (2007)
Innovativeness	x	x	x	x	x	x	x	x	x	x	x	x
Risk taking	x	x		x	x	x	x	x	x	x	x	x
Pro-activeness	x			x	x		x	x	x	x	x	x
Competitive aggressiveness						x	x			x	x	
Autonomy							x			x	x	

competitors and acting in anticipation of future demands to create change and shape the environment.

- *Competitive* aggressiveness reflects the intensity of a firm's efforts to outperform industry rivals, characterized by a combative posture and a forceful response to competitor's actions.

The original framework worked out by Covin and Slevin (1989) on the basis of the Miller and Friesen (1982) and Miller (1983) works, contains three dimensions: innovativeness, risk taking and pro-activeness. This scale has substantially determined the knowledge accumulation around the construct of entrepreneurial orientation (Brown et al., 2001). Lumpkin and Dess (1996) proposed to add two further dimensions: autonomy and competitive aggressiveness. Probably due to the absence of the questionnaire example in the initial paper, there have not been plenty of studies using them (see Table 10.3).

Although the scale used in the studies has remained more or less stable, the authors tended to use it in different ways (see Appendix B for a summary of different studies, including the definition and the scale used). Some researchers treated entrepreneurial orientation as a uni-dimensional construct and some proposed to look at dimensions of entrepreneurial orientation as varying independently (Wiklund and Shepherd, 2005). In this chapter we agree with Covin et al. (2006) who call these debates about dimensionality of the constructs 'somewhat misleading' (p. 80). Risk taking, innovation and pro-activeness could be manifested in organizations as distinct dimensions of behaviour, though being strong only on one of the dimensions would not make the firm entrepreneurial.

Considerable conceptual and empirical work has been done while investigating relationships between entrepreneurial orientation, related constructs and firm performance (Lyon et al., 2000). Other streams of research were directed to:

● identification of factors that predict entrepreneurial orientation or influence its relationship to company's performance (for example Miller and Friesen, 1982; Wiklund and Shepherd, 2003; Zahra, 1991);
● the identification of EO's effect on various dimensions of firm performance on samples of different sizes and life-cycle stages as well as in different environments (Hughes et al., 2007; Keh et al., 2007; Walter et al., 2006; Wiklund, 1999; Wiklund and Shepherd, 2005; Zahra and Covin, 1995);
● identification of variables that moderate the EO–firm performance relationship (for example, Covin and Slevin, 1988; Lumpkin and Dess, 2001).

Previous research has also supported the fact that entrepreneurial orientation has a positive influence on performance over some period of time (Madsen, 2007; Wiklund, 1999; Zahra and Covin, 1995). At the same time, the previous research on strategic entrepreneurship has treated the organization as a black box (Monsen and Boss, 2009).

Further, we focus on the influence of entrepreneurial orientation of the business as its climate for entrepreneurship, choosing this perspective rather than looking at individual influences of single organizational factors. We investigate what influence EO of the business might have on the beliefs, intentions and behaviours of employees. The next section is devoted to the conceptual model and development of propositions.

2. CONCEPTUAL FRAMEWORK AND PROPOSITIONS DEVELOPMENT

The first proposition stems from the observation that different individual organizational factors such as reward systems or management support are supportive for innovation and entrepreneurship only in combination. Therefore we argue that an interplay between different organizational factors should compose a climate for corporate entrepreneurship, or, specifically, perception of the entrepreneurial orientation of the business.

Proposition 1: The perceived EO of a business is a result of the interplay between individual organizational characteristics

Second, Lumpkin (2007) suggests that each of the dimensions of EO can contribute to any of the stages in the development of an entrepreneurial project. Such dimensions as pro-activeness, autonomy and innovativeness are well matched to the exploration of opportunities. Further, risk taking and competitive aggressiveness are fruitful for exploiting the opportunities. Thus, different dimensions of EO not only absorb the influence of individual organizational characteristics, but also create the environment and pre-conditions for different stages of the innovation process. In this chapter we are focusing on the early stages of the entrepreneurial process and therefore proceed with only one hypothesis regarding the exploration of opportunities.

Proposition 2a: Pro-activeness, autonomy and innovativeness of the business are conducive for exploration of entrepreneurial opportunities.

Proposition 2b: Pro-activeness, autonomy and innovativeness of the business are stimulating intentions of individual employees to engage in CE through stimulating exploration of entrepreneurial opportunities.

Further, Forbes (2005) argued that self-efficacy of employees could be promoted through providing them with a chance to participate in the decision-making process (autonomy dimension). Monsen and Boss (2009) have investigated the influence of strategic entrepreneurship on job stress and employee retention at management and staff levels. They found that the three dimensions of EO, contrary to their expectations, were generally associated with less role ambiguity and intention to quit. To some extent this was because supporting a culture of change and creativity helped to reduce fear, stress and ambiguity associated with risk taking, innovative and proactive activities.

Proposition 3: A strong EO of a business should positively affect the intentions of employees towards CE.

Proposition 3a: A strong EO of a business should positively affect the attitude component of intentions through clarifying the role of an entrepreneur.

Proposition 3b: A strong EO of a business should positively affect the perception of social support for entrepreneurship and innovation.

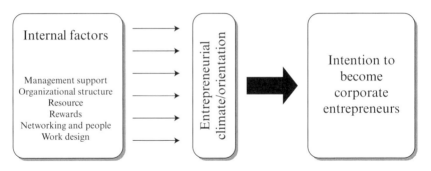

Figure 10.2　Conceptual model

Proposition 3c: Autonomy as a chance to participate in decision-making should positively affect the control dimension of intentions by influencing their self-efficacy.

Thus, based on our literature review, we can formulate the model shown in Figure 10.2, where intentions of employees towards corporate entrepreneurship are influenced by the entrepreneurial orientation of the company. EO is formed as a result of the interplay of organizational characteristics.

Verifying the hypotheses stated in this chapter would allow researchers to clarify the link between individual organizational characteristics and a more general, or strategic, construct of EO. Although entrepreneurial orientation is mostly studied at the organizational level, we provide some evidence, formulate several hypotheses, and argue that it should directly and positively influence the intentions of individual employees to engage in a corporate entrepreneurial process.

3.　CONCLUSION

Entrepreneurship and, in particular, corporate entrepreneurship is a multi-dimensional and complex phenomenon that cannot be easily described. Our in-depth literature review has shown that there are several aspects that are unique to corporate entrepreneurship as compared to conventional managers and independent entrepreneurs. These specific aspects make it necessary to avoid blind usage of concepts and tools from other domains without their adaptation to the field. Therefore, we discuss several approaches towards intentions of employees to engage in entrepreneurship and discuss a possible way to adjust them to the domain of corporate entrepreneurship.

Regarding the organizational context for corporate entrepreneurship our review has shown that numerous definitions and models of it are proposed within the field. This study has underlined the inner contradictions of the factor-by-factor organizational context analysis, arguing for the need to focus on a framework that will outline the factors by the nature of their influence on corporate entrepreneurship rather than the nature of the factors. We argue that the concept of entrepreneurial orientation could serve as a relevant framework: it reflects the basic processes regarding how corporate entrepreneurship is carried out within an organization, and has proven its reliability in connection with performance. Several researchers have already undertaken this path towards analysis of the influence of entrepreneurial orientation of the business on behaviours of employees, and have reported a positive link between this approach and the entrepreneurial spirit of staff.

A conceptual model is proposed. It delineates the relationships between different elements of organizational context and intentions. To test these relations, we formulate several propositions that need to be verified by future research.

NOTES

* The author would like to thank the Solvay Group for the support throughout this research project.
1. For references see Krueger (2007) and Downing (2005). The following papers are also notable for their contribution to this topic: Hoang and Gimeno (2010), Jain et al. (2009); Murnieks and Mosakowski (2007).
2. Organizational boundaries are the boundaries, real and imagined, that prevent people from looking at problems outside their own jobs like, for example, narrow job descriptions and rigid standards of performance.
3. Discretion of the workers to the extent that they are able to make decisions about performing their own work in the way that they believe is most effective.
4. For more details and references, see Appendix A.

BIBLIOGRAPHY

Abetti, P.A. (2000), 'Critical success factors for radical technological innovation: a case study', *Creativity and Innovation Management*, **9**(4), 208–21.
Ajzen, I. (2001), 'Nature and operation of attitudes', *Annual Review of Psychology*, **52**, 27–58.
Ajzen, I. and M. Fishbein (1980), *Understanding Attitudes and Predicting Social Behavior*, Englewood Cliffs: Prentice-Hall.
Aldrich, H. (1999), *Organizational Evolving*, London: Sage Publications.
Ancona, D., H. Bresman and K. Kaeufer (2002), 'The comparative advantage of x-teams', *MIT Sloan Management Review*, **43**(3), 33–9.
Anderson, N.R. and M.A. West (1998), 'Measuring climate for work group

innovation: development and validation of the team climate inventory', *Journal of Organizational Behavior*, **19**(3), 235–58.

Antoncic, B. and R.D. Hisrich (2001), 'Intrapreneurship: construct refinement and cross-cultural validation', *Journal of Business Venturing*, **16**, 495–527.

Antoncic, B. and R.D. Hisrich (2003), 'Clarifying the intrapreneurship concept', *Journal of Small Business and Enterprise Development*, **10**, 7–24.

Barringer, B.R. and A.C. Bluedorn (1999), 'The relationship between corporate entrepreneurship and strategic management', *Strategic Management Journal*, **20**(5), 421–44.

Bird, B. (1988), 'Implementing entrepreneurial ideas: the case for intention', *Academy of Management Review*, **13**(3), 442–53.

Birkinshaw, J. (1999), 'The determinants and consequences of subsidiary initiative in multinational corporations', *Entrepreneurship Theory and Practice*, **24**(1), 9–36.

Boyd, N.G. and G.S. Vozikis. (1994), 'The influence of self-efficacy on the development of entrepreneurial intentions and actions', *Entrepreneurship Theory and Practice*, **18**(4), 63–77.

Bresman, H. (2001), 'External sourcing of core technologies and the architectural dependency of teams', MIT Sloan Working Paper No. 4215–01.

Brown, T.E., P. Davidsson and J. Wiklund (2001), 'An operationalization of Stevenson's conceptualization of entrepreneurship as opportunity-based firm behavior', *Strategic Management Journal*, **22**(10), 953–68.

Burke, P.J. and J.C. Tully (1977), 'The measurement of role identity', *Social Forces*, **55**, 881–96.

Calantone, R.J., S.T. Cavusgil and Y. Zhao (2002), 'Learning orientation, firm innovation capability and firm performance', *Industrial Marketing Management*, **31**, 515–24.

Callero, P.L. (1992), 'The meaning of self in role: a modified measure of role identity', *Social Forces*, **71**, 485–501.

Charng, H.-W., J.A. Piliavin and P.L. Callero (1988), 'Role identity and reasoned action in the prediction of repeated behavior', *Social Psychology Quarterly*, **51**, 303–17.

Covin, J.G., K.M. Green and D.P. Slevin (2006), 'Strategic process effects on the entrepreneurial orientation–sales growth rate relationship', *Entrepreneurship Theory and Practice*, **30**(3), 57–82.

Covin, J.G., and D.P. Slevin (1986), 'The development and testing of an organizational-level entrepreneurship scale', in R. Ronstadt, J.A. Hornaday, R. Peterson and K.H. Vesper (eds), *Frontiers of Entrepreneurship Research*, Wellesley, MA: Babson College, pp. 628–39.

Covin, J.G. and D.P. Slevin (1988), 'The influence of organization structure on the utility of an entrepreneurial top management style', *Journal of Management Studies*, **25**, 217–34.

Covin, J.G. and D.P. Slevin (1989), 'Strategic management of small firms in hostile and benign environments', *Strategic Management Journal*, **10**(1), 75–87.

Covin, J.G. and D.P. Slevin (1991), 'A conceptual model of entrepreneurship as firm behavior', *Entrepreneurship Theory and Practice*, **16**(1), 7–25.

Davidsson, P. (1995), 'Determinants of entrepreneurial intentions', paper presented at RENT IX Conference, Piacenza, Italy, 23–24 November.

Dess, G.G., G.T. Lumpkin and J.G. Covin. (1997), 'Entrepreneurial strategy making and firm performance: tests of contingency and configurational models', *Strategic Management Journal*, **18**(9), 677–95.

Dougherty, D. and C. Hardy (1996), 'Sustained product innovation in large, mature organizations: overcoming innovation-to-organization problems', *Academy of Management Journal*, **39**(5), 1120–53.

Downing, S. (2005), 'The social construction of entrepreneurship: narrative and dramatic processes in the coproduction of organizations and identities', *Entrepreneurship Theory and Practice*, **29**(2), 185–204.

Ellis, R.J. and N.T. Taylor (1988), 'Success and failure in internal venture strategy: an exploratory study', *Frontiers of Entrepreneurship Research*, Wellesley, MA: Babson College.

Farmer, S.M., P. Tierney and K. Kung-McIntyre (2003), 'Employee creativity in Taiwan: an application of role identity theory', *Academy of Management Journal*, **46**, 618–30.

Fayolle, A., B. Gailly and N. Lassas-Clerc (2006), 'Assessing the impact of entrepreneurship education programmes: a new methodology', *Journal of European Industrial Training*, **30**(9), 701–20.

Forbes, D.P. (2005), 'The effects of strategic decision making on entrepreneurial self-efficacy', *Entrepreneurship Theory and Practice*, **29**(5), 599–626.

Hart, S. (1991), 'Intentionality and autonomy in strategy-making process: modes, archetypes, and firm performance', in P. Shrivastava, A. Huff and J. Dutton (eds), *Advances in Strategic Management, Vol. 7*, Greenwich, CT: JAI Press, pp. 97–127.

Hisrich, R.D. (1990), 'Entrepreneurship/intrapreneurship', *American Psychologist*, **45**(2), 209–22.

Hoang, H. and J. Gimeno (2010), 'Becoming a founder: how founder role identity affects entrepreneurial transitions and persistence in founding', *Journal of Business Venturing*, **25**(1), 41–53.

Hobson, E.L. and R.M. Morrison (1983), 'How do corporate start-up ventures fare?', in K.H. Vesper (ed.), *Frontiers of Entrepreneurship Research*, Wellesley, MA: Babson College.

Hornsby, J.S., D.F. Kuratko and S.A. Zahra (2002), 'Middle managers' perception of the internal environment for corporate entrepreneurship: assessing a measurement scale', *Journal of Business Venturing*, **17**(3), 253–73.

Hornsby, J.S., D.W. Naffziger, D.F. Kuratko and R.V. Montagno (1993), 'An interactive model of the corporate entrepreneurship process', *Entrepreneurship Theory and Practice*, **17**(2), 29–37.

Howell, J.M. and C.M. Shea (2006), 'Effects of champion behavior, team potency, and external communication activities on predicting team performance', *Group Organization Management*, **31**(2), 180–211.

Howell, J.M., C.M. Shea and C.A. Higgins (2005), 'Champions of product innovations: defining, developing, and validating a measure of champion behavior', *Journal of Business Venturing*, **20**(5), 641–61.

Hughes, M. and R.E. Morgan (2007), 'Deconstructing the relationship between entrepreneurial orientation and business performance at the embryonic stage of firm growth', *Industrial Marketing Management*, **36**, 651–61.

Hughes, M., P. Hughes and R.E. Morgan (2007), 'Exploitative learning and entrepreneurial orientation alignment in emerging young firms: implications for market and response performance', *British Journal of Management*, **18**, 359–75.

Hult, G.T.M. and D.J. Ketchen (2001), 'Does market orientation matter? A test of the relationship between positional advantage and performance', *Strategic Management Journal*, **22**, 899–906.

Ireland, R.D., J.G. Covin and D.F. Kuratko (2009), 'Conceptualizing corporate entrepreneurship strategy', *Entrepreneurship Theory and Practice*, **33**(1), 19–46.

Jain, S., G. George and M. Maltarich (2009), 'Academics or entrepreneurs? Investigating role identity modification of university scientists involved in commercialization activity', *Research Policy*, **38**(6), 922–35.

Jennings, R., C. Cox and C.L. Cooper (1994), *Business Elites: The Psychology of Entrepreneurs and Intrapreneurs*, London: Routledge.

Keh, H.T., T.T.M. Nguyen and H.P. Ng (2007), 'The effects of entrepreneurial orientation and marketing information on the performance of SMEs', *Journal of Business Venturing*, **22**, 592–611.

Khandwalla, P.N. (1976–77), 'Some top management styles, their context and performance', *Organization and Administrative Sciences*, **7**(4), 21–51.

Kollmann, T., J. Christofor and A. Kuckertz (2007), 'Explaining individual entrepreneurial orientation: conceptualisation of a cross-cultural research framework', *International Journal of Entrepreneurship and Small Business*, **4**(3), 325–40.

Kreiser, P.M., L.D. Marino and K.M. Weaver (2002), 'Assessing the psychometric properties of the entrepreneurial orientation scale: a multi-country analysis', *Entrepreneurship Theory and Practice*, **26**(4), 71–94.

Krueger, N.F. (2007), 'What lies beneath? The experiential essence of entrepreneurial thinking', *Entrepreneurship Theory and Practice*, **31**(1), 123–38.

Krueger, N.F. and A.L. Carsrud (1993), 'Entrepreneurial intentions: applying the theory of planned behaviour', *Entrepreneurship & Regional Development*, **5**, 315–30.

Krueger, N.F., M.D. Reilly and A.L. Carsrud (2000), 'Competing models of entrepreneurial intentions', *Journal of Business Venturing*, **15**(5–6), 411–32.

Kuratko, D.F., J.S. Hornsby, D.W. Naffziger and R.V. Montagno (1993), 'Implementing entrepreneurial thinking in established organizations', *Advanced Management Journal*, **58**(1), 28–39.

Kuratko, D.F., R.D. Ireland, J.G. Covin and J.S. Hornsby (2005), 'A model of middle-level managers' entrepreneurial behavior', *Entrepreneurship Theory and Practice*, **29**(6), 699–716.

Kuratko, D.F., R.V. Montagno and J.S. Hornsby (1990), 'Developing an intrapreneurial assessment instrument for an effective corporate entrepreneurial environment', *Strategic Management Journal*, **11**, 49–58.

Lawson, B. and D. Samson (2001), 'Developing innovation capability in organisations: a dynamic capabilities approach', *International Journal of Innovation Management*, **5**(3), 377–400.

Lee, S.M. and S.J. Peterson (2000), 'Culture, entrepreneurial orientation, and global competitiveness', *Journal of World Business*, **35**(4), 401–16.

Ling, Y., Z. Simsek, M. Lubatkin and J. Veiga (2008), 'Transformational leadership's role in promoting corporate entrepreneurship: examining the CEO–TMT interface', *Academy of Management Journal*, **51**(3), 557–76.

Lumpkin, G.T. (2007), 'Intrapreneurship and innovation', in J.R. Baum, M. Frese and R. Baron (eds), *The Psychology of Entrepreneurship*, Mahwah, NJ: Lawrence Erlbaum Associates, pp. 237–64.

Lumpkin, G.T. and G.G. Dess (1996), 'Clarifying the entrepreneurial orientation construct and linking it to performance', *Academy of Management Review*, **21**(1), 135–72.

Lumpkin, G.T. and G.G. Dess (2001), 'Linking two dimensions of entrepreneurial orientation to firm performance: the moderating role of environment and industry life cycle', *Journal of Business Venturing*, **19**, 429–51.

Lyon, D.W., G.T. Lumpkin and G.G. Dess (2000), 'Enhancing entrepreneurial orientation research: operationalizing and measuring a key strategic decision making process', *Journal of Management*, **26**(5), 1055–85.

MacMillan, I.C., Z. Block and P.N.S. Narasimha (1986), 'Corporate venturing: alternatives, obstacles encountered, and experience effects', *Journal of Business Venturing*, **1**, 177–91.

Madsen, E.L. (2007), 'The significance of sustained entrepreneurial orientation on performance of firms: a longitudinal analysis', *Entrepreneurship & Regional Development*, **19**(2), 185–204.

Markham, S.K. (1998), 'A longitudinal examination of how champions influence others to support their projects', *Journal of Product Innovation Management*, **15**(6), 490–504.

Marvel, M.R., A. Griffin, J. Hebda and B. Vojak (2007), 'Examining the technical corporate entrepreneurs' motivation: voices from the field', *Entrepreneurship Theory and Practice*, **31**(5), 753–68.

McCall, G.J. and J.L. Simmons (1978), *Identities and Interactions*, New York: The Free Press.

Miles, M.P. and D.R. Arnold (1991), 'The relationship between marketing orientation and entrepreneurial orientation', *Entrepreneurship Theory and Practice*, **15**(4), 49–65.

Miller, D. (1983), 'The correlates of entrepreneurship in three types of firms', *Management Science*, **29**, 770–91.

Miller, D. and P.H. Friesen (1982), 'Innovation in conservative and entrepreneurial firms: two models of strategic momentum', *Strategic Management Journal*, **3**(1), 1–25.

Miller, D. and P.H. Friesen (1983), 'Strategy-making and environment: the third link', *Strategic Management Journal*, **4**(3), 221–35.

Monsen, E.W. and W.R. Boss (2009), 'The impact of strategic entrepreneurship inside the organization: examining job stress and employee retention', *Entrepreneurship Theory and Practice*, **33**(1), 71–104.

Morgan, R.E. and C.A. Strong (2003), 'Business performance and dimensions of strategic orientation', *Journal of Business Research*, **56**, 163–76.

Morris, M.H., D.L. Davis and J.W. Allen (1994), 'Fostering corporate entrepreneurship: cross-cultural comparisons of the importance of individualism and collectivism', *Journal of International Business Studies*, **25**(1), 65–89.

Morris, M.H., S.A. Zahra and M. Schindehutte (2000), 'Understanding factors that trigger entrepreneurial behavior in established companies', in G. Libecap (ed.), *Entrepreneurship and Economic Growth in the American Economy* (vol. 12), New York: Elsevier Science, pp. 133–59.

Mumford, M.D. (2000), 'Managing creative people: strategies and tactics for innovation', *Human Resource Management Review*, **10**(3), 313–51.

Murnieks, C. and E. Mosakowski (2007), 'Who am I? Looking inside the "entrepreneurial identity"', paper presented at Babson College Entrepreneurship Research Conference (BCERC).

Quinn, J.B. (1979), 'Technological innovation, entrepreneurship and strategy', *Sloan Management Review*, **20**(Spring), 19–30.

Reichers, A.E. and B. Schneider (1990), 'Climate and culture: an evolution of constructs', in B. Schneider, (ed.), *Organizational Climate and Culture*, San Francisco: Jossey-Bass.

Schumpeter, J.A. (1939), *Business Cycles. A Theoretical, Historical, and Statistical Analysis of the Capitalist Process*, New York/Toronto/London: McGraw-Hill Book Company.

Scott, S.G. and R.A. Bruce (1994), 'Determinants of innovative behavior: a path model of individual innovation in the workplace', *The Academy of Management Journal*, **37**(3), 580–607.

Shapero, A. and L. Sokol (1982), 'The social dimensions of entrepreneurship', in C.A. Kent, D.L. Sexton and K.H. Vesper (eds), *Encyclopedia of Entrepreneurship*, Englewood Cliffs, NJ: Prentice-Hall, pp. 72–90.

Sharma, P. and J.J. Chrisman (1999), 'Toward a reconciliation of the definitional issues in the field of corporate entrepreneurship', *Entrepreneurship Theory and Practice*, **23**(3), 11–27.

Souder, W.E. (1981), 'Encouraging entrepreneurship in large corporations', *Research Management*, **24**(3), 18–22.

Stevenson, H.H. and D.E. Gumpert(1985), 'The heart of entrepreneurship', *Harvard Business Review*, **63**(2), 85–94.

Stevenson, H.H. and J.C. Jarillo (1990), 'A paradigm of entrepreneurship: entrepreneurial management', *Strategic Management Journal*, **11** (Special issue: Corporate Entrepreneurship, Summer), pp. 17–27.

Stryker, S. (1968), 'Identity salience and role performance: the relevance of symbolic interaction theory for family research', *Journal of Marriage and the Family*, **30**(4), 558–64.

Tang, J., Z. Tang, L.D. Marino, Y. Zhang and Q. Li (2008), 'Exploring an inverted U-shape relationship between entrepreneurial orientation and performance in Chinese ventures', *Entrepreneurship Theory and Practice*, **32**(1), 219–39.

Trafimow, D. and A. Duran (1998), 'Some tests of the distinction between attitude and perceived behavioural control', *British Journal of Social Psychology*, **37**, 1–14.

Turner, R.H. (1978), 'The role and the person', *American Journal of Sociology*, **84**, 1–23.

Vesper, K.H. (1984), 'Three faces of corporate entrepreneurship: a pilot study', in J.A. Hornaday, F.J. Tarpley, J.A. Timmons and K.H. Vesper (eds), *Frontiers of Entrepreneurship Research*, Wellesley, MA: Babson College.

Walter, A., M. Auer and T. Ritter (2006), 'The impact of network capabilities and entrepreneurial orientation on university spin-off performance', *Journal of Business Venturing*, **21**(4), 541–67.

Welbourne, T.M., D.E. Johnson and A. Erez (1998), 'The role-based performance scale: validity analysis of a theory-based measure', *Academy of Management Journal*, **41**(5), 540–55.

West, M.A. (2002), 'Sparkling fountains or stagnant ponds: an integrative model of creativity and innovation implementation in work groups', *Applied Psychology: An International Journal*, **51**, 355–424.

Wiklund, J. (1999), 'The sustainability of the entrepreneurial orientation–performance relationship', *Entrepreneurship Theory and Practice*, **24**, 37–48.

Wiklund, J. and D. Shepherd (2003), 'Knowledge-based resources, entrepreneurial orientation, and the performance of small and medium-sized businesses', *Strategic Management Journal*, **24**, 1307–14.

Wiklund, J. and D. Shepherd (2005), 'Entrepreneurial orientation and small business performance: a configurational approach', *Journal of Business Venturing*, **20**, 71–91.

Zahra, S.A. (1991), 'Predictors and financial outcomes of corporate entrepreneurship: an exploratory study', *Journal of Business Venturing*, **6**(4), 259–85.

Zahra, S.A. (2007), 'Contextualizing theory building in entrepreneurship research', *Journal of Business Venturing*, **22**(3), 443–52.

Zahra, S.A. and J.G. Covin (1995), 'Contextual influences on the corporate entrepreneurship–performance relationship: a longitudinal analysis', *Journal of Business Venturing*, **10**, 43–58.

APPENDIX A

Table 10A.1   Factors influencing corporate entrepreneurship: an overview

Authors (Year)	Management support	Organizational structure/ boundaries	Resources	Work design	Rewards	Networking and people	Other
Quinn, 1979	x	x	x	x	x	–/x	
Kuratko et al., 1990	x	x	x	x	x		
Zahra, 1991	x	x					Values
Covin and Slevin, 1991	x	x	x			–/x	Strategy, culture
Scott and Bruce, 1994	x			x			Team-member exchange, problem-solving style
Dougherty and Hardy, 1996		x	x				Strategic value and meaning
Birkinshaw, 1999	x	x	x	x			Subsidiary credibility
Mumford, 2000	x	x		t + i	x	x	Group structure and goals
Lawson and Samson, 2001		x		x	x	x	Org. intelligence, idea & technology management
Antoncic and Hisrich, 2001	x	x	t	x	x	x	Competition/ person related values
Hornsby et al., 2002	x	x	t	x	x		values
Ancona et al., 2002		x	i			x	Learning culture
West, 2002	x			x	x		External demands
Marvel et al., 2007	x	x	x	x			Risk-accept, company pride
Ling et al., 2008	x	x			x	x	Long-term compensation, behavioural integration

Note: The table presents the grouped factors on the basis of their definition; (**t**) denotes time resources; (**i**) denotes for informational resources; (**–x**) denotes approaches concentrated on human capital and not networking.

APPENDIX B

Table 10A.2   *Studies employing EO construct: an overview of definitions and measurement scales*

Authors	Year	EO definition	EO scale
Miller, Friesen	1982		Original scale
Zahra, Covin	1995	CE defined through dimensions of EO	Miller and Friesen (1982)
Dess, Lumpkin, Covin	1997	Entrepreneurial strategy-making	Hart (1991) 1) top-management intentionality 2) organizational actor autonomy
Wiklund	1999	Entrepreneurial strategic orientation	Miller and Friesen (1982) (8 items)
Barringer, Bluedorn	1999	Corporate entrepreneurship	Covin and Slevin (1986) (3 factors)
Brown, Davidsson, Wiklund	2001	Characteristic of the firm-level entrepreneurial behaviour	Covin and Slevin (1989), modified
Lumpkin, Dess	2001	Strategy-making processes and styles of firms that engage in entrepreneurial activities	Covin and Slevin (1986/1989) + 2 original sub-constructs for pro-activeness and competitive aggressiveness
Kreiser, Marino, Weaver	2002		Covin and Slevin (1988/1989)
Wiklund, Shepherd	2003	Firm's strategic orientation, capturing specific entrepreneurial aspects of decision-making styles, methods and practices (L&D,1996)	Covin and Slevin (1989)
Covin, Green, Slevin	2006	Strategic construct whose conceptual domain includes certain firm-level outcomes and management-related preferences, beliefs and behaviours as expressed among a firm's top-level managers.	Covin and Slevin (1989) Khandwalla (1976/77) Miller and Friesen (1982)

Entrepreneurship research in Europe

Table 10A.2   (continued)

Authors	Year	EO definition	EO Scale
Walter, Auer, Ritter	2006		Dess et al. (1997): proactiveness, innovation, risk taking, assertiveness (6 items)
Keh, Nguyen, Ng	2007		Covin and Slevin (1989) Miller and Friesen (1982)
Hughes, Hughes, Morgan	2007	Decision-making styles, processes and practices that specify how a firm intends to operate and compete	*Risk taking*: Barringer and Bluedorn (1999), Hult and Ketchen (2001), Morgan and Strong (2003) *Innovativeness:* Calantone, Çavuşgil and Zhao (2002) *Pro-activeness*: Hult and Ketchen (2001) Morgan and Strong (2003)
Madsen	2007	A way to see how management may discover and exploit opportunities	Original scale
Tang et al.	2008		Covin and Slevin (1989)

Index

Aaltio, I. 5, 8, 111, 116, 120, 121, 122–3
Abbott, A. 112, 115, 116, 117, 118–19
Abetti, P.A. 239
Academy of Management Conference (Aarhus, 2005) 116
Acs, Z.J. 56, 155, 156
Aguilar, F.J. 220
Aguilar, R. 90
Ahl, H. 114, 121
Åhlberg, M. 70
Ajzen, I. 34, 36, 37, 41, 42, 80, 232, 233, 235, 236
Aldrich, H. 34, 136, 145, 228
Alter, K. 154, 167
Alvarez, S.A. 86
American Social Enterprise School 6, 158, 161, 163–9, 178; *see also* social entrepreneurship
American Social Innovation School 158, 160–61, 163, 166–9; *see also* social entrepreneurship
Amit, R. 218
analogy/ies 8, 116, 117–19, 122, 127; *see also* heuristics; social capital
Ancona, D. 239
Andersen, O. 191
Anderson, A.R. 34
Anderson, C. 95
Anderson, N.R. 239
Antoncic, B. 134, 135, 136, 230
Ardichvili, A. 86, 87
Arenius, P. 57, 138
Armitage, C.J. 41, 42, 43
Aspelund, A. 35, 189, 190, 192, 194
Asper Biotech 199, 206–9
    compared with Regio and MicroLink 208–9
    focus and start of niche market strategy (2003–06) 208

product platform development (1999–2000) 206–7
start systematic sales network development (2001–02) 207–8
and usage of public funds for R&D (2003–04) 208
Audet, J. 35, 37
Audi, R. 60
Audretsch, D.B. 56, 155, 156
Austin, J. 160, 163, 164, 166
Autio, E. 34, 36, 39, 41, 135, 196, 216, 221

Bacq, S. 5, 6, 8
Baker, T. 121
Bandura, A. 36
Barney, J.B. 86
Baron, J.N. 136
Baron, R.A. 34
Barringer, B. 214, 216, 217
Bates, T. 138
Battle Anderson, B. 156, 158, 161, 166
Baum, J.R. 134, 138
Bell, J. 190, 217
Belousova, O. 7, 8
Benassi, M. 149
Bilen, S.G. 14
Bilkey, W.J. 189, 193
Bird, B. 36, 232
Birkinshaw, J. 237
Birley, S. 137, 146, 147
Black, P. 112, 115
Blackburn, R. 153
Blair, C. 63
Borch, O.J. 1
Borland, J. 94
Bornstein, D. 155, 161
Borzaga, C. 167
Boschee, J. 155, 165, 166
Bosma, N. 135
Bosman, C. 56